Hans Dieter Schaal
Stage Architecture / Bühnenarchitektur

Hans Dieter Schaal
Stage Architecture / Bühnenarchitektur

Introduction / Einführung
Gottfried Knapp

Interview
Frank R. Werner

Edition Axel Menges

© 2002 Edition Axel Menges, Stuttgart/London
ISBN 3-930698-86-2

Reproductions/Reproduktionen: Bild und Text
Joachim Baun, Fellbach
Printing/Druck: Druckhaus Münster GmbH, Korn-
westheim
Binding/Bindearbeiten: Ernst Riethmüller & Co.
GmbH, Stuttgart

Editorial supervision/Lektorat: Dorothea Duwe
Translation into English/Übersetzung ins Eng-
lische: Michael Robinson
Design: Axel Menges

Contents

Inhalt

Gottfried Knapp
Life – a space. Hans Dieter Schaal's stage sets

In order to characterize Hans Dieter Schaal's work as a stage designer and to set him apart from the mass production of everyday theatrical work, it is sensible to remember that Schaal – not just in terms of his training, but in every fibre of his artistic being – is an architect. We gained some sense of how unusual it still seems to be to include architects, despite the fact that it seems so obvious, in the visual world of our stages when architect and utopian Daniel Libeskind, a source of astonishment the world over, the designer of the Jewish Museum in Berlin, was first billed as the set designer by a theatre in spring 2001, and the international press set off with high expectations almost exclusively for this reason (and were then a little disappointed by the pale silhouette world that Libeskind had to offer here).

In fact, if major theatres decide they want to break away from their in-house do-it-yourself routine and bask in the glow emanating from an eminent guest, they usually start to look around in the world of painting, sculpture or the applied arts, or even go straight to the new leading aesthetic media of design, fashion and advertising, which says something about the role of the designer in today's theatre: they no longer need to produce versions of the buildings, rooms, squares, gardens and landscapes that are described for them in the plays and libretti, and they shouldn't enhance or offer counterpoint to the artistic work of directing the actors and singers, their function is usually reduced to a kind of atmospheric decoration, they are supposed to breathe an approximate sense of life into aesthetic trivia or striking individual objects or simply just spread something like splendour or chic.

Hans Dieter Schaal – and this is precisely what his directors like about his work – wants to express much more with his stage sets, convey very much more of the profundity of each particular piece, reveal very much more of the expressive forms into which the psyche of the people involved in each case takes refuge. And long before he started to work as an exhibition and set designer he had systematically analysed the expressive qualities of structures. In his early books of drawings, which he published himself, Schaal examines the primal forms of architecture in a highly entertaining and instructive way. He also reveals, in numerous humorous and satirical or surreal and fantastic variants, the emotional potential latent in constructed forms. Using the forms of architecture, he develops an amazingly rich typology of psychologically expressive forms, shows how cubes can be invested with a sensual and psychological charge, and what sort of wit and horror can lurk in our everyday buildings.

After these playfully audacious architectural studies in the late seventies, these intellectual experiments on architectural and town-planning themes, it was only a question of time before Schaal was able to try his applied building philosophies out on other arts, before museum directors, exhibition organizers and theatre peo-ple invited him to work with them and reflect on the aesthetic and psychological effects of presentation forms.

The first invitation to work in a theatre was also the most monumental individual commission. In 1983 the opera house in Frankfurt am Main decided to stage Hector Berlioz's monumental work *Les Troyens* on its gigantic revolve. This opera is seldom performed, but highly esteemed by connoisseurs, and is an enormous physical as well as intellectual challenge for any theatre. Klaus Zehelein, who later as director of the Stuttgart opera made it »opera house of the year«, was dramaturg in Frankfurt at the time. He showed extraordinary courage even in this role, and almost prophetic skills when he invited Hans Dieter Schaal to Frankfurt as a set designer – a starry-eyed architectural idealist who was very familiar with the arts but completely inexperienced in the theatre. Schaal was placed in harness with Ruth Berghaus, a highly individual interpreter-personality from the talent forges of the GDR, known for her uncompromising work as a director. This established an artistic partnership that constantly risked new interpretations of familiar works and thus made interpretative history in the late twentieth century, until the director's death. Schaal, like the author of this foreword, had his first major theatrical experiences in the sixties in the theatre in Ulm, when Kurt Hübner was artistic director there, employing directorial talents like Peter Zadek, Peter Palitzsch, Johannes Schaaf and Alfred Kirchner alongside and after each other to allow their artistic genius to shine, before moving on to the great, lucrative directorial and management posts in the German theatre. Wilfried Minks was responsible for the sets for many of these celebrated productions – and his minimalist style, tending to the abstract, often relying on the interplay of light and shade alone, must have made a great impression on Schaal's theatrical imagination. Schaal described these productions in a school magazine at the time, and even dreamed of pursuing a career as a stage designer at a later stage, when he was an architecture student in Hanover and Stuttgart. But it needed the imagination of a theatrical visionary and talent-spotter like Hübner – or in fact Zehelein, for this youthful dream to come true.

The revolve in the new opera house in Frankfurt is said to be the largest in Germany. Only an eighth of the gigantic circle fits into the proscenium opening at any given time. Schaal took over this huge area completely in his first job in the theatre, and divided it into an architectural structure that could be interpreted and used in such a way that every time the stage went through a turn of an eighth a new setting appeared in the foreground, but the architectural structures in the middle of the stage shifted effectively in their perspective and triggered a constant stream of new associations.

Two historically and mythologically significant locations have to be invoked for the evening of *Les Troyens*, and differentiated for the individual scenes: Troy and Carthage. For Troy, which was ground down after years under siege, at its historical nadir, indeed burning down in the course of the operatic action, Schaal came up with a deep shaft that acquired a very effective stage

Gottfried Knapp
Das Leben ein Raum. Die Bühnenbilder von Hans Dieter Schaal

Um das bühnenbildnerische Werk von Hans Dieter Schaal zu charakterisieren und aus der Massenproduktion des Bühnenalltags herauszuheben, ist es sinnvoll, daran zu erinnern, daß Schaal – nicht nur von der Ausbildung her, sondern mit seiner ganzen künstlerischen Überzeugung – Architekt ist. Wie ungewöhnlich die an sich so naheliegende Einbeziehung eines Architekten in das bildnerische Geschehen auf unseren Bühnen immer noch zu sein scheint, war zu ahnen, als der weltweit bestaunte Architektur-Utopist Daniel Libeskind, der Erbauer des Jüdischen Museums in Berlin, im Frühjahr 2001 zum ersten Mal von einem Theater als Bühnenbildner angekündigt wurde und die internationale Presse sich, fast ausschließlich dieser Pointe wegen, mit entsprechenden Erwartungen auf den Weg machte (um dann doch ein wenig enttäuscht zu sein von der blassen Scherenschnitt-Welt, die Libeskind in diesem Fall zu bieten hatte).

Tatsächlich halten die großen Theater, wenn sie beim Bühnenbild aus der häuslichen Bastelroutine ausbrechen und sich mit einem prominenten Gast schmücken wollen, meist bei der Malerei, der Bildhauerei und den angewandten Künsten, oder aber gleich bei den neuen ästhetischen Leitmedien Design, Mode und Werbung Ausschau, was einiges über die Rolle der Bühnenbildner auf dem heutigen Theater aussagt: Sie brauchen nicht mehr die in den Stücken und Libretti detailgenau vorgeschriebenen Bauten, Räume, Plätze, Gärten und Landschaften nachzubauen, sie sollen auch nicht mehr mit suggestiven Ausdrucksräumen die künstlerische Arbeit der Personenregie überhöhen oder kontrapunktieren, ihre Funktion reduziert sich meist auf eine Art von atmosphärischem Dekor, sie sollen mit ästhetischen Beiläufigkeiten oder auffälligen Einzelobjekten ein ungefähres Lebensgefühl vermitteln oder einfach nur etwas wie Glanz oder Chic verbreiten.

Hans Dieter Schaal will – und seine Regisseure schätzen genau das an seiner Arbeit – mit seinen Bühnenbauten sehr viel mehr ausdrücken, sehr viel mehr mitteilen von den Tiefendimensionen des jeweiligen Stücks, sehr viel mehr sichtbar machen von den Ausdrucksformen, in die sich die Psyche der jeweils handelnden Personen flüchtet. Und er hat, lange schon bevor er als Ausstellungsgestalter und Bühnenbildner zu arbeiten begann, systematisch die Ausdrucksmöglichkeiten von Gebautem studiert und analysiert. In seinen im Selbstverlag veröffentlichten frühen Zeichnungsbüchern untersucht Schaal auf höchst unterhaltsame und lehrreiche Weise die Urformen der Architektur und deckt in zahlreichen humoristisch-satirischen oder surreal-phantastischen Abwandlungen und Übersteigerungen das emotionale Potenzial auf, das in gebauten Formen steckt. Er entwickelt mit den Formen der Architektur eine reichhaltige Typologie psychologischer Ausdrucksformen und zeigt, wie kubische Formen sich sinnlich und seelisch aufladen lassen und was in den Bauten unseres Alltags an Witz und Grusel versteckt sein kann.

Nach diesen spielerisch verwegenen Architektur-Etüden aus den späten siebziger Jahren, diesen intellektuellen Versuchsanordnungen zu architektonischen und stadtplanerischen Themen, war es nur noch eine Frage der Zeit, bis Schaal seine angewandte Bau-Philosophie an anderen Künsten erproben durfte, bis Museumsleiter, Ausstellungsmacher und Theaterleute ihn zur Mitarbeit, zum Nachdenken über die ästhetischen und psychologischen Wirkungen von Präsentationsformen einluden.

Die erste Einladung an eine Bühne erbrachte gleich den monumentalsten Einzelauftrag. Im Jahr 1983 wollte die Oper in Frankfurt/Main auf ihrer gigantischen Drehbühne das von Kennern zwar hoch geschätzte, aber kaum je aufgeführte Monumentalwerk *Die Trojaner* von Hector Berlioz herausbringen, das für jedes Theater eine enorme physische wie geistige Herausforderung darstellt. Klaus Zehelein, der später als Intendant das Opernhaus in Stuttgart zum Seriensieger in der Kategorie »Opernhaus des Jahres« gemacht hat, war damals Dramaturg in Frankfurt. Er bewies schon in dieser Rolle außerordentlichen Mut und fast seherische Fähigkeiten, als er den theaterunerfahrenen, aber mit den Künsten sehr wohl vertrauten Architektur-Phantasten Hans Dieter Schaal als Bühnenbildner nach Frankfurt holte und mit Ruth Berghaus, der eigenwilligen Interpreten-Persönlichkeit aus den Talentschmieden der DDR – sie war für ihre kompromißlose Regie-Arbeit bekannt –, zusammenspannte. Er stiftete damit eine künstlerische Partnerschaft, die bis zum Tod der Regisseurin immer wieder komplexe Neudeutungen bekannter Werke gewagt und so ein Stück Interpretationsgeschichte am Ende des 20. Jahrhunderts geschrieben hat. Schaal hat – wie der Autor dieses Vorworts – seine ersten großen Theatererlebnisse in den sechziger Jahren im Ulmer Theater gehabt, als Kurt Hübner dort Intendant war, und in seinem Haus neben- und nacheinander Regiebegabungen wie Peter Zadek, Peter Palitzsch, Johannes Schaaf und Alfred Kirchner ihr Genie blitzen ließen, bevor sie die großen einträglichen Regie- und Intendantensessel im deutschen Theater eroberten. Wilfried Minks hat bei vielen dieser gefeierten Inszenierungen die Bühnenbilder geschaffen – und sein minimalistisch abstrahierender Stil, der oft allein auf die Wechselwirkung von Licht und Schatten setzte, dürfte Schaals Bühnenphantasie stark geprägt haben. Schaal beschrieb die Aufführungen damals in einer Schülerzeitung und träumte auch noch später, während des Architekturstudiums in Hannover und Stuttgart, von einer Karriere als Bühnenbildner. Doch es bedurfte der Intuition eines Theatervisionärs und Talentsuchers wie Hübner – oder eben Zehelein, daß der Jugendtraum in Erfüllung gehen konnte.

Die Drehbühne in der neuen Oper in Frankfurt gilt als die größte in Deutschland. Jeweils nur ein Achtel des riesigen Kreisrunds paßt in die Öffnung des Bühnenportals. Schaal hat diese gigantische Fläche in seiner ersten Arbeit für das Theater bis an die Ränder in Beschlag genommen und mit einem vielfältig deut- und nutzbaren Architekturgebilde so unterteilt, daß sich bei jeder Achteldrehung der Bühne ein neuer Schauplatz in den Vordergrund schob, die Aufbauten in der Mitte der Scheibe aber sich perspektivisch wirkungsvoll verschoben und immer neue Assoziationen hervorriefen.

Zwei historisch und mythologisch bedeutsame Orte mußten am *Trojaner*-Abend evoziert und für die einzelnen Auftritte differenziert werden: Troja und Karthago. Für Troja, die von der jahrelangen Belagerung zermürbte, auf dem Tiefpunkt ihrer

appearance in one of his preliminary drawings, powerfully summing up the emotions of the scene: the shaft looked as though it had been dug in the earth by cruel gods with a monstrous spade. Thus Schaal developed one aspect of his emotional stage architecture from a spontaneously associative drawing that would have fitted in well with one of the earlier volumes of drawings. The fluted, steep, high walls of the shaft, into which light could penetrate directly only from the top, gave the impression of total hopelessness, threat, captivity. And the idea of being at the bottom of a gigantic lock gate that could open to devastating effect at any time also conveyed itself uncannily to the spectators. The Trojans' sense of being at the end of everything, which despite Cassandra's warnings is turned into hysterical rejoicing when the Greeks withdraw and the wooden horse is left behind, was reflected vividly and directly in the built surroundings, indeed it seemed to take on physical shape in and to condense into architectural forms. This »cut of the spade« translated monumentally into stage reality did not only represent the start of the great romantic ancient melodrama about the Trojans in the Frankfurt opera house, but also the start of the career of Hans Dieter Schaal, space dramatist.

Carthage, where the Trojans land up in Berlioz's opera, is at a first glance the dazzlingly bright, flourishing counter-world to the claustrophobically gloomy, charred final condition of Troy. After seven years of peace and rising to be a maritime country richly blessed by nature, Queen Dido and her people are able to enjoy an exuberant party and later celebrate victory in a war that had been forced upon them with their battle-tested Trojan guests. For these elated events, Schaal had designed a broad ramp that rose evenly over the full depth of the revolve, fringed with graphically striking railings for ever sprouting bridges and flights of steps at the sides, leading to other settings and ending at the top end in a tangle of walkways, deck-rails and bridges thrusting out freely into the air, and so making a bizarre play with the insignia of ship's architecture and homesickness, adventure and farewells associated with this. At the end, when the Trojans set off for Rome, the sloping plane will be transformed into a kind of ship's deck on which Dido, abandoned by Aeneas, will say farewell to the world with the vision that her Carthage, so radiant for a time, will be outshone by the brilliance of Aeneas's future Rome. The culmination of this private tragedy against the background of world history, suicide by the founders of Rome on their fast armoured craft as they sail towards their destiny, is reached via a series of transitional scenes for which Schaal provided an almost inexhaustible abundance of eloquent locations in his revolving, multipartite, all-embracing structure. Thus the intimate confrontations between Dido and Aeneas were set in a love-pit on the edge of the Carthaginian plateau. Nautical trappings made it possible to see the pit as a side-deck on the aircraft-carrier »Carthage«. At the other end of the long, upward-sloping ramp, under the gangways and bridges that thrust freely into the sky, bizarre labyrinths that could be expressively illuminated and interpreted opened up, blocked with scaf-

folding. They suggested a modern building site, which could readily be interpreted in terms of the mythological events.

Thus each built section was ambiguous; it had a clearly defined front and a back that was just as effective, and a shape that could be interpreted from both the top and the bottom. For example, the high walls of the Trojan shaft play a different, entirely contrasting role as palace battlements on the Carthage side.

Although Schaal never subsequently had an opportunity to exploit the potential of a large revolve so exhaustively, even here, in his first stage set, it is possible to see the powerfully developed ideas about architecture and space that distinguish his designs from those by his colleagues working with their paintbrushes and drawing on their modelling skills. Clearly recognizable three-dimensional structures constantly assume new states as the light changes, coming now from the front or the back, now from the top or the bottom, now from the right or the left; they mutate from one psychological condition into the next. So there is no final or unambiguous condition. A second plane of depth, a behind or an underneath, is always opening up. The chambers and landscapes of the soul are unfathomable.

Ten years after *Les Trojans* in Frankfurt, Schaal designed another artistic interpretation of the drama of *Dido and Aeneas* for the Komische Oper in Berlin. The melodramatic love episode from the Odyssey, retold by Vergil in the *Aeneid* – it depicts the contrasting roles of the sexes as larger-than-life archetypes – had to be captured in images for Arila Siegert's ballet *Circe and Odysseus*, to music by Gerald Humel (1993). To do this, Schaal stated the basic architectural motif of the Carthage scenes more precisely: an area rising towards the back of the stage (in Schaal's own words »ship's deck, mountain, wave, house and roof terrace in one«) defined two action spaces for the choreographic movements clearly: the space at the bottom in the foreground, representing anything that was close by, for example the sandy shore of the island, and the plateau at the top at the end of the slope, which indicated the distance, formed a horizon and could be interpreted as a ship's deck. A third space, a framed rectangle, was let into the slope; this sometimes functioned as house, sometimes as a love-hollow, and illustrated in three-dimensional form, indeed in a form that could almost be interpreted anatomically, the female and seductive component, but also the paralysingly settled way of life of the eponymous heroine, the fact that she was rooted in her own home soil. The changing light separated out the individual locations from the uniform set one after the other and guided associations in the desired direction.

Schaal had one more opportunity to intensify the psychological state of abandoned mythical female figures in a single scene. When Georg Anton Benda's two melodramas *Ariadne auf Naxos* and *Medea*, dating from the time the palace was built, were performed on the little stage of the Schloßtheater in the Neues Palais in Potsdam in 1996 (director: Jürgen Tamchina), the shamefully abandoned and deceived heroines' outbursts of despair, rage and revenge

Geschichte angekommene Stadt, die noch während der Opernhandlung abbrennt, hat Schaal einen tiefen Schacht konzipert, der in einer seiner suggestiv die Emotionen der Szene einkreisenden Vorzeichnungen auch gleich sein bühnenwirksames Aussehen bekam: Der Schacht sah so aus, als sei er von grausamen Göttern mit einem monströsen Spaten in die Erde getrieben worden. Aus einer spontan assoziierenden Zeichnung, die gut in einen der früheren Zeichnungsbände gepaßt hätte, entwickelte Schaal also ein Element seiner emotionalen Bühnenarchitektur. Die geriffelten, steilen, hohen Wände des Schachts, in den nur Licht direkt von oben einfiel, suggerierten totale Ausweglosigkeit, Bedrohung, Gefangenschaft. Auch die Vorstellung, an den Fuß eines überdimensionalen Schleusentors, das sich jederzeit vernichtend öffnen könnte, verbannt worden zu sein, schwang in den Empfindungen des Betrachters unheimlich mit. Die Endzeitstimmung der Trojaner, die, trotz der Warnungen Kassandras, beim Abzug der Griechen und beim Anblick des hinterlassenen Holzpferds zeitweilig in hysterischen Jubel umschlägt, spiegelte sich drastisch direkt in der gebauten Umgebung, ja sie schien selber physische Gestalt anzunehmen, sich zu architektonischen Formen zu verdichten. Mit diesem monumental in die Bühnenrealität übersetzten »Spatenstich« begann nicht nur das große romantische Antiken-Melodram über die Trojaner in der Frankfurter Oper, sondern auch die Laufbahn des Raum-Dramatikers Hans Dieter Schaal.

Karthago, wohin es die Trojaner in der Oper von Berlioz verschlägt, ist auf den ersten Blick die strahlend helle, blühende Gegenwelt zum klaustrophobisch düsteren, verkohlten Endzustand Trojas. Nach sieben Jahren Frieden und Aufbau in einem von der Natur reich gesegneten Land am Meer kann Königin Dido mit ihrem Volk ein ausgelassenes Fest und später mit den kampferprobten trojanischen Gästen den Sieg in einem aufgezwungenen Krieg feiern. Für diese hochgestimmten Ereignisse hat Schaal eine über die ganze Tiefe der Drehbühne hinweg gleichmäßig ansteigende breite Rampe entworfen, die, von graphisch einprägsamen Geländern gesäumt, immer wieder seitlich Brücken und Treppenläufe zu anderen Schauplätzen hin aussandte und am oberen Ende in ein Gewirr von frei in die Luft hinausstoßenden Laufgängen, Relings und Brücken auslief, also auf bizarre Weise mit den Insignien von Schiffsarchitektur und den damit verbundenen Assoziationen Fernweh, Abenteuer und Abschied spielte. Am Ende, wenn die Trojaner nach Rom aufbrechen, wird sich die schiefe Ebene dann tatsächlich in eine Art Schiffsdeck verwandeln, auf dem Dido, von Äneas verlassen, sich aus der Welt mit der Vision verabschiedet, daß ihr zeitweilig so strahlendes Karthago untergehen, vom Glanz des kommenden äneischen Rom überstrahlt werden wird. Bis zur Kulmination dieser privaten Tragödie vor dem Hintergrund der Weltgeschichte, diesem Selbstmord auf dem Schnellboot der ihrer Bestimmung entgegenziehenden Gründer Roms, gibt es einige Übergangsszenen, für die Schaal in seinem drehbaren, vielteiligen Rundumbauwerk eine kaum ausschöpfbare Fülle sprechender Örtlichkeiten bereitstellte. So ereigneten sich die intimen Begegnungen zwischen Dido und Äneas in einer

Liebesgrube am Rand des karthagischen Plateaus, die man ihrer nautischen Bestückung wegen auch als ein Seitendeck auf dem Flugzeugträger »Karthago« empfinden konnte. Am anderen Ende der langen, ansteigenden Rampe taten sich unter den frei in den Himmel vorstoßenden Gangways und Brücken bizarre, mit Gerüsten verstellte Labyrinthe auf, die expressiv ausgeleuchtet und ausgedeutet werden konnten. Sie suggerierten eine moderne Baustelle, die sich gut auf das mythologische Geschehen hinüberdeuten ließ.

Jedes gebaute Teil war demnach mehrdeutig; es hatte eine klar definierte Vorder- und eine ebenso wirksame Rückseite, eine Form, die mal von oben, mal von unten interpretiert werden konnte. Die hohen Wände des Troja-Schachts zum Beispiel spielten auf der Karthago-Seite als Palastzinnen eine zweite, durchaus gegensätzliche Rolle.

Obwohl Schaal später keine Gelegenheit mehr hatte, die Möglichkeiten einer großen Drehbühne so ausgiebig einzusetzen, lassen sich schon hier, beim ersten Bühnenbild, die kräftig ausgeprägten Architektur- und Raumvorstellungen erkennen, die seine Entwürfe von denen der pinselnden und bastelnden Kollegen unterscheiden. Deutlich erkennbare, dreidimensionale Bauten nehmen im Wechsel des Lichts, das mal von vorne oder von hinten, mal von oben oder von unten, mal von rechts oder von links kommt, ständig neue Aggregatzustände an; sie mutieren aus einer psychischen Befindlichkeit in die nächste. Es gibt also keinen endgültigen oder eindeutigen Zustand. Immer tut sich eine zweite Tiefenschicht, ein Dahinter oder Darunter auf. Die Kammern und die Landschaften der Seele sind unergründlich.

Zehn Jahre nach den *Trojanern* in Frankfurt hat Schaal an der Komischen Oper in Berlin eine weitere Interpretation des Dido-Äneas-Dramas bildnerisch gestaltet. In Arila Siegerts Ballett *Circe und Odysseus* zur Musik von Gerald Humel (1993) war die melodramatische Liebesepisode aus der Odyssee, die Vergil in der *Aeneis* nachgedichtet hat – sie malt in archetypischer Übergröße die gegensätzlichen Rollen der Geschlechter aus –, in Bilder zu fassen. Schaal hat dafür das architektonische Grundmotiv der Karthago-Szenen präzisiert: Eine nach hinten ansteigende Fläche (nach Schaals eigenen Worten »Schiffsdeck, Berg, Welle, Haus und Dachterrasse in einem«) definierte deutlich zwei Handlungsräume für die choreographischen Bewegungen: den Raum unten im Vordergrund, der das Naheliegende, etwa die sandigen Ufer der Insel meinte, und das Plateau oben am Ende der Schräge, das die Ferne andeutete, einen Horizont bildete und als Schiffsdeck gedeutet werden konnte. In die schiefe Ebene war ein dritter Raum, ein Rahmenrechteck eingelassen; es fungierte mal als Haus, mal als Liebesmulde und setzte in plastisch einprägsamer, ja fast anatomisch deutbarer Form die weiblich-verführerische Komponente, aber auch die lähmende Seßhaftigkeit der weiblichen Titelfigur, das Verwurzeltsein in der Heimaterde, ins Bild. Das wechselnde Licht separierte die einzelnen Orte nacheinander aus dem Einheitsbühnenbild und lenkte die Assoziationen in die gewünschte Richtung.

Noch einmal hat Schaal die psychische Befindlichkeit verlassener mythischer Frauenfiguren in einem einzigen Bild zuspitzen können. Als

took place in front of a gigantic (slightly tilted) rectangular door let into the back wall. A colossal wedge thrust aggressively through this open picture frame from the back right down to the orchestra pit at the front – a three-dimensional figure of injury, a monument to psychological and physical penetration, whose consequences were apparent from the rocky ruins lying around at the sides.

Thus once more there was a disturbing depth in the image; once again the eye was drawn into uncertainty by an aperture; and once again it was the light that gave this two-layered world, this close-up image of defloration, its diverse interpretations and opened up the depths of the stage individually for the two plays. When the title characters moved on the wedge through the time- and space-gate, the brutal stereometric structure could become a kind of tongue lapping into the present and linking the two spheres that were separated by hostilities with each other. For Gluck's *Orpheus and Euridice* in Lübeck in 1998 (director: Jürgen Tamchina), there were several large rectangular gates present at the same time, tilted out of the vertical to different degrees, on one axis after the other. They made the existential thresholds on the way into the next world and back again into a visual event. Orpheus went through the gates to the worlds beyond this world, he looked deep into the framed, shattered mirror that was held up to him by the next world.

When staging Puccini's *Turandot* in the Hessisches Staatstheater Wiesbaden in 1998 (director: Dominik Neuner), Schaal gave the motif of the gate, which is open to a large number of interpretations, a particularly striking, erotically based slant: the gigantic Chinese round gate in the centre of the stage, which had a kind of walkway or ramp leading to it, was not just a way through to the forbidden realms of the imperial palace, a peephole into the cruelly icy, bizarrely jagged psychological landscape of the man-destroying princess, it was also a clear symbol of the three murderous riddles posed by Turandot, which seemed easy to solve, but cost everyone who took the risk their heads. And so as the plot unfolded the huge round hole changed into a guillotine, then into a bodily aperture that could swallow people up; but the ramp in front of it became a walkway for the battle of the sexes. On its detached height the cruelly beautiful, bloodthirsty female creature, coming forward from her psychological Arctic, mingled with people, paraded with obvious relish through the forest of skewered men's heads and revelled in the attention paid by her next victims. Schaal also condensed the various locations for *Der Prinz von Homburg* in 1997 – again in Wiesbaden – when he designed the set for Hans Werner Henze's operatic version of Kleist's play (director: Dominik Neuner). Brutalist exposed concrete walls, floors and ceilings, which came together to form a piece of the Siegfried Line, offered a framework for the prince's father's strictly military regime, whose laws the prince infringes both privately and as a soldier. All that could be seen when looking through the crenel into the open air was the battlefield. And the round aperture in the floor did not provide a means of evading one's duty either. The narrow strip of stage in front of and behind the monumental bunkered barracks worked as a counter-world, as the garden in Fehrbellin, as a bed of Brandenburg sand, on which the prince lost himself in his fateful dreams. Thus the hierarchies of society and the abysses yawning between the principal characters were manifested in the successions and stacks of the built elements.

The set for *Patmos*, a co-production by the Munich Biennale and the Staatstheater Kassel (director: Ruth Berghaus) in 1990, provides a particularly fine example of the way in which Schaal places his architectural imagination, his three-dimensional thinking at the disposal of the story that is to be told. In order to collect impressions for this musical and theatrical version of the Revelation of St. John undertaken by the composer Wolfgang von Schweinitz, Schaal travelled to the supposed site from which these apocalyptic insights originated and examined the terrain like an archaeologist. His depiction of the cave John lived in with a crack revealing the sky, in which fragments of reality or of nature, in the form of birds flying to and fro, could be seen from time to time when looking through, reads like a description of one of his own stage sets. Then, in his first drawings for the actual set, Schaal defined his archaeological method and his three dimensional pictorial idea quite unambiguously: square shafts were let into the floor of the stage that led into another, long past era of time, as at an archaeological dig, bringing to light all sorts of objects that triggered a number of associations. The religious and mythological depths of the ancient text were thus translated into a spatial, a three-dimensional and pictorial, a tangible form: Schaal himself described the experiment as »the text of Revelation in Braille«.

You could literally get hold of the dual layers of the construction, the top and bottom, today and yesterday. The set designer as archaeologist, as a myth researcher, as an interpreter of the past and of events that have been buried; built space as a research station. The visions of the Apocalypse rising from the depths acquired an oppressive topicality in the top time layer, representing today: at times the ditches started to look like military trenches; the excavation site became a battlefield. So here architecture functions as a probe, as an instrument for revealing hidden, forgotten or suppressed dimensions. In Richard Strauss's one-act music drama *Salome*, the deep layer – the meta-level, the counter-world – is already present in the symbolic scenery taken over from Oscar Wilde. The terrace in the palace of King Herod, a location that has been taken out of normality, is the venue for a bloody drama of lust and passion. The voice of Jokanaan, the warning voice of the new Christianity, comes from the lower level, from the cistern, as if from another world, sounding eerily in the morally degenerate world of the old ruling powers. The complexity that Schaal discovers in so much material is an architectural donné from the dramatist Wilde here, and so in the stage set it has only to be copied or interpreted further.

For the performance at the Staatstheater Braunschweig in 1994 (director: Dominik Neuner), Schaal turned the whole of the terrace into a danger area: large shafts gaped in the

1996 auf der kleinen Bühne des Schloßtheaters im Neuen Palais in Potsdam die beiden Melodramen *Ariadne auf Naxos* und *Medea* von Georg Anton Benda aus der Erbauungszeit des Schlosses aufgeführt wurden (Regie: Jürgen Tamchina), ereigneten sich die Verzweiflungs-, Wut- und Racheausbrüche der schmählich verlassenen und hintergangenen Heldinnen vor einem riesigen (leicht gekippten) rechteckigen Tor, das in die abschließende Wand gebrochen war. Durch diesen geöffneten Bilderrahmen schob sich von hinten ein kolossaler Keil mit der Spitze aggressiv nach vorne bis zum Orchestergraben – ein dreidimensionales Symbol der Verletzung, ein Monument der physischen wie psychischen Penetration, dessen Folgen an den seitlich herumliegenden Felstrümmern abzulesen waren.

Wieder tat sich also eine irritierende Tiefe im Bild auf; wieder wurde der Blick durch eine Öffnung ins Ungewisse hinausgezogen; und wieder war es das Licht, das dieser zweischichtigen Welt, diesem nahegerückten Bild der Defloration, seine vielfältigen Deutungen gab und den Tiefenraum für die beiden Bühnenstücke individuell erschloß. Wenn die Titelfiguren sich auf dem Keil durch das Zeit- und Raumtor bewegten, konnte aus dem brutalen stereometrischen Gebilde eine Art Zunge werden, die in die Gegenwart hereinlappte und die zwei feindlich getrennten Sphären miteinander verband. Bei Glucks *Orpheus und Eurydike* in Lübeck 1998 (Regie: Jürgen Tamchina) standen dann gleich mehrere große rechteckige Tore, unterschiedlich aus der Senkrechten gekippt, in einer Achse hintereinander. Sie machten die existenziellen Schwellen auf dem Weg ins Jenseits und zurück ins Diesseits zum visuellen Ereignis. Orpheus durchschritt die Tore zu den Welten hinter unserer Welt, er tat tiefe Blicke in die gerahmten, zerbrochenen Spiegel, die ihm das Jenseits entgegenhielt.

Bei der Realisierung von Puccinis *Turandot* 1998 im Hessischen Staatstheater Wiesbaden (Regie: Dominik Neuner) gab Schaal dem vielfältig deutbaren Motiv des Tores eine besonders markante, erotisch grundierte Deutung: Das riesige chinesische Rundtor in der Mitte der Bühne, auf das eine Art Laufsteg, eine Rampe zuführte, war nicht nur der Durchlaß in die unerreichbaren Gefilde des kaiserlichen Palastes, das Guckloch in die grausam vergletscherte, bizarr gezackte Seelenlandschaft der männervernichtenden Prinzessin, es war auch ein handgreifliches Symbol für die von Turandot gestellten drei mörderischen Rätsel, die scheinbar leicht zu lösen waren, aber alle Wagemutige den Kopf kosteten. Das riesige runde Loch mutierte also im Fortgang der Handlung mal zur Guillotine, mal zur verschlingenden Körperöffnung; die Rampe davor aber wurde zum Laufsteg des Geschlechterkampfs, auf dessen abgehobener Höhe das grausam schöne, blutdürstige Weibswesen, aus seiner psychischen Arktis nach vorne kommend, sich unter die Menschen mischte, genüßlich durch den Wald der aufgespießten Männerköpfe promenierte und die Blicke der nächsten Opfer einheimste. Zu einem ähnlich dynamischen Bild hat Schaal auch die verschiedenen Handlungsorte in *Der Prinz von Homburg* verdichtet, als er 1997 – ebenfalls in Wiesbaden – für Hans Werner Henzes Opern-Version des Kleist-Dramas (Regie: Dominik Neuner) das Bühnenbild schuf. Brutalistische Sichtbeton-Wände, -Böden und -Decken, die sich zu einem Stück Westwall zusammenschoben, bildeten den Rahmen für die militärisch streng reglementierte Welt des Vaters, gegen deren Gesetze der Prinz privat, aber auch als Soldat verstößt. Der Blick durch den Schießschartenschlitz hinaus ins Freie brachte nur das Schlachtfeld ins Bild. Und auch die runde Öffnung im Boden bot keine Möglichkeit, den Pflichten zu entkommen. Der schmale Bühnenstreifen vor und unterhalb der monumentalen Bunkerkaserne fungierte als Gegenwelt, als Garten von Fehrbellin, als Bett aus märkischem Sand, auf dem der Prinz seinen verhängnisvollen Träumen nachhing. Im Hinter- und Übereinander der gebauten Elemente manifestierten sich also die Hierarchien der Gesellschaft und die Abgründe, die zwischen den Hauptfiguren klaffen.

Wie direkt Schaal seine architektonische Vorstellungskraft, sein dreidimensionales Denken in den Dienst der zu erzählenden Geschichte stellt, läßt sich besonders schön am Bühnenbild zu *Patmos*, einer Koproduktion der Münchner Biennale und des Staatstheaters Kassel (Regie: Ruth Berghaus) aus dem Jahr 1990, studieren. Um für die musikalisch-theatralische Umsetzung der Apokalypse des Johannes, die der Komponist Wolfgang von Schweinitz unternommen hatte, Eindrücke zu sammeln, hatte sich Schaal an den mutmaßlichen Ort der Endzeit-Eingebungen, auf die Insel Patmos begeben und wie ein Archäologe das Terrain sondiert. Seine Schilderung der Wohnhöhle des Johannes mit dem Spalt zum Himmel, in dem man ab und zu Vögel kreuzen sieht, also beim Durchblick Fragmente der Realität oder der Natur erkennen kann, liest sich wie die Beschreibung eines Schaalschen Bühnenbilds. In den ersten Zeichnungen zum realen Bühnenbild definierte Schaal dann schon eindeutig seine archäologische Methode und seine dreidimensionale Bildvorstellung: In den Bühnenboden waren quadratische Schächte eingelassen, die wie auf einer archäologischen Ausgrabungsstätte in eine andere, längst vergangene Zeitschicht hinunterführten und allerlei assoziationsreich sprechende Gegenstände ans Licht beförderten. Die mythologischen und die religiösen Tiefendimensionen des antiken Texts wurden also in eine räumliche, eine dreidimensional-bildhafte, eine tastbare Form übersetzt: »Der Text der Apokalypse in Blindenschrift« hat Schaal selbst das Experiment beschrieben.

Die Doppelschichtigkeit der Konstruktion, das Oben und Unten, das Heute und Gestern, war buchstäblich mit Händen zu greifen. Der Bühnenbildner als Archäologe, als Mythen-Forscher, als Deuter des Vergangenen und Interpret der verschütteten Ereignisse; der gebaute Raum als Forschungsstation. Die aus der Tiefe aufsteigenden Visionen der Apokalypse bekamen in der oberen, der heutigen Zeitschicht eine bedrückende Aktualität: Die Gruben nahmen zeitweilig das Aussehen von Schützengräben an; aus der Ausgrabungsstätte wurde ein Schlachtfeld. Architektur fungiert hier also als Sonde, als Instrument zum Erschließen verborgener, vergessener oder verdrängter Dimensionen. Im einaktigen Musikdrama *Salome* von Richard Strauss ist die Tiefenschicht – die Metaebene, die Gegenwelt – schon in der von Oscar Wilde übernommenen Symbol-Szenerie physisch präsent. Die Terrasse im Pa-

floor in several places, with an alarmingly alien quality forcing its way up through them. The figures from the world above – except Salome – were unsettled by the sounds from under the floor. The bitonality that Strauss, in a unique compositional experiment, developed from the stark contrasts in emotion, dimension and rank offered by the piece, was reflected by Schaal's set architecturally, in three dimensions.

When Dominik Neuner directed the opera again at the opera house in Wiesbaden, four years later (1998), Schaal reduced the apertures in the floor to slits, cut the palace architecture down to a tilted cube and used a telescope pointing into the background to indicate the incipient world of the new faith that Jokanaan – John the Baptist – proclaimed before his horrifying death.

In Richard Strauss's second world-wide operatic success, *Elektra*, to a libretto by Hugo von Hofmannsthal, the set is almost identical with that of *Salome* according to the stage directions: it consists of a palace courtyard, the buildings around it and a well. Hofmannsthal himself, in his notes on the piece – Schaal quotes the passage – hoped that the set would create an impression of being »constricted: it is not possible to escape, the characters are isolated«. In the 1986 Berghaus production at the Semperoper in Dresden, where *Elektra* had its world première in 1909, Schaal projected the eponymous heroine's desperate longing for her father's avenger, her brother Orestes, into a high tower, a three-tier diving-platform that seemed to promise a view of Orestes as he arrived in the distance. It vividly represented the huge psychological distance between the principal characters on the vertical plane, but also the danger of the deadly downward plunge, of suicide.

At the Zurich opera house – again in working with Ruth Berghaus (1991) – Schaal translated the disassociation of the characters, reflected in vertical architecture in Dresden, into a bewildering horizontal spatial continuum: the open walls of the palace gave a sense, varying with the lighting angles, of an eerily constructed labyrinth in which the characters were trapped. And so in Zurich the abysses did not lead into the depths, but backwards, into another of the three dimensions. Places of confusion, of ambiguity, reminiscent of the nightmare scenes in Piranesi's imagined *Carceri*, are a recurrent feature of Hans Dieter Schaal's work as a stage designer. He created an architecture of surveillance, traps and prisons of depressing hopelessness, a symbol and sense-image of psychological states, to represent the terrible ideological aberrations of the Anabaptists, which lead to a dictatorship and a horrifying end in Azio Corghi's opera *Divara – Wasser und Blut* (»Divara – Water and Blood«, Teatro Nacional de São Carlos, Lisbon, 2001, director: Christof Nel).

For Lars Norén's play *Nacht, Mutter des Tages* (»Night, Mother of Day«) in the Akademietheater in Vienna (1991, director: Guy Joosten), which portrays the decline of a family in several gloomy scenes, Schaal designed a combined kitchen and living room that contracted claustrophobically in the course of the action, gradually revealing the parents' bedroom, the source of the whole disaster.

Another endgame by Norén, *Eintagswesen*, (»Epemeral Beings«) his play about death and decay (Ghent 1986, director: Guy Joosten), took place amidst surreally distorted domestic architecture from which there was no escape; at the end the only life was on the television: a dog endlessly leaping at a wire fence.

Theatre directors who seek their salvation largely on the surface would have difficulty with Schaal's self-confidently interventionist, analytical stage sets; they would be afraid that their own interpretation would not stand up to the demands of the set. But Schaal was able to become a creative partner for a personality like Ruth Berghaus; she was able to build his interpretatively advanced architectures into her complex readings. When Berghaus and Schaal worked together on Schönberg's *Moses und Aron* at the Berlin Staatsoper Unter den Linden in 1987, they were compelled by the material itself to reflect on the function of what they were doing, about the power of words alone, about the seductive powers of images and music and about the fatal abuse of the two extremes. Moses, the lawgiver, the fanatical man of words, the earthly representative of a stern, invisible God, thought that he had to forbid all images and everything sensual. He condemns his brother Aaron to death because he tried to pacify the people with idols and sensual pleasures in Moses's absence, but unleashed a dangerous orgy. Here two extreme opposites collide. Schönberg, who wrote the libretto and the music, positioned himself morally on the side of Moses the man of words, who is only allowed to express himself in dry Sprechgesang in the opera – Moses would of course have forbidden an opera about his mission; but as a composer Schönberg imbued the heathen opposite position, which indulges itself in music and dance, with an almost ecstatic abundance of sensual presence. Berghaus and Schaal, who had to illustrate the contrast vividly on stage, inevitably sided with Aaron, the sensual artist. They invented actions and images for the detached movements of the music, without which any performance of the work on stage would be pointless. Schaal, the creator of images, was thus the Aaron of this production. He revealed the deficiencies of the opposite point of view, used his visual resources to unmask the inhumanity of religious fundamentalism, showed where fanatical literalism and uncompromising adherence to the law would lead: not to the »land flowing with milk and honey« that Moses promised, but from collective captivity into a new prison, into the dictatorship of bans, into the sterility of order: in Berlin Moses's world of law coagulated into the interior of a massive bank vault whose walls were made up of closed lockers. Later a stepped pyramid appeared, with familiar and yet mysterious scenes of horror from the recent past appearing in its windows. Towards the end a gigantic electric coil – an energy block, a fuel element? – started to glow disturbingly above the human beings: the disaster conjured up by the militancy and inhumanity of a mind bent on absolutism was taking its course.

Hans Dieter Schaal has thought more carefully than any of his professional colleagues at the preliminary stages of devising his stage sets,

last des Königs Herodes, ein aus der Normalität herausgehobener Ort, bildet den Schauplatz für ein blutiges Drama der Lüste und der Leidenschaften. Aus der Ebene darunter, aus der Zisterne, tönt die Stimme Jochanaans, die mahnende Stimme des jungen Christentums, wie aus einer anderen Welt kommend, unheimlich herauf in die moralisch verkommene Welt der herrschenden alten Mächte. Die Mehrschichtigkeit, die Schaal in so vielen Stoffen entdeckt, ist hier eine vom Dramatiker Wilde gestiftete architektonische Gegebenheit, muß also im Bühnenbild nur nachgebaut oder weiterinterpretiert werden.

Bei der Aufführung im Staatstheater Braunschweig (1994, Regie: Dominik Neuner) hat Schaal die ganze Terrasse zu einem gefährlichen Pflaster werden lassen: An mehreren Stellen klafften große Schächte im Boden, durch die das Fremde verunsichernd heraufdrang. Die Figuren der Oberwelt – außer Salome – reagierten beunruhigt auf die Töne aus dem Boden. Die Bitonalität, die Strauss in einem einmaligen kompositorischen Experiment aus den schrillen emotionalen, räumlichen und standesmäßigen Gegensätzen entwickelt hat, fand bei Schaal ihre dreidimensional-architektonische Entsprechung im Bühnenbild.

Als vier Jahre später (1998) Dominik Neuner die Oper in Wiesbaden noch einmal inszenierte, ließ Schaal die Öffnungen im Boden zu Schlitzen verkleinern. Er reduzierte die Palastarchitektur auf einen gekippten Würfel und deutete mit einem in den Hintergrund gerichteten Fernrohr jene heraufziehende Welt des neuen Glaubens an, die Jochanaan – Johannes der Täufer – vor seinem grausigen Tod verkündet hat.

Im zweiten Opern-Welterfolg von Richard Strauss, in *Elektra* nach einem Libretto von Hugo von Hofmannsthal, ist das Bühnenbild laut Anweisungen fast identisch mit dem der *Salome*: Es besteht aus dem Hof eines Palastes, den umliegenden Gebäuden und einem Ziehbrunnen. Hofmannsthal selber hat sich in seinen Anmerkungen zum Stück – Schaal zitiert die Stelle – vom Bühnenbild den Eindruck von »Enge, Unentfliehbarkeit, Abgeschlossenheit« erhofft. Bei der Berghaus-Inszenierung 1986 an der Semperoper in Dresden, also in dem Haus, in dem *Elektra* 1909 uraufgeführt worden ist, hat Schaal die verzweifelte Sehnsucht der Titelfigur nach dem Rächer des Vaters, nach dem Bruder Orest, in einen hohen Turm hineinprojiziert, in einen Sprungturm mit drei Ebenen, der eine Fernsicht auf den Ankömmling zu versprechen schien und die riesigen seelischen Abstände zwischen den Hauptfiguren in einer Vertikale bildhaft vor Augen führte, aber auch die Gefahr des tödlichen Absturzes, des Selbstmords, sichtbar machte.

Im Opernhaus Zürich – wieder in Zusammenarbeit mit Ruth Berghaus (1991) – hat Schaal dann die Dissoziation der Figuren, die in Dresden in einer vertikalen Architektur gespiegelt war, in ein verwirrendes horizontales Raumkontinuum übersetzt: Die offenen Wände des Palastes ließen je nach Lichteinfall ein unheimliches, gebautes Labyrinth erahnen, in dem die Figuren gefangen waren. Die Zürcher Abgründe führten also nicht in die Tiefe hinab, sondern nach hinten, in eine andere der drei Dimensionen. Orte der Verwirrung, der Vieldeutigkeit, die an die Alptraum-Szenerien der imaginierten *Carceri* von Piranesi erinnern, finden sich immer wieder im bühnenbild-

nerischen Werk von Hans Dieter Schaal. Für die in der Oper *Divara* von Azio Corghi dargestellten schaurigen ideologischen Verirrungen der Wiedertäufer, die in eine Diktatur münden und ein grauenhaftes Ende finden, hat Schaal eine Überwachungs-, Fallen- und Gefängnisarchitektur von bedrückender Ausweglosigkeit, ein Sinn-Bild psychischer Zustände, geschaffen (Teatro Nacional de São Carlos, Lissabon, 2001, Regie: Christof Nel).

Für Lars Noréns Stück *Nacht, Mutter des Tages* im Akademietheater Wien (1991, Regie: Guy Joosten), das den Untergang einer Familie in düsterste Bilder faßt, hat Schaal als Einheitsraum eine Wohnküche entworfen, die sich im Laufe der Aufführung klaustrophobisch zusammenschob und dabei allmählich das Elternschlafzimmer, den Ursprung des ganzen Unheils, sichtbar machte.

Ein anderes Endspiel von Norén, das Sterbe- und Verwesungsspiel *Eintagswesen* (Gent 1986, Regie: Guy Joosten), ereignete sich in einer surreal verbauten Wohnarchitektur, aus der es kein Entrinnen gab; am Ende war nur noch im Fernseher Leben: Auf dem Bildschirm sprang ein Hund endlos an einem Gitter hoch.

Theaterregisseure, die ihr Heil vorwiegend an der Oberfläche suchen, dürften mit den selbstbewußt sich einmischenden, analytischen Bühnenbildern Schaals Schwierigkeiten haben; sie müssen befürchten, daß ihre eigene Deutung dem Anspruch des Bühnenbilds nicht standhält. Für eine Persönlichkeit wie Ruth Berghaus aber konnte Schaal zum kreativen Partner werden; sie hat seine interpretatorisch avancierten Architekturen geschickt in ihre komplexen Deutungskonzepte eingebaut. Als Berghaus und Schaal an der Staatsoper Unter den Linden in Berlin 1987 Schönbergs *Moses und Aron* gestalteten, waren sie schon durch den Stoff gezwungen, über die Funktion ihres Tuns, über die Macht des puren Wortes, über die Verführungskraft der Bilder und der Musik und über den verhängnisvollen Mißbrauch beider Extreme nachzudenken. Moses, der Gesetzgeber, der fanatische Mann des Wortes, der irdische Vertreter eines strengen, unsichtbaren Gottes, glaubt alle Bilder verbieten und die Sinne unterdrücken zu müssen. Er verurteilt seinen Bruder Aron zum Tode, der das Volk in seiner Abwesenheit mit Götzenbildern und sinnlichen Genüssen ruhigstellen wollte, aber einen gefährlichen orgiastischen Furor provozierte. Zwei extrem gegensätzliche Prinzipien prallen hier aufeinander. Schönberg, der Textautor und Komponist, stellte sich moralisch zwar auf die Seite des Wortmenschen Moses, der sich in der Oper ausschließlich im spröden Sprechgesang äußern darf – Moses hätte die Oper über seine Mission selbstverständlich verboten –; als Komponist aber spendierte Schönberg der heidnischen Gegenseite, die sich in Musik und Tänzen ergeht, eine geradezu rauschhafte Fülle an sinnlichster Gegenwart. Berghaus und Schaal, die den Gegensatz bildhaft auf die Bühne bringen mußten, stellten sich zwangsläufig noch entschiedener auf die Seite Arons, des Künstlers und Sinnenmenschen. Sie erfanden die Aktionen und Bilder zu den gegenstandsfreien Bewegungen der Musik, ohne die Aufführungen des Werks auf Bühnen sinnlos wären. Schaal, der Bildermacher, war also der Aron der Aufführung. Er legte die Mängel der Gegenseite bloß, entlarvte mit seinen visuellen Mitteln die Inhumanität des reli-

and also when realizing his designs, about the nature of the theatre and the effective force of built scenes. An opera that itself tries to tell the story of the theatre and theatrical performance in telling examples must have been like a challenge for him to think about and explain his own craft. So for the world première of Franz Hummel's opera *Der Intendant* (»The Director«) in the Bundeskunsthalle in Bonn he designed a demonstratively simple primal stage that could have been interpreted in a number of ways. It was a slightly inclined round disc, raised above the level of the main stage, a stage on the stage, a podium made of boards, signifying »the world«. There have been simple playing areas in all the theatre's great epochs. The old idea that the world was a floating disc lives on here symbolically. Wieland Wagner, when reviving the Bayreuth festival after the Second World War, reduced his grandfather's stage cosmos to similarly abstract basic forms, thus writing a chapter of theatrical history: the circular area marked out as if by a compass on the stage became a place for mythical events, it was like an altar table raised above the profane everyday world. In Bonn, Schaal grouped all kinds of everyday objects ironically around this central round cultic disc and had all the characters from the composed historical parade – the legendary heroes of theatrical history – emerge and disappear again through a round hole in the middle of the disc, from one of those shafts that we know from Schaal's other stage sets. This shaft leading into the depths of history was thus the birth channel through which the protagonists came from the past into the present. But the round disc was like an island on which the cultic event – the theatrical ceremony – could happen; it embodied every conceivable stage set, it was the abstract primal form of all rooms. Geometrical discs like this, islands, floe-like earth structures as places on which action can happen occur again and again in Schaal's work.

Die Entführung aus dem Serail (Il Seraglio) in the Lübeck theatre (1999, director: Jürgen Tamchina) took place on a round podium like this, slightly rising towards the back of the stage; it was symmetrically equipped with well trimmed, spherical hedges and a trough to sit in, and thus suggested a well-tended garden, an ordered world, an island of the blessed, though admittedly it had become a prison for the protagonists. It was only at the end that a view opened up over the edge of the dish to the horizon, to the rescuing distance.

The next step in the objectification process takes us firmly into the third dimension in Schaal's case, producing the sheltering hollow cube, the primal house, the cubic symbol of architecture, the city and the built world. Schaal drew a great deal of significance from this type in his early drawings and then later in the theatre as well. For example, he brought the large number of ostentatiously ancient Roman settings for Mozart's *La Clemenza di Tito* (»The Clemency of Titus«) to life in the theatre in Ulm (2000, director: Arila Siegert) by using what was effectively a kinetic stage set: two mobile, revolving cubic buildings, closed on three sides, and offering a view of a rising flight of steps on the fourth side, were turned to relate to each other or pulled apart by stagehands during the production in such a way that they seemed to suggest all sorts of urban situations – alleyways, courtyards, palaces. squares. The stage set became a self-confident partner of the music; the ballet of the buildings brought the stage into a vibrant state, and provided the third dimension for the continuing movement of the music and the performers.

In another Mozart opera, Schaal made the elements of the stage set develop further in terms of their own laws in the course of the performance, in fact the audience sometimes had the impression that the architectural items were coupling on the open stage and creating offspring, which gave the effect of a humorous and surreal paraphrase of the openly expressed desires of the principal characters. In *The Magic Flute* in the Wiesbaden Staatstheater (1996, director: Dominik Neuner), an abstract, empty building that could have derived from the librettist Schikaneder's summerhouse or from the cage used by the bird-catcher Papageno, became the starting point for an extremely pleasurable proliferation of motifs. A constant stream of new birdhouses, nesting boxes, little temples and summerhouses, all of which seemed to come from the same architectural family, shot up out of the earth next to each other like mushrooms, and the happily united couples finally moved into them. Architecture that proliferates and breeds naturally, as a creative counterpart to a stage plot that portrays young people growing up and starting to fall in love – a stage set could hardly respond in a more lively fashion to the emotional events that are being acted out on stage.

In the two performances of Wagner's *Tannhäuser* in Braunschweig and Wiesbaden (1993 and 2001, director: Dominik Neuner) a cubic building, rising through the full height of the stage and suggested by walls completely filled with windows, became the setting for the courtly events on the Wartburg and at the same time a dividing wall between the incompatible worlds of the Wartburg and the Venusberg, which existed almost next door to each other. The duality of earthly existence, as portrayed by Wagner, thus became almost physically tangible on the stage. In fact in Wiesbaden, *Tannhäuser* additionally demonstrated frantic lurching between the zones by trying to drag the instrument he needed as singer – a grand piano – between the two areas. Stage sets as psychological spaces, as symbols of exploding or imploding passion.

For Verdi's *Rigoletto* in Münster (1995, director: Dominik Neuner), Schaal built a »space trap«, a shaft tapering in a wedge-shape towards the bottom, additionally distorted by furniture, ladders and horizontal beams. Its light apertures offered no sort of view into the open air, a cauldron of lust and cynicism, in which the master of ceremonies, the court jester Rigoletto, has trapped himself. In Debussy's operatic fragment *The Fall of the House of Usher*, after Edgar Allan Poe, the main character, Roderick, compares his own physical condition with the rotting stones of his ruinous dwelling, within whose walls fate takes its cruel course. So even Poe himself expressly celebrated architecture as the mirror of the soul, as the unfeeling accomplice of decline and fall. Debussy identified himself with

giösen Fundamentalismus, deutete an, wohin die fanatische Wortgläubigkeit und die kompromißlose Gesetzestreue führen: nicht in das von Moses versprochene »Land, wo Milch und Honig fließen«, sondern aus der kollektiven Gefangenschaft in ein neues Gefängnis, in die Diktatur der Verbote, in die Sterilität der Ordnung: Die Gesetzeswelt des Moses gerann in Berlin zum Inneren eines riesigen Banktresors, dessen Wände aus verschlossenen Schließfächern bestanden. Später tauchte eine Stufenpyramide auf, in deren Fenstern bekannte und doch rätselhafte Schreckensbilder aus unserer jüngeren Vergangenheit aufschienen. Gegen Ende dann begann eine riesige Elektrospule – ein Energieblock, ein Brennstabelement? – beunruhigend über den Menschen zu strahlen: Das Verhängnis, das durch die Militanz und die Inhumanität des verabsolutierten Geistes heraufbeschworen worden war, nahm seinen Lauf.

Hans Dieter Schaal hat wie kein anderer seiner Berufskollegen in den theoretischen und bildnerischen Vorüberlegungen zu seinen Bühnenbildern, aber auch bei der Bühnengestaltung selber über die Daseinsformen auf dem Theater und über die Wirkungskräfte gebauter Szenen reflektiert. Eine Oper, die selber die Geschichte des Theaters und der theatralischen Darbietungsformen in andeutenden Beispielen nachzuerzählen versucht, mußte für ihn wie eine Aufforderung sein, sich des eigenen Gewerbes in besonderer Weise reflektierend und klärend zu versichern. So hat er für die Uraufführung von Franz Hummels Oper *Der Intendant* ,1997, in der Bundeskunsthalle in Bonn eine demonstrativ einfache und vielfältig deutbare Ur-Bühne entworfen, eine aus dem Bühnenboden herausgehobene, leicht geneigte runde Scheibe, eine Bühne auf der Bühne, ein Podium aus Brettern, das »die Welt bedeutet«. In allen großen Epochen des Theaters hat es solche schlichte Spielpodien gegeben. Die alte Vorstellung, daß die Welt eine schwimmende Scheibe sei, lebt hier symbolisch weiter. Auch Wieland Wagner hat nach dem Zweiten Weltkrieg bei der Wiederbelebung der Bayreuther Festspiele den Bühnenkosmos seines Großvaters auf ähnlich abstrahierte Grundformen reduziert und damit Theatergeschichte geschrieben: Die geometrisch ausgezirkelte Fläche auf der Bühne wurde zum Ort des mythischen Geschehens, sie war wie die Mensa eines Altars herausgehoben aus der profanen Alltagswelt. Schaal gruppierte in Bonn alle möglichen Gebrauchsgegenstände ironisch locker um diese zentrale runde Scheibe des Kults und ließ alle Figuren der komponierten historischen Parade – die legendären Heroen der Theatergeschichte – durch ein rundes Loch in der Mitte der Scheibe, einen jener Schächte, die wir aus anderen Bühnenbildern von Schaal kennen, auftreten und wieder verschwinden. Dieser Schacht in die Tiefe der Geschichte war also der Geburtskanal, durch den die Protagonisten aus der Vergangenheit in die Gegenwart hinaufstiegen. Die runde Scheibe aber war wie eine Insel, auf der sich das kultische Ereignis – die Theaterzeremonie – ereignen konnte; sie verkörperte alle nur denkbaren Bühnenbilder, war die abstrakte Urform aller Räume. Immer wieder tauchten solche geometrischen Scheiben, solche Inseln, solche schollenartigen Erdgebilde als Spielorte in den Bühnenbildern von Schaal auf.

Die Entführung aus dem Serail im Theater Lübeck (1999, Regie: Jürgen Tamchina) fand auf einem solchen nach hinten leicht ansteigenden Rundpodium statt; es war mit wohlbeschnittenen Heckenkugeln und einer Sitzmulde symmetrisch bestückt, suggerierte also einen gepflegten Garten, eine wohlgeordnete Welt, eine Insel der Seligen, die freilich für die Protagonisten zum Gefängnis geworden war. Erst am Ende öffnete sich der Blick über den Schüsselrand hinaus auf den Horizont, in die rettende Ferne.

Die nächste Stufe der Vergegenständlichung führt bei Schaal entschieden in die dritte Dimension, sie bringt den bergenden hohlen Würfel hervor, das Ur-Haus, das kubisch stilisierte Sinn-Bild für Architektur, Zivilisation, Stadt und gebaute Welt. Schaal hat diesem Typus schon in seinen frühen Zeichnungen und dann später auch auf dem Theater immer wieder neue Deutungen abgewonnen. Die Vielzahl bombastischer altrömischer Spielorte in Mozarts *La clemenza di Tito* etwa wurde von Schaal im Ulmer Theater (2000, Regie: Arila Siegert) durch ein quasi kinetisches Bühnenbild lebendig gemacht: Zwei bewegliche, drehbare Würfelhäuser, die auf drei Seiten geschlossen waren und auf der vierten Seite jeweils Einblick auf einen ansteigenden Treppenlauf gewährten, wurden während der Aufführung von Bühnenarbeitern so aufeinander zugedreht oder auseinander gezogen, daß sie alle möglichen städtischen Situationen – Gassen, Höfe, Paläste, Plätze – zu suggerieren schienen. Das Bühnenbild wurde zum selbstbewußten Partner der Musik; das Häuser-Ballett brachte den Bühnenraum in Schwingung, es lieferte die dritte Dimension zu den fortlaufenden Bewegungen der Musik und der Darsteller.

In einer anderen Oper von Mozart ließ Schaal die Elemente des Bühnenbilds im Lauf der Aufführung sich nach eigenen Gesetzen märchenhaft weiterentwickeln, ja der Zuschauer hatte zeitweilig den Eindruck, daß die Architekturstücke sich auf offener Bühne paaren und Nachwuchs zeugen, was wie eine humoristisch-surreale Paraphrase auf die offen geäußerten Sehnsüchte der Hauptfiguren wirkte. In der *Zauberflöte* im Staatstheater Wiesbaden (1996, Regie: Dominik Neuner) wurde ein abstrahiertes, offenes leeres Haus, das sich äußerlich vom Gartenhaus des Librettisten Schikaneder oder aber vom Vogelkäfig des Vogelfängers Papageno ableiten ließ, zum Ausgangspunkt für eine höchst vergnügliche Motiv-Vermehrung. Immer neue Vogelhäuser, Nistkästen, Tempelchen und Lustgebäude, die der gleichen architektonischen Familie zu entstammen schienen, sprossen wie Pilze neben- und hintereinander aus der Erde und wurden am Ende von den glücklich vereinten Paaren bezogen. Architektur, die naturhaft wuchert und sich vermehrt, als bildnerisches Pendant für eine Märchenhandlung, die das Erwachsenwerden und die aufkeimende Liebe junger Menschen schildert – lebendiger kann ein Bühnenbild kaum reagieren auf die emotionalen Ereignisse einer Bühnenhandlung.

In den beiden Aufführungen von Wagners *Tannhäuser* in Braunschweig und Wiesbaden (1993 und 2001, Regie: Dominik Neuner) wurde jeweils ein mit bühnenhohen, durchfensterten Wänden angedeuteter Hauskubus zum Schauplatz für das höfisch gesittete Geschehen auf der Wartburg und gleichzeitig zur Trennwand

the decadent male leading figure, his ruinous existence and bizarre inclinations. And so Schaal must have felt that he was confirmed in his method of psychological illustration by the material; at the Stuttgart Staatsoper (1996, director: Christof Nel), all he had to do was set up the crumbling walls that are celebrated in such detail, in order to capture the psychological condition of the characters visually. He built a disturbing three-dimensional cross-bred structure, a dark, inhospitable cube behind whose walls a second, lighter layer of space with windows rose up into nowhere. It was never quite clear from all this where the empire of the dead began and where it ended. Rooms as transitional places, as zones that belong first to one and then to another world, according to the lighting – in Schaal's work we always encounter them where death or the hereafter overshadow the present. »Every man is an abyss. It makes you dizzy to look down into it.« Schaal and Ruth Berghaus made this terrible statement from Büchner's *Woyzeck* the key to their expressive interpretation of Alban Berg's *Wozzeck*. For them, Wozzeck had finally arrived in the present, in the nightmare world of the modern city. The absurdity of human existence was manifested in solid concrete, in vertiginous perspectives and stumbling new buildings. Architecture as aggression, as a real threat.

In the version at the Staatsoper in Berlin (1984) the wall that sealed everything off at the beginning rose to reveal a labyrinth of tilting façades, balconies, terraces, gaps and courtyards to the spectator; one of the buildings was torn apart in the middle, and a motorway bridge thrust forward out of the background like a tank. In the version for the Opéra de Paris (1985) it was a monumental sculpture of a staircase structure suspended on the outside that opened up and revealed the expressionist tangle of buildings. Thus the city became a vessel for human fears.

But architecture is also capable of movements of great lightness and playful comedy for Schaal. For Verdi's *Falstaff* at the Frankfurt opera house (2000, director: Katrin Hilbe) Schaal built a kind of hotel lobby, a transit area that seemed to give quite natural access to all the locations needed, and with the most elegant logic made Falstaff the proprietor of an establishment that had seen better days.

Büchner's comedy *Leonce und Lena* at the Nationaltheater in Mannheim (1989, director: Nicolas Brieger) was set in an open hall in which a series of functionally meaningless, confusingly mirrored revolving doors invite the characters to involve themselves in absurd, game-like actions. This made the stage into a gigantic pinball machine in which the characters were hurled aimlessly to and fro like balls. But it was also possible to see the whole thing as a gigantic playground for adults with a lot of roundabouts. In any case, the fanciful, bored nihilism of the characters found a lavish setting in which to be brought into play in Schaal's stage design.

Schaal also found a powerfully eloquent image for his Leipzig interpretation (1999, director: Nicolas Brieger) of the splendid range of cheerful folk characters displayed by Smetana in his comic opera *The Bartered Bride*. He shifted the

events in the village out of 19th century Bohemia into the post-socialist Czech Republic, and allowed it to blossom in satirical cheerfulness in an atmosphere that seemed strange at a first glance but soon opened up a whole range of comic possibilities. The public festival took place under a half-finished motorway bridge; capitalism was starting to overwhelm the old orders. The young people of the village cruised around on upright motorbikes. The piles of tar-barrels changed into beer barrels where necessary, and the pushy marriage-broker Kezal became a Western investment advisor who turned out to be no less tiresome. So the stage set was a central component of the interpretation, and not just a pleasing and inconspicuous foil in front of which events could develop at will.

Some particularly powerful pictorial metaphors from other operas remain to be mentioned: the space ship, for example, in whose vaulted belly Ferruccio Busoni's *Doktor Faustus* set off on a fantastic journey through time (Nuremberg 1998, director: Jürgen Tamchina); or the surreal urban collage with the slanting marble plane, the concrete furniture let into it, the escalator going upwards and the gigantic porch that Schaal created for the sexual drama in Alban Berg's *Lulu* (Brussels opera house 1988, director: Ruth Berghaus).

But finally we would like to turn to the cosmos of Wagner's *The Ring of the Nibelung*, which any man of the theatre would be bound to see as one of the greatest artistic challenges, in order to convey something of Schaal's interpretative method once more.

For his first confrontation with the material – 1996 at the Nuremberg opera house (director: Niels-Peter Rudolph) – only *The Rhinegold*, in other words the one-act »preliminary evening« of the stage festival play was to be designed. Here Schaal designed his look back into mythical prehistory as an archaeological section through the accumulated layers of material and consciousness: the various places in which the action takes place are like illuminated mole tunnels cut alongside, above and below each other in the piece of dark earth that has been opened up in front of the spectators. The Rhine Maidens moved in a long tube with naturally soft curves, like a glowing condom in the dark belly of the earth. The underground world of Nibelheim was suggested by a vertical slit in the wall of earth, a small light-shaft thrusting down from above. And here Valhalla was a vaulted niche in the mountain wall, with a ramp leading up to it.

For the full *Ring* cycle in Mannheim (1999/ 2000, director: Martin Schüler), which managed to acquire the status of a secret tip among the travelling Wagner fraternity – because of the conductors as well –, Schaal designed a uniform frame that revealed new insights into the phases of decline on each evening. A brutalist concrete wall, quite clearly a product of Modernism, and triggering associations with bunkers and the Siegfried Line, rose and fell in front of the action. A concrete seat was inset in front of the wall, and here gods waited from time to time for their appearance inside in the realm of myth. And then the natural settings of the tetralogy appeared behind the concrete wall. They were all framed architecturally and geometrically, and

zwischen den unvereinbaren Welten Wartburg und Venusberg, die quasi Tür an Tür existierten. Durch die vielen Öffnungen in der Wand nahmen die beiden polarisierten Bereiche aufeinander Bezug. Die Doppelschichtigkeit der irdischen Existenz, wie sie Wagner schildert, wurde auf der Bühne also geradezu physisch greifbar. Ja in Wiesbaden stellte Tannhäuser sein verzweifeltes Hin- und Hertaumeln zwischen den Zonen zusätzlich drastisch zur Schau, als er versuchte, sein Sänger-Instrument – einen Flügel – aus der einen Zone in die andere hinüberzuzerren. Bühnenbilder als Räume der Seele, als Sinnbilder explodierender oder implodierender Leidenschaften.

Für Verdis *Rigoletto* in Münster (1995, Regie: Dominik Neuner) hat Schaal eine »Raumfalle« gebaut, einen keilartig sich nach unten verengenden, durch Möbel, Leitern und querlaufende Balken zusätzlich verstellten Schacht, der durch seine Lichtluken keinen Ausblick ins Freie gewährte, einen Kessel der Lüste und der Zynismen, in dem sich der Zeremonienmeister, der Hofnarr Rigoletto, selber verfing. In Debussys Opernfragment *Der Untergang des Hauses Usher* nach Edgar Allan Poe vergleicht die Hauptfigur Roderick ihren eigenen physischen Zustand mit den verotteten Steinen des ruinösen Schlosses, in dessen Mauern das Schicksal seinen grausigen Lauf nimmt. Schon Poe hat also ausdrücklich die Architektur als den Spiegel der Seele, als den gefühllosen Kumpan des Untergangs besungen. Debussy identifizierte sich mit der dekadenten männlichen Hauptfigur, ihrer ruinösen Existenz und ihren bizarren Neigungen. Schaal mußte sich also schon durch den Stoff in seiner psychologisierenden Bebilderungsmethode bestätigt sehen; er mußte an der Staatsoper Stuttgart (1996, Regie: Christof Nel) nur die ausführlich besungenen maroden Mauern hinzustellen, um die psychischen Zustände der Figuren ins Bild zu bannen. Er baute einen irritierenden Raumzwitter, einen dunklen, unwohnlichen Kubus, hinter dessen Wänden sich eine zweite, hellere Raumschicht mit Fenstern ins Nirgendwo auftat. Wo das Totenreich begann und wo es aufhörte, wurde dabei nicht ganz geklärt. Räume als Orte des Übergangs, als Zonen, die je nach Beleuchtung mal zur einen, mal zur anderen Welt gehören – wir sind ihnen bei Schaal immer dort begegnet, wo der Tod oder das Jenseits die Gegenwart überschatteten. »Jeder Mensch ist ein Abgrund. Es schwindelt einem, wenn man hinabsieht.« Dieser ungeheuerliche Satz aus Büchners *Woyzeck* wurde für Schaal und Ruth Berghaus zum Anspruch für ihre hochexpressiven Ausdeutungen des *Wozzeck* von Alban Berg. Wozzeck war bei ihnen endgültig in der Gegenwart, in der Alptraumwelt der modernen Großstadt angekommen. Die Absurdität des menschlichen Daseins wurde in massivem Beton, in stürzenden Perspektiven und strauchelnden Neubauten manifest. Architektur als Aggression, als reale Bedrohung.

Bei der Fassung an der Staatsoper Berlin (1984) tat sich, sobald die abriegelnde Betonwand des Anfangs in die Höhe gefahren war, ein Labyrinth von kippenden Fassaden, Balkonen, Terrassen, Durchlässen und Höfen vor dem Betrachter auf; eines der Häuser wurde in der Mitte auseinandergerissen, und aus dem Hintergrund schob sich eine Autobahnbrücke wie ein Panzer nach vorn. In der Fassung für die Opéra de Paris

(1985) war es die monumentale Skulptur eines außen hängenden Treppenbauwerks, die sich im Lauf der Aufführung teilte und den Blick auf das expressionistische Bautengewirr freigab. Der Stadtraum wurde so zum Gefäß der menschlichen Ängste.

Architektur ist bei Schaal aber auch zu Bewegungen von hoher Leichtigkeit und verspielter Komik fähig. Für Verdis *Falstaff* in der Oper Frankfurt (2000, Regie: Katrin Hilbe) hat Schaal eine Art Hotellobby gebaut, einen Durchgangsraum, der alle benötigten Örtlichkeiten ganz natürlich zu erschließen schien und Falstaff in schönster Logik zum Insassen eines Etablissements machte, das seine besten Tage schon hinter sich hat.

Büchners Lustspiel *Leonce und Lena* im Nationaltheater Mannheim (1989, Regie: Nicolas Brieger) ereignete sich in einer offenen Halle, in der eine Reihe funktional sinnloser, verwirrend spiegelnder Drehtüren die Figuren zu absurden spielerischen Aktionen einluden. Die Bühne wurde so zu einem riesigen Flipperautomaten, in dem die Figuren wie Kugeln ziellos hin- und hergeschleudert wurden. Man konnte das Ganze aber auch als einen großen Kinderspielplatz für Erwachsene mit vielen Karussells empfinden. Der verspielte, gelangweilte Nihilismus der Figuren jedenfalls fand ein reiches Betätigungsfeld auf der Schaalschen Bühne.

Auch für den herrlichen Reichtum volkstümlich heiterer Charakterbilder und Szenen, den Smetana in seiner Komischen Oper *Die verkaufte Braut* ausbreitet, hatte Schaal bei seiner Umsetzung in Leipzig (1999, Regie: Nicolas Brieger) ein kraftvoll sprechendes Bild gefunden. Er verlegte das dörfliche Geschehen aus dem Böhmen des 19. Jahrhunderts in das postsozialistische Tschechien und ließ es in einem auf den ersten Blick befremdlichen Ambiente, das aber bald schon eine Fülle komischer Möglichkeiten offenbarte, satirischheiter erblühen. Das Volksfest fand unter einer halbfertigen Autobahnbrücke statt; der Kapitalismus begann also die alten Ordnungen zu überrollen. Die jungen Dorfbewohner kreuzten auf steilen Motorrädern durch die Szene. Die aufgestapelten Teertonnen mutierten nach Bedarf zu Bierfässern; und aus dem aufdringlichen Heiratsvermittler Kezal wurde ein nicht weniger lästiger westlicher Anlageberater. Das Bühnenbild war also zentraler Bestandteil der Interpretation, nicht nur eine gefällig-unauffällige Folie, vor der sich das Geschehen beliebig entwickeln konnte.

Ein paar besonders kräftige Bildmetaphern aus anderen Inszenierungen wären noch zu erwähnen: das Raumschiff etwa, in dessen gewölbtem Bauch Ferruccio Busonis *Doktor Faustus* eine phantastische Zeitreise antritt (Nürnberg 1998, Regie: Jürgen Tamchina); oder die surreale Stadtcollage mit der schiefen Marmorebene, den eingelassenen Betonmöbeln, der hinaufführenden Rolltreppe und dem riesigen Windfang, die Schaal für das Drama des Sexus in Alban Bergs *Lulu* geschaffen hat (Opernhaus Brüssel 1988, Regie: Ruth Berghaus).

Doch zum Abschluß wollen wir am Kosmos von Wagners *Ring des Nibelungen*, den jeder Theatermensch als eine der größten künstlerischen Herausforderungen empfinden dürfte, noch einmal etwas von Schaals interpretatorischer Methode vermitteln.

rarely vouchsafed a glimpse of real nature beyond them.

This time the bottom of the Rhine was simulated by an oval opening, a cross-section through an underground canal, in whose watery light the Rhine Maidens tussled with Alberich. The theft of the Rhinegold and its conversion into a ring here marked a primal ecological outrage that damaged the balance between the existing orders and triggered the final decline. Nibelheim was a futuristic factory hall and Valhalla an art deco skyscraper projected on to the sky and approached via a rainbow-coloured ceremonial carpet and a gangway.

In *The Valkyrie* as well the characters moved in an extremely artificial world, wrenched into shape by engineers, star architects and designers. These surroundings helped to show the danger the characters were in and made the end that threatened them comprehensible. Hunding's hut in the first act could have been built by Richard Meier or Oswald Mathias Ungers as a villa for an industrial magnate; this made the naturally towering trunk of an ash tree, not yet used for firewood, with the heroic sword Nothung stuck into it, seem all the more strange. The »wild rocky mountains« in the second act were a rubble-strewn slanting podium behind which a precisely rounded arch segment suggested the mountains. A door in this rounded eminence afforded a glimpse from time to time beyond the artificial geometrical world to the naturally jagged mountain-tops and the setting sun.

The Valkyries' rock of the third act, which also had an important part to play in the other two evenings, was not the mildly implausible mountain-top that Wagner asked for with an entrance to a cave at the side, but the cave itself, a kind of air-bubble in the summit of the mountain, with an oval aperture looking up at the sky; a protecting container that became a prison for some of its inhabitants. This place triggered a number of interpreting associations: it figured as an observatory, as an artillery battery, a bunker, fortress, germ cell and – when the fire was flickering around it – even as a yawning crater; with its shaft leading to the open air and the tunnel with steps leading upwards it made a particularly clear and impressive statement about the complexities of this world.

Even Mime's cave in the wood (in the first act of *Siegfried*) was almost architecturally framed by the tree-trunks piled one on top of the other. The closed wall of firewood then parted in Act Two to reveal the dragon's cave. Then finally in *The Twilight of the Gods*, the hall of the Gibichungs, which already reflects the power relationships after the fall of the gods, was a cold marble hotel lobby of Bauhaus-like austerity. The little pile of wood by the fireplace was a further ironic reference to the pictorial motif that made its first appearance in Hunding's hut, where Siegfried was conceived, and was then further spun out in Mime's cave, where Siegfried was brought up. A large window opened on to the landscape of the Rhine, but finally also revealed a tilted version of Mies van der Rohe's Seagram Building: so as the skyscraper of architectural Utopia was visibly collapsing, so were the machinations and Utopias of the gods and their earthly henchmen.

And so Schaal keeps hot on the heels of Wagner's gloomy ideological message with his distinctive stage pictures, but he also repeatedly risks breaking away and shifting the stage events unmistakably into the present, and looking for ways of interpreting the material that certainly not all directors would feel able to follow.

Thus it is not surprising that Schaal – significantly on the stage of the Bauhaus in Dessau – conceived a stage work in 1998 in which the action is no longer determined by words and music, but by the surrounding architecture, the empty pictorial space, the stage set. In *Stadträume* (»Urban Spaces«, director: Arila Siegert), an empty space seems to breathe life into the three characters who enter one after the other and gravitate slowly towards each other, and in combination with the force of gravity they are stimulated in a way that finally leads to a highly charged ballet. And so all the emotions develop from the built opposite number that surrounds them, from the almost electrical tension in the closed space of the stage. The space shapes the life. Or, put poetically: life – a space.

And so it would be only natural if Schaal's stage sets were to determine the movements of the people involved some time at a performance in an opera house, if Hans Dieter Schaal himself were to take over the role of director on one of his stages.

Bei der ersten Konfrontation mit dem Stoff – 1996 an der Oper in Nürnberg (Regie: Niels-Peter Rudolph) – war nur *Das Rheingold*, also der einaktige »Vorabend« des Bühnenfestspiels, zu gestalten. Hier hat Schaal den Blick zurück in die mythische Vorzeit als einen archäologischen Schnitt durch die angelagerten Stoff- und Bewußtseinsschichten gestaltet: Die verschiedenen Handlungsorte sind wie beleuchtete Maulwurfsgänge neben- und übereinander in das vor dem Zuschauer aufgeschnittene dunkle Stück Erde hineinmodelliert. Die Rheintöchter bewegten sich in einem langen, naturhaft weich geschwungenen Schlauch, einem lichthaltigen Riesenkondom durch den dunklen Bauch der Erde. Die Unterwelt von Nibelheim wurde durch einen senkrechten Schlitz in der Erdwand, einen von oben herunterstürzenden schmalen Lichtschacht suggeriert. Und Walhall war hier eine gewölbte Nische in der Bergwand, zu der eine Rampe emporführte.

Für die Gesamtaufführung des *Rings* in Mannheim (1999/2000, Regie: Martin Schüler), die sich bei der reisenden Wagner-Gemeinde – auch der Dirigenten wegen – den Ruf eines Geheimtips erwerben konnte, hat Schaal einen einheitlichen Rahmen entworfen, der an jedem Abend neue Ausblicke in die Phasen des Untergangs freigab. Eine brutalistische Betonwand, die eindeutig der Moderne zugehörte und Assoziationen an Bunker und Westwall auslöste, hob und senkte sich über dem Geschehen. Vor ihr war seitlich eine Sitznische hinbetoniert, in der ab und zu Götter auf ihren Auftritt drinnen im Reich des Mythos warteten. Hinter der Betonwand taten sich dann die Naturschauplätze der Tetralogie auf, die allesamt architektonisch-geometrisch gefaßt waren, nur vereinzelt Ausblicke in die reale Natur dahinter zuließen.

Der Grund des Rheins wurde diesmal durch eine ovale Öffnung simuliert, einen Querschnitt durch einen unterirdischen Kanal, in dessen wässrigem Schein die Rheintöchter sich mit Alberich balgten. Der Raub des Rheingolds aus seiner Umgebung und die Umarbeitung zum Ring markierten hier einen ökologischen Ur-Frevel, der das Gleichgewicht zwischen den bestehenden Größenordnungen beschädigte und den Untergang auslöste. Nibelheim war eine futuristische Fabrikhalle und Walhall ein Art-Déco-Wolkenkratzer, der an den Himmel projiziert war und über einen regenbogenfarbigen Ehrenteppich und eine Gangway angesteuert wurde.

Auch in der *Walküre* bewegten sich die Figuren in einer von Ingenieuren, Stararchitekten und Designern gewaltsam zurechtgezwungenen, extrem künstlichen Welt, die ihre Gefährdung mit ausstellte, ihr drohendes Ende verständlich machte. Hundings Hütte im ersten Aufzug hätte von Richard Meier oder Oswald Mathias Ungers als Villa für einen Industriemagnaten errichtet worden sein können; umso befremdlicher nahm sich der noch nicht im Kamin verfeuerte naturhaft ragende Eschenstamm in der Mitte des Salons aus, in dem das Heldenschwert Nothung steckte. Das »Wilde Felsgebirge« im zweiten Aufzug war ein trümmerbedecktes schiefes Podium, hinter dem ein exakt gerundeter Segmentbogen das Gebirge andeutete. Eine Tür in dieser runden Erhebung ließ hin und wieder den Blick aus der geometristischen Kunstwelt hinaus auf natürlich gezackte Berggipfel und Sonnenuntergänge entweichen.

Der Walkürenfels des dritten Aufzugs, der auch an den beiden übrigen Abenden noch eine bedeutsame Rolle spielte, war nicht der von Wagner gewünschte, etwas unglaubwürdige Berggipfel mit dem seitlich gelegenen Höhleneingang, sondern die Höhle selber, eine Art Luftblase im Gipfel des Bergs, mit einer ovalen Öffnung nach oben zum Himmel; ein schützendes Behältnis, das für einige seiner Bewohner zum Gefängnis wurde. Dieser Ort löste viele interpretierende Assoziationen aus: Er figurierte als Observatorium, als Geschützbatterie, Bunker, Festung, Keimzelle und – wenn das Feuer um ihn loderte – sogar als Kraterschlund; er machte mit seinem Schacht ins Freie und mit dem hinaufführenden Treppentunnel die Doppelschichtigkeit dieser Welt besonders eindrucksvoll deutlich.

Selbst Mimes Höhle im Wald (im ersten Aufzug des *Siegfried*) wurde durch die übereinandergestapelten Baumstämme quasi architektonisch gefaßt. Die geschlossene Wand aus Brennholz teilte sich dann im zweiten Aufzug und brachte die Drachenhöhle ins Blickfeld. Die Halle der Gibichungen in der *Götterdämmerung* schließlich, die schon die Machtverhältnisse nach dem Untergang der Götter widerspiegelte, war eine marmorkalte Hotellobby von bauhausstrengen Formen. Der kleine Holzstapel am Kamin nahm noch einmal ironisch Bezug auf das Bildmotiv, das in Hundings Hütte, dem Ort der Zeugung Siegfrieds, angestimmt und in Mimes Höhle, dem Ort von Siegfrieds Jugend, weitergesponnen wurde. Ein großes Fenster öffnete sich hinaus auf die Rheinlandschaft, ließ am Ende aber das gekippte Seagram Building von Mies van der Rohe aufscheinen: So wie die Architektur-Utopie Hochhaus sichtbar scheiterte, so scheiterten auch die Machenschaften und Utopien der Götter und ihrer irdischen Handlanger.

Schaal bleibt der düsteren ideologischen Botschaft Wagners mit seinen ausgeprägten Bühnenbildern also dicht auf den Fersen, er riskiert aber auch immer wieder Ausbrüche, die das Bühnengeschehen in die Gegenwart herüberreißen und Wege der Interpretation suchen, auf denen sicher nicht alle Regisseure zu folgen vermögen.

So wundert es einen nicht, daß Schaal – bezeichnenderweise auf der Bühne am Bauhaus in Dessau – 1998 ein Bühnenwerk konzipiert hat, in dem nicht mehr Worte und Musik die Handlung bestimmen, sondern die umgebende Architektur, der leere Bildraum, das Bühnenbild. In *Stadträume* (Regie: Arila Siegert) scheint ein leerer Raum die nacheinander auftretenden und sich aufeinanderzubewegenden drei Figuren langsam mit Leben zu füllen und im Verein mit der Schwerkraft zu Bewegungen zu animieren, die schließlich in ein erotisch hochgespanntes Bewegungsballett münden. Alle Emotionen entwickeln sich also aus dem gebauten Gegenüber, aus der quasi elektrischen Spannung in dem geschlossenen Raum der Bühne. Der Raum formt das Leben. Oder, poetisch ausgedrückt: Das Leben – ein Raum.

Es wäre also nur natürlich, wenn die Schaalschen Bühnenbilder irgendwann auch bei einer Aufführung in einem Opernhaus die Bewegungen der handelnden Personen bestimmen würden, wenn Hans Dieter Schaal selber auf einer seiner Bühnen die Regie übernehmen würde.

The way things are

»I can take any empty space and call it a bare stage. A man walks across this empty space, whilst someone else is watching him, and this is all that is needed for an act of theatre to be engaged.« (Peter Brook)

Every morning when we wake up, when we open our eyes, the world with all its objects, spaces and images presents itself to us as a real exterior. Inside ourselves we are still clinging on to the night's dreams. This simultaneous existence of the inside and the outside world runs through our days and indeed our whole lives as a basic drama. And it is at this intersection point that the origins of culture, religion and science also lie. Intellectual ideas occur subjectively. They are invisible to other people. A cosmos of possibilities in the subjunctive. Making them visible is one of the tasks of culture, of the fine arts, of the theatre, opera and film.

While we are asleep, and later while we are walking about and working in our own home, we are all on our own, but any move out into the street, into the public eye, has a theatrical aspect: in other people's eyes we become performers of a person who is walking out into the street. We are playing a part: when shopping, at the doctor's, in chance conversations. We can be friendly or surly, according to the mood we are in and the way we see our role.

Actor or voyeur: the everyday world with its random theatrical events is enough to keep a lot of people amused. In addition the expectations are raised that something exciting might happen that we could get involved in, so that we can forget the pressures of the world with all its subjec-

tive worries. Sporting events and pop concerts act as surrogates. Here there is no sense of conveying meaning, but excitement is guaranteed. We ask: who's won? at a sporting event right up to the last whistle. Once there's an answer to that question, the crowd disperses and we go home.

At pop concerts the communal experience is crucial; we have the same taste in music as all the people around us. The rhythm keeps all our bodies throbbing to the same beat.

Watching films in cinemas is also a mass phenomenon as a collective orientation medium, public spaces to dream in that have started to shape subjective taste and ideals.

Television has taken over the role of the prime organ for conveying information and knowledge. Almost everything, important and trivial, that happens in the world is shown there. The average American spends about seven hours per day watching television.

Nowadays going to concerts, museums, theatre, opera or ballet performances has become a habit involving the educated minority. Cultural events like these need a certain amount of effort and a readiness to concentrate hard. Anyone who goes to them will perhaps be able to avoid the endless storm of images and deluge of information that comes from the media. By addressing the experience of art, visitors are checking their own interpretation of reality. There is a chance that the conflict between inside and outside will be lifted, that both aspects will come together, and perhaps we are closer to the pulse of the world for a short moment.

Theatrical space is artificial space. Reality appears only to the extent that it applies to the action. The notion of opera goes back to the Italian

Zustandsbeschreibung

»Ich kann jeden leeren Raum nehmen und ihn eine nackte Bühne nennen. Ein Mann geht durch den Raum, während ihm ein anderer zusieht, das ist alles, was zur Theaterhandlung notwendig ist.« (Peter Brook)

Jeden Morgen, wenn wir aufwachen, wenn unsere Augen sich öffnen, stellt sich uns die Welt mit ihren Objekten, Räumen und Bildern als reales Außen entgegen. Innerlich hängen wir noch an den Träumen der Nacht. Diese gleichzeitige Existenz von Außen- und Innenwelt zieht sich als Grunddrama durch unseren Alltag und unser ganzes Leben. Hier an dieser Schnittstelle liegt auch der Ursprung der Kultur, der Religion und der Wissenschaft. Die geistigen Vorstellungen ereignen sich subjektiv. Für andere Menschen sind sie unsichtbar. Ein Möglichkeitskosmos im Konjunktiv. Ihm zur Sichtbarkeit zu verhelfen, ist eine der Aufgaben der Kultur, der bildenden Künste, des Theaters, der Oper und des Films.

Während man beim Schlafen und später beim Umhergehen und Arbeiten in der eigenen Wohnung ganz bei sich selbst ist, hat jedes Sich-Hinausbegeben auf die Straße, in die Öffentlichkeit der Stadt, einen theatralischen Aspekt: In den Augen der anderen wird man zum Darsteller eines Menschen, der die Straße betritt. Man spielt eine Rolle: beim Einkaufen, beim Arzt, beim zufälligen Gespräch. Man ist freundlich oder unwirsch, je nach Tageslaune und Rollenverständnis.

Darsteller oder Voyeur: Die Alltagswelt mit ihren zufälligen theaternahen Ereignissen reicht vielen zur Zerstreuung aus. Es wächst jedoch auch die Erwartung, daß etwas Spannendes sich ereignen möge, an dem man teilnehmen kann, um darüber das Gewicht der Welt mit all seinen subjektiven Sorgen zu vergessen. Als Surrogat dienen Sportveranstaltungen und Popkonzerte. Hier werden keine Inhalte vermittelt, nur Spannung garantiert. Beim Sport stellt sich bis zum Schlußpfiff die Frage: Wer ist der Sieger? Ist diese Frage beantwortet, geht man auseinander.

In Popkonzerten ist das Gemeinschaftserlebnis entscheidend; man hat den gleichen Musikgeschmack wie alle Umstehenden. Der Rhythmus läßt die Körper simultan beben.

Auch das Betrachten von Filmen in Kinos ist als kollektives Orientierungsmedium ein Massenphänomen, öffentliche Traumräume, die prägend für den subjektiven Geschmack und die Lebensideale geworden sind.

Informations- und Wissensvermittlung hat heute primär das Fernsehen übernommen. Nahezu alles, was sich an großen und kleinen Dingen ereignet, wird gezeigt. Etwa sieben Stunden täglich verbringt ein Durchschnittsamerikaner vor dem Fernseher.

Der Besuch von Konzerten, Museen, Theater-, Opern- oder Ballettaufführungen ist heute eher eine Gewohnheit gebildeter Minderheiten. Kulturelle Veranstaltungen wie diese erfordern eine gewisse Anstrengung und die Bereitschaft zu hoher Konzentration. Wer sie besucht, will sich vielleicht für einige Stunden dem unendlichen Bildergewitter und der Informationsflut der Medien entziehen. Durch die Auseinandersetzung mit dem Kunstereignis überprüft der Besucher seine Interpretation der Realität. Es besteht die Chance, daß sich der Gegensatz zwischen dem Innen und dem Außen aufhebt, daß beide Aspekte zusammenfließen, und vielleicht ist man für einen kurzen Moment näher am Herzschlag dieser Welt.

Der Theaterraum ist ein Kunstraum. Realität erscheint nur, sofern sie für die Handlung gebraucht wird. Der Begriff Oper geht auf das italienische Wort »opera musicale« zurück, was Musikwerk bedeutet. Es handelt sich um ein Kunstwort, das aus dem lateinischen »opus«, »opera« gebildet wurde und mit »Mühe«, »Arbeit«, aber auch mit »erarbeitetes Werk« übersetzt werden kann. Stück und Werk, herausgebrochen aus der Totalität der Realität, konzentriert, komprimiert, mit Anfang und Ende, mit einer Form wie eine plastische Figur. Das eigentliche Werk ist vor der Aufführung allerdings nur als Text oder Partitur lesbar und sonst noch ungeboren. Im Theater haucht man ihm durch die Inszenierung Leben ein, es wird sichtbar und hörbar gemacht.

phrase »opera musicale«, formed from the Latin »opus – opera«, which can be translated as »effort«, »work« or also »achieved work«. Piece and work, broken away from the totality of reality, concentrated, compressed, with a beginning and an end, with a shape and a three-dimensional figure. Of course the actual work can be read only as a text or score before the performance, and is otherwise still unborn. In the theatre life is breathed into it by the staging, it is made audible and visible.

»But the décor, the actors and the points made in the dialogue create a completely closed world in the mean time, because we cannot force our way into it, we can only see it, a unique world and a world that is a type of the human world at the same time: it is simply the world in which I live, but I am suddenly driven out of it; put in another way: I am outside. Normally a person is in the world, in the midst of things and outside it at the same time, as he can look at it.

In the case of the theatre the opposite is true: I am completely outside and I can only watch what is happening; in short, all there is here is an immediate fulfilment of the human desire to get out of oneself in order to be able to see oneself better, not as other people see one, but as one is … here on the one hand things are realized, immediate, I exist only as mere seeing, and the world as a presence is a world that has closed over itself, and I am merely its witness: I no longer have hands because I cannot seize the actor to stop him stabbing himself to death.

And so it seems to me to be the origin, the meaning of the theatre itself, to show the human world at an absolute distance, an insurmountable distance, the distance that separates me from the stage; and the actor is such a distance away that I can in fact see him, but I can never touch him or influence him in any way. …

On the other hand, when we are distanced from the décor we are also distanced from the human being, in other words, the human being we have before us and who is acting is someone whom we are aware of only through his actions, we can only get to know a character through his actions; it is precisely this that on the one hand allows us to understand the significance of the actor in the theatre, and on the other hand the very fact that we are watching the action liberates us from psychology.« (Jean-Paul Sartre)

The theatre

»The theatres are simply there, like an empty hole that has to be filled. One is afraid that the hole will become visible.« (Heiner Müller)

Two entirely different spaces face each other: the soft upholstered auditorium landscape and the empty stage encrusted with technical equipment at the periphery. Here an ordered army of seats, balconies one on top of the other, there a technoid cave, a blackish-brown stage floor with scratches, tracks and marks, walls with cables, switches, spotlights, struts, steps, lift and revolve equipment, and above this the flies as a possible sky.

Between these two spaces is the crucial, linking, framed hole that can be opened or closed by a curtain: window, door, gate, picture, eye, looking in, looking through, looking out. The proscenium arch is also an interface, the curtain plays the part of the anatomical knife and the scaffold. At the beginning the knife moves backwards. When the interface opens the spectators look into the inside of the events. They see how ideas, blood and desires are circulating.

While in the city people are almost always on the move, allowing their eyes to wander, so that new perspectives are constantly produced, theatre- and opera-goers sit in a seat that is screwed to the floor and watch the events from the same angle all the time. Seen in terms of film, theatre can offer nothing but a long shot.

As neither the auditorium nor the stage has windows, it is completely dark inside the building. Parts of the stage set and the people acting on it are picked out of this night. The light becomes a crucial fellow player. It comes in through cracks and windows, doors and holes, weak and pale or dazzlingly bright. It falls on a seated group, warm and yellow, or finds its way through invisible cracks in the ceiling in a ghostly blue. Within seconds it is possible to switch the mood from romantic to banal, common to comfortable or dramatic to objective. The theatre is not just an experimental space for the human psyche, for the expressive forms of architecture, but also for the moods that the light creates, for atmospheres.

Transitions, truth and lie. Reality and fiction. Actors pretend to be something. They are not playing themselves, but other characters. Masks as symbols of transformation. I become you, you become me. What is the truth of spaces? Do spaces act as well? People enjoy being deceived. The fascination of something that is made artificially, of the workshop character.

Surfaces are broken open in the theatre. Illusions, expressions and dreams glow. In opera, music adds sounds to the event. Then love really does exist – here and now –, and so does redemption. The structure of the intrigues becomes comprehensible, it is always other people who are tormented, tortured and killed – on our behalf. We see our life as clear as glass for a short moment, in this illuminated showcase, this shop-window at the front there.

The stage becomes a mirror: the observer can break out of the constraints of his own ego and take part in a large number of lives and events. Spectating as an expansion of the ego and also as a classification ritual in the overall flow of the world, of lives and of fates. We are no longer alone in a state of inner turmoil between good and evil, between longing for happiness and depression. The tragedies take their course. At the end everyone is a winner, because he has survived and can walk out into the street, alive.

The stage set

The space created by the stage set is above all an expressive space, built expression. It defines the atmosphere of the production.

The language of pictorial architecture is an artificial one: geometrical construction and questions of reality confront each other. People and spaces are seen as a unity. Each one suffers and distorts architecture in his own way: between a prison and a homely snail shell, between glitter-

»Aber das Dekor, die Schauspieler und die Hinweise des Dialogs bilden indessen eine vollkommen geschlossene Welt, weil wir nicht in sie eindringen können, weil wir sie nur sehen, eine einmalige Welt und eine Welt, die zugleich Typus der menschlichen Welt ist: es ist einfach die Welt, in der ich lebe, aber plötzlich bin ich daraus vertrieben; anders gesagt, ich bin draußen. Normalerweise ist ein Mensch zugleich in der Welt, mittendrin, und draußen, da er sie ja ansehen kann.

Im Fall des Theaters haben wir die Negation: ich bin völlig außerhalb und kann nur zuschauen; kurz, es gibt da einzig eine unmittelbare Erfüllung des menschlichen Verlangens, aus sich herauszukommen, um sich besser sehen zu können, nicht wie ein anderer Mensch einen sieht, sondern wie man ist. ... hier ist es auf der Stelle realisiert, unmittelbar, ich existiere nur noch als bloßes Sehen, und die Welt als Anwesenheit ist eine über sich geschlossene Welt, deren bloßer Zeuge ich bin: ich habe keine Hände mehr, da ich dem Schauspieler ja nicht in den Arm fallen kann, um ihn daran zu hindern, daß er sich ersticht.

So scheint es mir der Ursprung, der Sinn des Theaters selbst zu sein, die menschliche Welt mit einer absoluten Distanz, einer unüberwindlichen Distanz zu zeigen, der Distanz, die mich von der Bühne trennt; und der Schauspieler befindet sich in einer solchen Distanz, daß ich ihn zwar sehen, aber nie berühren noch auf ihn einwirken kann. ...

Andererseits haben wir, wenn wir uns in Distanz zum Dekor befinden, auch Distanz zum Menschen, das heißt, der Mensch, der vor uns ist und der spielt, ist jemand, den wir nur durch seine Handlungen wahrnehmen, wir können eine Figur nur durch ihre Handlungen kennenlernen; genau das bringt uns nun einerseits auf die Bedeutung des Mimen im Theater, und andererseits befreit uns eben die Tatsache, daß wir die Handlung betrachten, von der Psychologie.« (Jean-Paul Sartre)

Das Theater

»Die Theater sind eben da wie ein leeres Loch, das gefüllt werden muß. Man hat Angst, daß das Loch sichtbar wird.« (Heiner Müller)

Zwei grundverschiedene Räume stehen sich gegenüber: die weiche Polstersessel-Landschaft des Zuschauerraums und der leere, an den Rändern mit Technik überkrustete Bühnenraum. Hier eine geordnete Sesselarmee, übereinanderhängende Ränge, dort eine technoide Höhle, schwarzbrauner Bühnenboden mit Schrammen, Spuren und Zeichen, Wände mit Kabeln, Schaltern, Scheinwerfern, Gestängen, Treppen, Hebe- und Drehvorrichtungen, darüber der Schnürboden als Möglichkeitshimmel.

Zwischen diesen beiden Räumen befindet sich das entscheidende, verbindende, gerahmte, mit einem Vorhang zu öffnende und zu schließende Loch: Fenster, Tür, Tor, Bild, Auge, Einblick, Durchblick, Ausblick. Die Bühnenöffnung ist auch eine Schnittfläche, der Vorhang nimmt die Rolle des anatomischen Messers und des Schafotts ein. Am Anfang bewegt sich das Messer rückwärts. Mit dem Öffnen der Schnittfläche blickt der Zuschauer in das Innere des Geschehens. Er sieht, wie die Gedanken, das Blut und die Sehnsüchte kreisen.

Während man sich in der Stadt fast immer bewegt, die Blicke wandern läßt, so daß sich ununterbrochen neue Perspektiven ergeben, sitzt der Theater- und Opernzuschauer in einem festgeschraubten Sessel und hat stets den gleichen Blickwinkel auf das Geschehen. Filmisch gesehen, gibt es im Theater nur die Totale.

Da Zuschauer- und Bühnenraum fensterlos sind, herrscht hier vollkommene Dunkelheit. Aus dieser Nacht werden Teile des Bühnenbildes mit den handelnden Personen herausgehoben. Das Licht wird zum entscheidenden Mitspieler. Es fällt durch Ritzen und Fenster, durch Türen und Löcher, schwach und bleich oder blendend hell, warm und gelb legt es sich über eine Sitzgruppe oder dringt gespenstisch blau durch unsichtbare Spalten in der Decke ein. Innerhalb von Sekun-

ing elegance and exhausted decay. The walls, doors and windows remain indifferently silent and cold, or they join in with the events in a tiresome fashion. In each case the pictorial architecture is not alone and lonely, but it is used, caressingly or full of hatred. Surrealism is possible: black cubes are lowered, filled with snow, walls lean to the side or crown in on the figures erotically. Strange tubes crawl across floors, split walls and coil around helpless cupboards. Things live, breathe and behave obstinately. The rooms can be ancient, and have absorbed an enormous number of stories, or they are brand new, with shiny surfaces without a patina. They tell us almost nothing, except that they are young and unused.

Firmly established realities are cut to pieces and reassembled. Places for thought. Spaces that seem to be floating between the world of pedestrian zones, homes and the open space of the imagination.

Other times. Clear views. Unfocused views. Views as if through a telescope, views as if through a microscope. Trapped in a glass building, surrounded by concrete furniture, under the arch of the sky and the horizon. Stones fall down like thoughts. Birds fly through the image.

Each piece is a defined laboratory instruction: you have to be able to see whether the actors are coming into the room for the first, the tenth or the hundredth time. You have to sense whether they are strangers paying a visit or whether they live there and are comfortable there.

Exhibitionism: revealing everything without shame, emotion, sexuality, fear.

Rooms as light traps.
Patches of light on the walls. Flickering, shimmering, or rigid, precise, exact, geometrical.
Picture spaces.
Light spaces.
Shadow spaces.
Light corridors.

Shadow corridors.
Lanes of meaning.
Paths and spaces leading through things.
Consciousness spaces.
Subconscious spaces.
Classical prisons.

»… the figures have to choose a particular space for themselves in the artificial space that they define as their own, that they give up, to whom they return, in which they leave traces behind, so that they can find them again, even if they are not present themselves. If the composer surrounds his thoughts with an aura of sound, Ruth Berghaus creates a spatial aura for them. She creates a character-related sound space. Then a character reveals himself among other things by the way in which this person walks out of and through spaces, touches upon them, whether he approaches them as if to open them tentatively or blow them up violently, which way he goes and which places he avoids.«
(Sigrid Neef on Ruth Berghaus)

Perhaps the space is too confined, a vessel, a case, whose constraints the actors resist; they want to break out, they hate the walls, they work at them with their hands and feet, or the space is too big, then they feel lost and lonely. Freezing, they form their own body zone in the middle of the space.

In any case the stage architecture is staged apparent space, provisional artificial space, open for experiments on reality, fiction, inside and outside.

den lassen sich Stimmungswechsel erzeugen zwischen romantisch und banal, gemein und gemütlich oder dramatisch und sachlich. Das Theater ist nicht nur ein Experimentierraum für die menschliche Psyche, für die Expressionsformen der Architektur, sondern auch für die Stimmungslagen, die das Licht erzeugt, für Atmosphären.

Übergänge, Wahrheit und Lüge. Realität und Fiktion. Schauspieler täuschen etwas vor. Sie spielen nicht sich selbst, sondern andere Figuren. Masken als Symbole der Verwandlung. Ich werde du, du wirst ich. Was ist die Wahrheit von Räumen? Spielen Räume auch? Man läßt sich gern täuschen. Faszination des künstlich Gemachten, des Werkstatt-Charakters.

Im Theater brechen die Oberflächen auf. Illusionen, Expressionen, Träume glühen. In der Oper bringt die Musik die Ereignisse zum Klingen. Es gibt sie dann wirklich, die Liebe – hier und jetzt – die Erlösung auch. Die Struktur der Intrigen wird überschaubar, immer sind es andere, die – stellvertretend – gequält, gefoltert und getötet werden. In dieser beleuchteten Vitrine, diesem Schaufenster dort vorn, sehen wir unser Leben für einen kurzen Moment glasklar.

Der Bühnenraum wird zum Spiegel: Der Betrachter kann aus seiner eigenen Ich-Befangenheit ausbrechen, an vielen Leben und Ereignissen teilnehmen. Zuschauen als Ich-Erweiterung und auch als Einordnungritual in den Gesamtfluß der Welt, der Leben und der Schicksale. Man ist nicht mehr allein in seiner Zerrissenheit zwischen Gut und Böse, zwischen Glückssehnsucht und Niedergeschlagenheit. Die Tragödien nehmen ihren Lauf. Am Ende ist jeder ein Sieger, weil er überlebt hat und als Lebender hinaus auf die Straße treten kann.

Das Bühnenbild

Der Bühnenbildraum ist vor allem Ausdrucksraum, gebaute Expression. Er definiert die Atmosphäre der Inszenierung.

Die Sprache der Bildarchitektur ist künstlich: Geometrische Konstruktion und Realitätsfragmente begegnen einander. Strukturen entstehen und zerfallen. Personen und Räume werden als Einheit verstanden. Jeder erleidet und verzerrt die Architektur in seinem Sinne: zwischen Gefängnis und wohnlichem Schneckenhaus, zwischen spiegelnder Eleganz und marodem Zerfall. Die Wände, Türen und Fenster bleiben teilnahmslos stumm und kalt, oder sie mischen sich lästig in die Abläufe ein. In jedem Fall steht die Bildarchitektur nicht allein und einsam da, sie wird benutzt, liebkosend oder haßerfüllt. Surrealismus ist möglich: Schwarze Kuben senken sich herab, gefüllt mit Schnee, Wände neigen sich zur Seite oder bedrängen erotisch die Bewohner. Fremdartige Rohre kriechen über Fußböden, spalten Wände und umschlingen hilflose Schränke. Dinge leben, atmen und verhalten sich eigensinnig. Die Räume können uralt sein, schon viele Geschichten in sich aufgenommen haben, oder sie sind nagelneu, mit blitzenden Oberflächen ohne Patina. Sie erzählen fast nichts, außer daß sie jung und unbenutzt sind.

Festgefügte Realitäten werden zerschnitten und neu zusammengesetzt. Denkorte. Räume

wie schwebend zwischen der Welt der Fußgängerzonen, den Wohnungen und dem offenen Raum der Vorstellung.

Andere Zeiten. Klare Blicke. Unscharfe Blicke. Blicke wie durch ein Fernrohr, Blicke wie durch ein Mikroskop. Gefangen im Glasbau, umstellt von Betonmöbeln, überwölbt von Horizont und Himmel. Steine fallen herab wie Gedanken. Vögel fliegen durch das Bild.

Jedes Stück ist eine beschriebene Laboranordnung: Man muß den Darstellern anmerken, ob sie den Raum zum ersten, zum zehnten oder zum hundertsten Mal betreten. Man muß spüren, ob sie dort als Fremde zu Besuch sind, oder ob sie dort wohnen und sich wohl fühlen.

Exhibitionismus: ohne Scham alles offen legen, die Emotion, die Sexualiät, die Angst.

Räume als Lichtfallen.
Lichtflecken auf den Wänden. Flackernd, flimmernd oder starr, genau, exakt, geometrisch.
Bilderräume.
Lichträume.
Schattenräume.
Lichtkorridore.
Schattenkorridore.
Bedeutungsschneisen.
Wege und Räume durch die Dinge hindurch.
Bewußtseinsräume.
Unterbewußtseinsräume.
Klassische Gefängnisse.

»... die Figuren haben sich im Kunstraum einen bestimmten Ort zu wählen, den sie als den ihrigen kennzeichnen, den sie aufgeben, zu dem sie zurückkehren, in dem sie Spuren hinterlassen, so daß sie auffindbar bleiben, auch wenn sie selbst nicht anwesend sind. Gibt der Komponist seinen Gedanken eine klangliche Aura, verleiht die Berghaus ihnen eine räumliche. Sie schafft einen figurenbezogenen Klang-Raum. Ein Charakter offenbart sich dann unter anderem auch dadurch, wie der Mensch Räume aus- und durchschreitet, umkreist, tangiert, ob er sich ihnen vorsichtig öffnend oder gewaltsam sprengend nähert, welche Wege er geht und welche Orte er meidet.« (Sigrid Neef über Ruth Berghaus)

Vielleicht ist der Raum zu eng, ein Gefäß, eine Schatulle, gegen dessen Enge die Handelnden sich wehren; sie wollen ausbrechen, hassen die Wände, bearbeiten sie mit Händen und Füßen, oder der Raum ist zu weit, dann fühlen sie sich verloren und einsam. Frierend bilden sie ihre eigene Körperzone mitten im Raum.

In jedem Fall ist die Bühnenarchitektur inszenierter Scheinraum, provisorischer Kunstraum, offen für Experimente über Realität, Fiktion, Innen und Außen.

Der Intendant (»The Director«)
Opera by Franz Hummel based on a text by
Thomas Körner
  Kunst- und Ausstellungshalle der Bundesre-
publik Deutschland, Bonn, 1997; director: Jürgen
Tamchina, sets: Hans Dieter Schaal, costumes:
Judith Fischer, dramaturgy: Klaus Peter Kehr

This opera tries to tell the whole story of the
theatre in a witty and reflective way. Individual
aspects, images and people involved in the
enormous number of events and developments
are picked out and presented in the piece.

A slightly sloping, circular area made of
boards and resting on ruined walls was constructed as a stage in the theatre in the Bundeskunsthalle. Showcases and raised seats
grew out of the rest of the floor, which was covered with granulated material. A built collage
of archaeology and circus.

The area made up of boards is reminiscent
of the stamped-down clay on which the story
of the theatre started in prehistoric times. The
struggle between good and evil spirits was
danced out and sung here, in the middle of
the village community and to the rhythm of the
drums. As the people all watched the shamans'
ritual movements they were brought together in
a common view of the world, a collective culture.

In the Greek theatre the dancing area with the
altar of Dionysus was also central. Rites, cult,
worship, play and theatre formed a unit from the
outset. The fact that events developed alongside

this that were less weighted down with a particular view of the world (sporting events, Olympic
games, chariot races, gladiatorial sights, bull-
fights) is evidence of man's rooted desire for entertainment at all periods. The presence and the
conflict between Apollo and Dionysus, between
high and low, between great art and banal farce
determined the whole of theatrical history. Theatre was used to present power, religion and political events. As courtly entertainment it offered
living images that were able to assert themselves
against yawning emptiness and grinding boredom. At popular entertainments people laughed
themselves into a noisy community. The step to
instruction and agitation was not a large one. In
the Middle Ages, when the theatre was firmly in
the hands of the Church, the Passion plays that
were all that was on offer were intended to
strengthen the community in a Christian way of
life. In the late Middle Ages, the farcical German
Shrovetide plays, which contained every dirty
joke in the book, acted like a liberating force.

In many places, theatrical performances were
forbidden during the Reformation period as the
work of the devil. In the 16th century the Shake-
spearean stage established the bourgeois theatre and the new profession of acting. It was
from this point at the latest that written plays
were seen as high-class literature.

When opera was invented in the year 1600,
Italian noblemen and artists wanted to forge a
link with Greek tragedy and create a universal
work of art made up of literature, music, the per-

forming arts, dance, stage play, song, architecture and painting. The first opera is by Jacopo
Peri and was performed on 6 October 1600 in
Florence on the occasion of the celebrations of
the marriage of Maria de Medici to King Henry IV
of France. It is called *Eurydice*.

Since then about 50000 operas have been
written, of which only about 200 are regularly
performed today.

But back to the opera *Der Intendant* in the
Kunsthalle in Bonn. There was a hole in the middle of the central boarded area. Seen emotion-
ally, it could be equated with a dark primeval
belly giving birth. But a disrespectful and ironic
eye demoted it to a privy. As the centre of the
world, it fits in with the idea of a cosmos circling
around the ego. Equally it could stand for death,
who lies in wait everywhere, suddenly devouring
his victims.

They all appeared from this hole: Dionysus,
Harlequin, Hans Wurst, the Neuberin, characters
created by Lessing, Schiller and Goethe. And
they all disappeared back into it again, after they
had had their fun and spoken their stilted lines.

History brought back to life. Memory-space.
Ghosts. Some fleeting, fanciful, merely breaths,
other rough, coarse and unambiguous. The
great, heavy lines demand marble, and want to
be put in the museum, the others, more frivo-
lous, are swallowed up by the rubbish-bin of the
everyday.

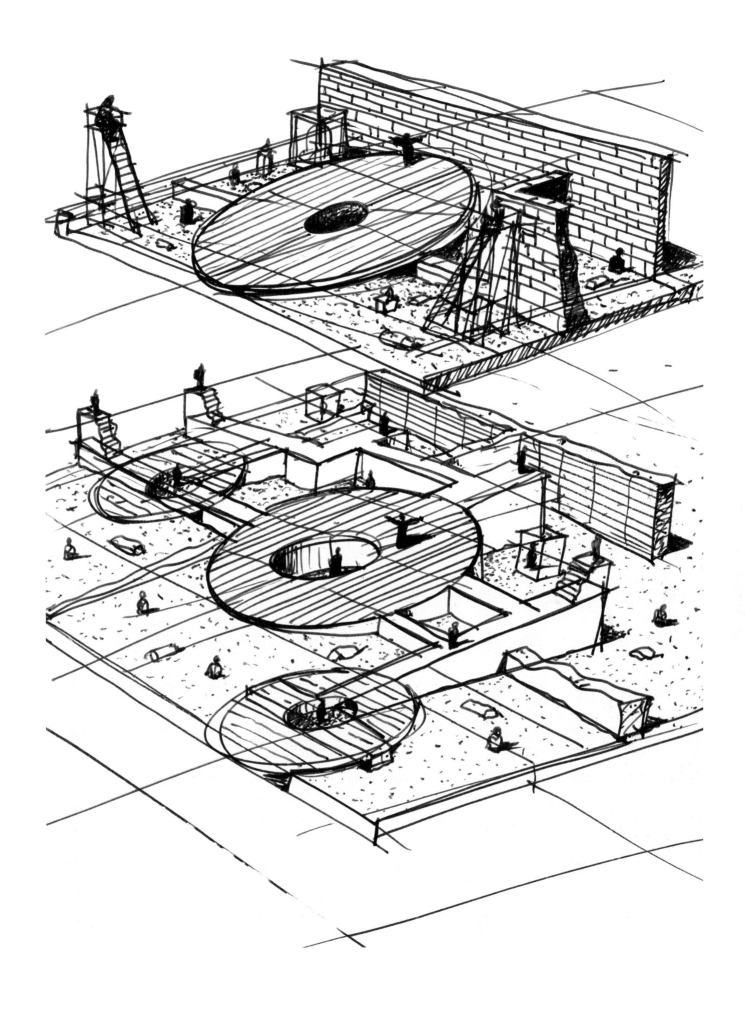

Der Intendant

Oper von Franz Hummel nach einem Text von Thomas Körner

Kunst- und Ausstellungshalle der Bundesrepublik Deutschland, Bonn, 1997; Inszenierung: Jürgen Tamchina, Bühne: Hans Dieter Schaal, Kostüme: Judith Fischer, Dramaturgie: Klaus Peter Kehr

Die Oper unternimmt auf witzige und nachdenkliche Weise den Versuch, die gesamte Theatergeschichte zu erzählen. Aus der Fülle der Ereignisse und Entwicklungen werden einzelne Aspekte, Bilder und Personen herausgehoben und dargestellt.

Im Theaterraum der Bundeskunsthalle wurde als Bühne eine leicht geneigte, kreisrunde Fläche aus Brettern aufgebaut, welche auf Mauerruinen ruhte. Aus der restlichen Bodenfläche, die mit Granulat bedeckt war, wuchsen Vitrinen und Hochsitze. Eine Baucollage aus Archäologie und Zirkus.

Die Bretterfläche erinnert an den gestampften Lehmbodenplatz, auf dem in archaischer Vorzeit die Theatergeschichte ihren Anfang nahm. Hier inmitten der Dorfgemeinschaft und im Rhythmus der Trommeln wurde tanzend und singend der Kampf zwischen den guten und bösen Geistern dargestellt. Die gemeinsamen Blicke auf die rituellen Bewegungen der Schamanen führten zu einer gemeinsamen Weltanschauung, zu einer kollektiven Kultur.

Im griechischen Theater befand sich der Tanzplatz mit dem Altar des Dionysos ebenfalls im Zentrum. Ritus, Kult, Gottesdienst, Spiel und Theater bildeten von Anfang an eine Einheit. Daß sich daneben Darbietungen entwickelten, die weniger weltanschaulich belastet waren (Sportveranstaltungen, Olympiaden, Wagenrennen, Gladiatorenkämpfe, Stierkämpfe) spricht für die geerdete Unterhaltungssehnsucht der Menschen zu allen Zeiten. Die Anwesenheit und der Streit zwischen Apollo und Dionysos, zwischen Hohem und Niedrigem, zwischen großer Kunst und banaler Posse bestimmte die gesamte Theatergeschichte. Theater diente der Inszenierung von Macht, Religion und politischen Vorgängen. Als höfische Unterhaltung bot es lebendige Bilder, die sich gegen gähnende Leere und quälende Langeweile stellten. Bei der Volksbelustigung lachten sich alle zu einer lauten Gemeinschaft zusammen. Der Schritt zu Belehrung und Agitation war nicht groß. Im Mittelalter, als sich das Theater fest in der Hand der Kirche befand, sollten die ausschließlich dargebotenen Passionsspiele zu einem christlichen Lebenswandel anregen. Wie eine Befreiung wirkte daher im ausgehenden Mittelalter das Possentreiben der Fasnachtsspiele, bei denen keine Zote ausgelassen wurde.

An manchen Orten wurde Theaterspielen während der Reformationszeit als Teufelswerk verboten. Im 16. Jahrhundert begründete die Shakespearebühne das bürgerliche Theater und den neuen Berufsstand des Schauspielers. Spätestens ab jetzt galten auch die geschriebenen Stücke als hohe Literatur.

Mit der Erfindung der Oper im Jahr 1600 wollten italienische Adlige und Künstler an die griechischen Tragödien anknüpfen und ein Gesamtkunstwerk aus Literatur, Musik, darstellender Kunst, Tanz, Schauspiel, Gesang, Architektur und Malerei schaffen. Die erste Oper stammt von Jacopo Peri und wurde am 6. Oktober 1600 in Florenz anläßlich der Feierlichkeiten zur Vermählung von Maria de Medici mit König Heinrich IV. von Frankreich aufgeführt. Sie trägt den Titel *Eurydice*.

Seitdem sind etwa 50 000 Opern geschrieben worden, von denen heute nur etwa 200 immer wieder zur Aufführung kommen.

Doch zurück zur Oper *Der Intendant* in der Bonner Kunsthalle. In der Mitte der zentralen Bretterfläche befand sich ein Loch. Pathetisch betrachtet, konnte man es mit einem dunklen gebärenden Urbauch gleichsetzen. Die despektierlich-ironische Perspektive würdigt es hingegen zu einem WC-Abtritt herab. Als Mittelpunkt der Welt entspricht es der archaischen Vorstellung einer um das Ich kreisenden Welt. Ebenso könnte es den überall lauernden Tod darstellen, der plötzlich seine Opfer verschlingt.

Aus diesem Loch erschienen sie alle: Dionysos, der Harlekin, Hans Wurst, die Neuberin, die Figuren Lessings, Schillers und Goethes. Und darin verschwanden sie auch wieder, nachdem sie ihre Späße getrieben und ihre gespreizten Sätze gesprochen hatten.

Wiederbelebte Geschichte. Erinnerungsraum. Geister. Flüchtig, verspielt und hingehaucht die einen, derb, zotig und eindeutig die andern. Die großen schweren Sätze verlangen nach Marmor und wollen ins Museum gestellt werden, die anderen, die leichtsinnigen verschluckt der Mülleimer des Alltags.

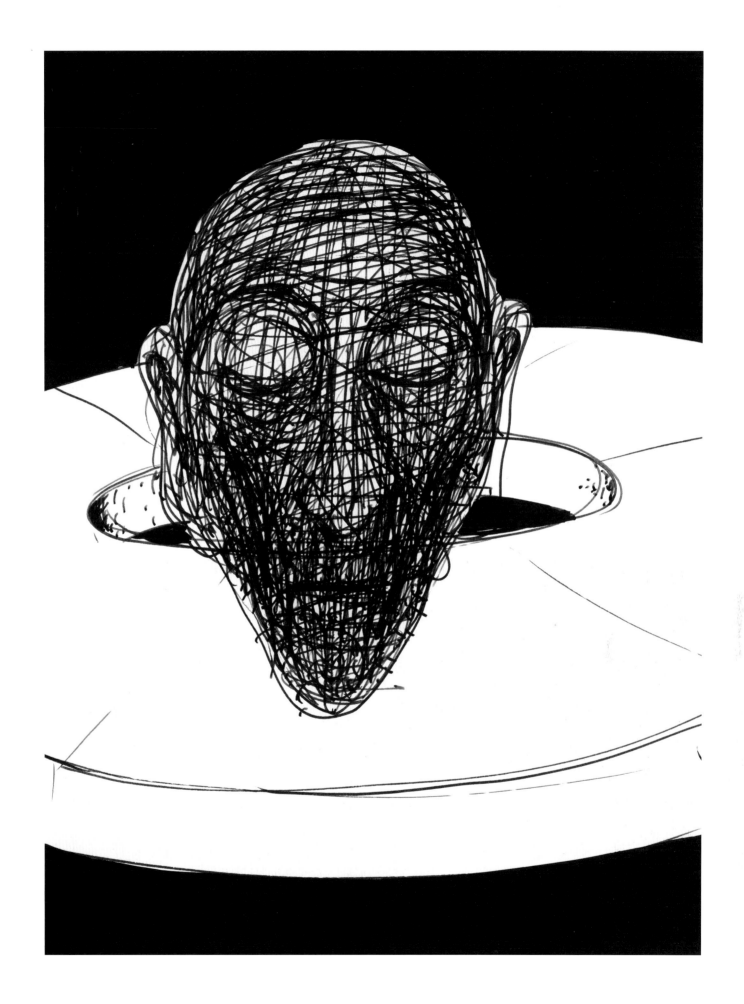

Stadträume (»Urban Spaces«)

Theatre in the Bauhaus, Dessau, 1998; texts, sets, video projection: Hans Dieter Schaal, music/composition: Lutz Glandien, staging and choreography: Arila Siegert, costumes: Marie-Luise Strandt

We walk into a large, dark hall. There are a number of closed cells distributed around the space, like container snail-shells, like gigantic sleeping tortoises. Light peeps through the cracks, we have a sense of some hidden internal life. Sleeping spaces with closed eyelids. When waking up, after we have opened our eyes, these spaces will look at us like breathing and thinking living creatures.

As theatregoers we sit in front of the closed curtain and wait excitedly for the secret that will soon be revealed to us. We sense the prickle of anticipatory joy that also seized us as children on Christmas Eve, in the hour before the presents were given out. Then the theatre goes dark, the curtain moves slowly to one side or rises, as if pulled upwards by a ghostly hand. The stage lights come on, and the theatre space becomes visible.

And there it now is, the simple space cell, brightly lit. There is no fourth wall. The secret is revealed. We look into the space and discover a man who is lying asleep on the floor. His chest is rising and falling. He is alive. Light is coming in through a window. It slowly gets brighter. The room is not quite empty, there is a coat hanging on the wall, and a stool by the window.

Then the man moves, he turns ponderously over on to his back, stretches, flexes his fingers and arms, and then his legs. He stands up, bemused, as if he is neither awake nor asleep.

We see the man moving out into the space, watch him walking around, feeling the walls, touching them, breathing. He is conscious of his own weight. He has difficulty in walking. Gravity is working.

We will never understand the simultaneity of all space events. We observe only one event, and the event observes us. We are a dedicated community: the cell, the performers, the spectators, Schrödinger's cat, quantum theory, space fields, the clock is ticking, this evening as well. The movements are planned. Where is chance in this, where is the openness of the next moment?

We move into the next moment with the dancer. Now. From one moment to the next. Action.

A stage play carved out of reality, out of a dream, out of the idea, carved out of the night, of fear, of depression, of hope, carved out of the labyrinth.

Then the images of the city come flickering in. Projections like patches of sunlight. Camera obscura. Plato's cave. The wounds were opened, feelings shown. Movements made.

Now the camera eye tracks back and the world outside the action becomes visible.

Stadträume

Bühne am Bauhaus, Dessau, 1998; Texte, Bühne, Video-Projektion: Hans Dieter Schaal, Musik/Komposition: Lutz Glandien, Inszenierung und Choreographie: Arila Siegert, Kostüme: Marie-Luise Strandt

Wir betreten eine große dunkle Halle. Im Raum verteilt liegen viele verschlossene Raumzellen, wie Container-Schneckenhäuser, wie riesige schlafende Schildkröten. Licht fällt durch Ritzen, Man ahnt etwas vom verborgenen Innenleben. Schlafende Räume mit geschlossenen Lidern. Wenn wir erwachen und die Augen geöffnet haben, werden uns die Räume anschauen wie atmende und denkende Lebewesen.

Als Theaterbesucher sitzen wir vor dem geschlossenen Vorhang und warten gespannt auf das Geheimnis, das sich uns bald auftun wird. Wir spüren die prickelnde Vorfreude, wie Kinder am Weihnachtsabend in der Stunde vor der Bescherung. Dann wird das Theater dunkel, der Vorhang bewegt sich langsam zur Seite oder fährt, wie von Geisterhand gezogen, nach oben. Das Licht auf der Bühne erstrahlt, und der Theaterraum wird sichtbar.

Da steht sie nun, die einfache Raumzelle, hell erleuchtet. Die vierte Wand fehlt. Das Geheimnis ist enthüllt. Wir schauen hinein und entdecken einen Mann, der schlafend am Boden liegt. Sein Brustkorb hebt und senkt sich. Er lebt. Durch ein Fenster fällt Licht. Langsam wird es heller. Der Raum ist nicht ganz leer, ein Mantel hängt an der Wand, neben dem Fenster steht ein Hocker.

Dann bewegt sich der Mann, schwerfällig dreht er sich auf den Rücken, reckt sich, dehnt seine Finger und Arme, dann die Beine. Er steht auf, benommen, wie auf der Grenze zwischen Schlafen und Wachen.

Wir sehen den Mann in den Raum greifen, sehen wie er umhergeht, die Wände befühlt, betastet, atmet. Er spürt sein Gewicht. Es fällt ihm schwer zu gehen. Die Schwerkraft arbeitet.

Nie werden wir die Gleichzeitigkeit aller Raumereignisse verstehen. Wir observieren nur einen Vorgang, und der Vorgang observiert uns. Wir sind eine verschworene Gemeinschaft: die Zelle, die Darsteller, die Zuschauer, Schrödingers Katze, die Quantentheorie, die Raumfelder, die Uhr tickt, auch an diesem Abend. Die Bewegungen sind geplant. Wo bleibt der Zufall, wo die Offenheit des nächsten Moments?

Mit dem Tänzer greifen wir hinein in die nächsten Momente. Jetzt, von einem Augenblick zum nächsten: Handlung.

Ein Theater-Stück herausgeschnitten aus der Realität, aus dem Traum, aus der Vorstellung, herausgeschnitten aus der Nacht, der Angst, der Depression, der Hoffnung, herausgeschnitten aus dem Labyrinth.

Dann flackern die Bilder der Stadt herein. Projektionen wie Sonnenlichtflecken. Camera obscura. Platons Höhle. Die Wunden wurden geöffnet, Gefühle gezeigt. Bewegungen durchgeführt.

Jetzt fährt das Kamera-Auge zurück, und die Welt außerhalb der Handlung wird sichtbar.

The formless space of thought and feeling set against the networks of constructed and built space. Suddenly looks and thoughts acquire geometrical structures. The perspective turns out to be a trap like the spider's web. Noises get tangled up in it, hang there and are spun in by invisible space spiders. Words collide with walls, drip from tables and chairs, creep stickily across floors and sink over the edge of the space into the past.

Der formlose Raum des Denkens und Fühlens gegen die Netzwerke des konstruierten und gebauten Raums. Plötzlich erhalten Blicke und Gedanken geometrische Strukturen. Die Perspektive entpuppt sich als Falle wie ein Spinnennetz. Geräusche verfangen sich, bleiben hängen und werden eingesponnen von unsichtbaren Raumspinnen. Worte prallen gegen Wände, tropfen von Tischen und Stühlen, kriechen zäh über Fußböden und versinken über die Raumkante in der Vergangenheit.

Orpheus and Eurydice

Azione teatrale per musica in three acts by Christoph Willibald Gluck. Libretto by Raniero Simone Francesco Maria de Calzabigi

Theater Lübeck, April 1998; conductor: Rüdiger Bohn, direction and costumes: Jürgen Tamchina, sets: Hans Dieter Schaal

Orpheus, the Thracian singer, is mourning the death of his wife Eurydice, who died from a snakebite. He cannot come to terms with fate, and decides to fetch his beloved back from the Underworld. He is able to calm the Furies who guard the gates of death with his music.

He is allowed to lead Eurydice out of Hades into the visible world on condition that he neither looks at her nor speaks to her. But as they are escaping through the labyrinths of the Underworld, Eurydice is unable to understand her lover's cold attitude, and asks him to turn round. When their eyes meet, she finally dies.

By finally sacrificing his beloved, Orpheus is able to compose and sing for ever. The dead Eurydice is his ally in the afterlife.

Art almost always deals with an absence, with the longing for presence and mourning for what has not been achieved. Herein lies the drama of the artist: he needs mourning and pain, as the greatest works of art emerge from unhappiness.

As a happy ending was desirable in Gluck's day, the composer has Eurydice come back to life again and the couple to escape into the visible world. This distortion of the myth takes the profoundly tragic element out of the story.

The settings for the action are these: »1. A grove with the tomb of Eurydice. 2. Entrance to the Underworld with the Styx. 3. Transformation: the Elysian Fields. 4. A gloomy cave, inside a labyrinth of fallen rocks and ruins, the ground covered with wild shrubs and plants. 5. Transformation: a magnificent temple, dedicated to Eros.«

The set in Lübeck treated only the first scene literally, and then it took another route that has something to do with the world of today: we move into a whirlpool of images leading to a mythical tunnel: a number of painted gates, tilted against each other, are built into the depths of the space.

Penetrating into the counter-world, into the beyond was presented as penetrating the surface of a picture. The world behind the world, behind the world …

The surface is not the boundary. Orpheus reaches into the mirror, as in Cocteau's film *Orphée*.

The event of love has congealed into a picture that is slowly fading and starting to decay. The grid atoms become visible, and ultimately reveal themselves to be stars in the blue-black night sky.

Oprheus wanders out into the nocturnal city, lonely and sad. He has lost Eurydice for ever. Sometimes he turns up somewhere by the harbour or in a tatty suburban cinema – alone, abandoned.

Orpheus und Eurydike

Azione teatrale per musica in drei Akten von Christoph Willibald Gluck, Libretto von Raniero Simone Francesco Maria de Calzabigi

Theater Lübeck, April 1998; musikalische Leitung: Rüdiger Bohn, Inszenierung und Kostüme: Jürgen Tamchina, Bühne: Hans Dieter Schaal

Orpheus, der thrakische Sänger, beklagt den Tod seiner Gattin Eurydike, die an einem Schlangenbiß gestorben ist. Er will sich mit dem Schicksal nicht abfinden und die Geliebte aus der Unterwelt zurückholen. Es gelingt ihm, die Furien, die das Todestor bewachen, durch seine Musik zu besänftigen.

Unter der Bedingung, daß er Eurydike weder anspricht noch ansieht, ist es ihm erlaubt, sie aus dem Hades in die sichtbare Welt zu führen. Auf der Flucht aus der labyrinthischen Unterwelt versteht diese die abweisende Haltung ihres Geliebten jedoch nicht und bittet ihn, sich umzudrehen. Als sich ihre Blicke treffen, stirbt sie endgültig.

Indem er seine Geliebte opfert, kann Orpheus für immer komponieren und singen. Sie wird zu seiner Verbündeten im Jenseits.

Kunst handelt sehr häufig von Abwesendem, von der Sehnsucht nach Anwesenheit und von der Trauer um das nie Erreichte. Darin besteht das Drama des Künstlers: Er bedarf der Trauer und des Schmerzes, da die größten Kunstwerke im Unglück entstehen.

Da zu Glucks Zeiten ein Happy-End erwünscht war, läßt der Komponist Eurydike wiederauferstehen und das Liebespaar lebendig in die sichtbare Welt entkommen. Diese Entstellung des Mythos nimmt der Geschichte ihre tiefe Tragik.

Die Bühnenbild-Orte der Handlung: »1. Ein Hain mit Grabmal der Eurydike. 2. Eingang zur Unterwelt mit der Styx. 3. Verwandlung: die elysischen Gefilde. 4. Eine finstere Höhle, im Inneren ein Labyrinth von herabgestürzten Felsblöcken und Trümmern, der Boden bedeckt von wildem Strauchwerk und Pflanzen. 5. Verwandlung: ein prächtiger Tempel, dem Eros geweiht.«

Die Bühne in Lübeck erfüllte nur das erste Bild wortwörtlich, dann wählte sie einen anderen Weg, der mit unserer heutigen Welt zu tun hatte: Wir begeben uns in einen Bilderstrudel, der in einen mythischen Tunnel hineinführt: In die Tiefe des Raums sind viele, gegeneinander verkippte Bildtore hineingebaut.

Das Eindringen in die Gegenwelt, in das Jenseits wurde als Eindringen in eine Bildfläche dargestellt. Die Welt hinter der Welt, hinter der Welt …

Die Oberfläche ist nicht die Grenze. Orpheus faßt hinein in den Spiegel wie in Cocteaus Filmtitel *Orphée*.

Das Ereignis der Liebe ist zu einem Bild geronnen, das langsam verblaßt und zu verwesen beginnt. Die Rasteratome werden sichtbar, entpuppen sich am Ende als Sternpunkte am blauschwarzen Nachthimmel.

Einsam und traurig wandert Orpheus hinaus in die nächtliche Stadt. Für immer hat er Eurydike verloren. Manchmal sieht man ihn irgendwo am Hafen oder in einem vergammelten Vorortkino auftauchen – allein, verlassen.

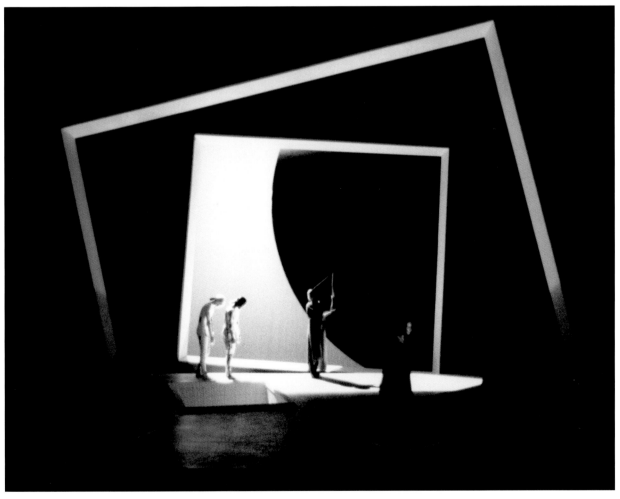

Orpheus

Ballet in three scenes by Edward Bond, music by Hans Werner Henze

Staatsoper, Vienna, 1986; conductor: Ulf Schirmer, choreography and direction: Ruth Berghaus, sets: Hans Dieter Schaal, costumes: Marie-Luise Strandt, dramaturgy: Karl Mickel

I was talking to Hans Werner Henze in 1985 in Vienna, and asked him how he imagined the after-world. He said – without thinking about it for very long: »Pedestrian precincts, our present pedestrian precincts ...« And I thought of the echoing footsteps at night, the shop-windows shining through the rain, and agreed with him. Perhaps we are already living in the after-world and will only be in this world after we have died.

A few weeks later we met again, in Paris. It was one of those days that inscribe themselves on the memory like photographs. The Café Flore was the meeting-point. When I got there at about two in the afternoon no one had arrived. I walked up and down in front of the café. A short time later a taxi drew up and Hans Werner Henze got out. He greeted me warmly. We went into the café and up to the first floor. There was very little room downstairs, but there were plenty of seats upstairs. We sat down in a corner at the back of the room. Henze sat down under a large mirror on the red artificial leather banquette that ran along the wall. After we had ordered and were waiting for Ruth Berghaus, he told me about the time he had spent here after the war. Jean Paul Sartre was sitting in the corner at the front, with René Leibowitz at the same table. I listened to Henze fascinated, and felt that for a while I was very close to the past intellectual centre of the world. I said that I saw Orpheus as an artist's drama. Orpheus tried to move the world with his music in order to bring Eurydice back to life again. The realism of the world made him into a martyr. The world could tolerate only the functional body, not the dreamer. The casing of laws, opinions, conventions, uniforms, tests and rituals had petrified to become a concrete bunker. Anyone who dreamt here, of a woman or of immortal fame, was condemned to death. This narrow-minded society knew only one law: that of conformity. Anyone who was not prepared to submit to this process would be walled up for ever, or wander through the dreary pedestrian precincts of this world, for ever lonely. Henze agreed.

By now, Ruth Berghaus had arrived. She sat down next to Henze on the artificial leather banquette. I got my camera out and shot a whole film. It was a beautiful and memorable image: this bald man with his strikingly round skull and next to him this woman whose unruly hair was standing up as though it wanted to declare independence. Embodiments of obstinacy, remorselessly close and yet a long way away at the same time. Secret dandies, perhaps, who want the world to love them and at the same time despise it in its present condition.

Orpheus

Ballett-Geschichte in drei Bildern von Edward Bond, Musik von Hans Werner Henze

Staatsoper, Wien, 1986; musikalische Leitung: Ulf Schirmer, Choreographie und Inszenierung: Ruth Berghaus, Bühne: Hans Dieter Schaal, Kostüme: Marie-Luise Strandt, Dramaturgie: Karl Mickel

Als ich Hans Werner Henze 1985 bei einem Gespräch in Wien fragte, wie er sich das Jenseits vorstelle, sagte er – ohne lange nachzudenken: »Die Fußgängerzonen, die heutigen Fußgängerzonen ...« Und ich dachte an das nächtliche Hallen der Schritte, an die leuchtenden Schaufenster im Regen und gab ihm recht. Vielleicht leben wir bereits im Jenseits und kommen erst nach unserem Tod ins Diesseits.

Einige Wochen später trafen wir uns in Paris wieder. Es war einer jener Tage, die sich wie Photographien ins Gedächtnis eingraben. Treffpunkt war das Café Flore. Als ich gegen 14.00 Uhr dort eintraf, war noch niemand da. Ich ging vor dem Café auf und ab. Nach kurzer Zeit fuhr ein Taxi vor, und Hans Werner Henze stieg aus. Er begrüßte mich freundlich. Wir betraten das Café und stiegen in den ersten Stock hoch. Während unten fast alle Stühle besetzt waren, gab es oben noch genügend freie Plätze. Wir ließen uns in der hintersten Raumecke nieder. Henze setzte sich unter einem großen Spiegel auf die rote, an der Wand entlanglaufende Kunstlederbank. Nachdem wir bestellt hatten und auf Ruth Berghaus warteten, erzählte er von seiner Zeit, die er hier nach dem Kriege verbracht hatte. Vorne in der Ecke habe Jean Paul Sartre gesessen und bei ihm, am Tisch, René Leibowitz. Ich hörte Henze gebannt zu und hatte das Gefühl, eine Weile dem vergangenen Gedankenzentrum der Welt ganz nahe zu sein. Ich sagte, daß ich Orpheus als Künstlerdrama sähe. Orpheus versuche, mit seiner Musik die Welt zu rühren, um Eurydike wiederzubeleben. Der Realismus der Welt mache aus ihm einen Märtyrer. Die Welt dulde nur den funktionalen Körper, nicht den Träumer. Das Gehäuse aus Gesetzen, Meinungen, Konventionen, Uniformen, Prüfungen und Ritualen sei zum Betonbunker versteinert. Wer hier träume, von einer Frau oder von unsterblichem Ruhm, sei zum Tode verurteilt. Diese borniere Gesellschaft kenne nur ein Gesetz: das der Anpassung. Wer sich diesem Vorgang nicht unterwerfe, werde für immer eingemauert sein, oder für immer einsam durch die trostlosen Fußgängerzonen der Welt irren. Henze stimmte mir zu.

Inzwischen war Ruth Berghaus eingetroffen. Sie setzte sich neben Henze auf die Kunstlederbank. Ich holte meinen Photoapparat heraus und verknipste einen ganzen Film. Es war ein schönes eindrucksvolles Bild: dieser kahlköpfige Mann mit seinem runden markanten Schädel und daneben diese Frau, deren Haare widerborstig in die Höhe standen, als wollten sie sich selbständig machen. Verkörperungen des Eigensinns, unerbittlich nah und fern zugleich. Insgeheime Dandys vielleicht, die von der Welt geliebt werden wollen und sie zugleich in ihrem jetzigen Zustand verachten.

At the centre of this ballet, in which no one sings or speaks, is Orpheus.

About the set: Orpheus has arrived in the twentieth century. We are looking back.

1. History revived in the everyday quarry-backyard. Petrified remains of civilization. The story is the same. Eurydice dies and passes over, beyond the edge of the world and through the great gate.

2. Orpheus dances the world into the abyss in rage and despair. He forces his way through into the realm of Hades.

This world is no paradise, a quite everyday hell, made up of fragments of pedestrian precincts, railway platforms and carriages, and bunkers that have burst open.

Hades lives with Persephone in a gleamingly bright cell.

3. Eurydice appears at the train window. Their eyes meet, and she finally dies in the middle of the ruins and rubble. Orpheus dances his lament and his mourning. The music sounds hard and painful now, steeped in the blood of a cruel century.

Im Zentrum dieses Ballets, in dem weder gesungen noch gesprochen wird, steht Orpheus.

Zur Bühne: Orpheus ist im zwanzigsten Jahrhundert angekommen. Wir blicken zurück.

1. Wiederberlebung der Geschichte im alltäglichen Steinbruch-Hinterhof. Versteinerte Zivilisationsreste. Die Geschichte ist die gleiche. Eurydike stirbt und geht hinüber, über den Rand der Welt, hinter das große Tor.

2. Orpheus tanzt die Welt in Wut und Verzweiflung in den Abgrund. Er erzwingt sich den Übergang, hinein in das Reich des Hades.

Diese Welt ist kein Paradies, eine ganz alltägliche Hölle, aus Fragmenten von Fußgängerzonen, Bahnsteigen, Zugwaggons und aufgeplatzten Bunkern.

Hades wohnt mit Persephone in einer strahlend hellen Zelle.

3. Eurydike taucht am Zugfenster auf. Die Blicke treffen sich und mitten im Trümmerfeld stirbt sie endgültig. Orpheus tanzt seine Klage und seine Trauer. Die Musik klingt jetzt hart und schmerzvoll, getränkt mit dem Blut eines grausamen Jahrhunderts.

Circe and Odysseus

Ballet in two acts, music by Gerald Humel after a text by Thomas Höft

Komische Oper, Berlin, 1993; conductor: Michail Jurowski, libretto, choreography and direction: Arila Siegert, sets: Hans Dieter Schaal, costumes: Jutta Harnisch, dramaturgy: Karin Schmidt-Feister

The ballet tells the story of one of the many adventures that Odysseus experienced on his ten-year journey home from Troy to Ithaca.

One day he and his soldiers land on a lonely island where the sorceress Circe lives with her little entourage. Odysseus falls in love with this beautiful woman. But the happiness is not to last. He moves on, and Circe remains behind alone. »The tortuous journey from Troy to Ithaca is the way through the myths taken by the personal self, infinitely weak and just forming in resistance to the violence of nature … The adventures that Odysseus undergoes are all dangerous lures that draw the self away from the path of its logic.« (Max Horkheimer and Theodor Adorno)

The set appears as a mysterious place, half the deck of a ship, half island with a rolling, shifting floor.

Anyone who steps on to this white landscape deck is lured in by a light-coloured building stuck in the earth, with a door glowing in its front wall. This is where Circe will appear with her little army of seductresses. The complications begin. »He walked past a house through lonely fields. She was looking through the half-open door. She smiled. And this smile was so powerful that the eternal laws of life began to shake. The earth

bowed down. The trees, the grass, everything pushed Odysseus to the door, which opened quietly. He came in. Inside it was cool and dark, it smelled like juicy fruit that had been cut up. The thin thread of a spring splashed quietly. The woman was called Circe.« (Jean Giono)

Going and staying. Going and staying. Going and staying. First a place for travelling and sailing. Flow in the flux. There is no escape, everything is washed along, bodies, arms, heads, thoughts, music and desires. Pasts crop up, mysterious memories. The weathered image of a stone figure. Looks wander off, search downwards, along the walls, search upwards. Rubble on the floor. Are these parts of our own bodies, are they thoughts that have broken free? The water trembles all around and glitters promisingly.

Going and staying. Then this door, which opens slowly, this landing, this arriving, this conquering and exploring an island. The lures increase. The seduction begins. The landscape that emerges now is a ship's deck, mountain, wave, house and roof terrace in one. In the middle is the hollow, the entrance to the house, to the earth, to the womb.

Going and staying. The dream of the beginning rises, of a time with no distinction between tree and man, between stone and hand, between bird and mouth. Thoughts stir slowly in the wind. In the distance, time rocks over the sea. The strange world is conquered and has swallowed up the intruders. Man and woman hurl themselves at each other. The wound of sexuality bleeds. Inside and outside. Nature. Experience as explosion. The whole of creation passes. After

this paradise will be a zoo, the cushions will be plumped up in the living pits, the catalogues of possible journeys will be looked through and the mythological sea will flicker on the screens. Going and staying. Going and staying. Going and staying.

Odysseus is looking for adventure and wants to be on the move the whole time. But Circe is the settled one, the sorceress who is rooted to the spot. For a while her erotic power tames the man's restlessness. But he is not created for hearth and home and for the comfortable living pit.

The horizon beckons. The ocean calls. »There are …, probably this was said by Borges, only two stories, the one about the man on the cross and the one about the man who came home without arriving. The women's Odyssey has only just begun.« (Annette Meyhöfer)

Circe und Odysseus

Ballett in zwei Akten, Musik von Gerald Humel
nach einem Text von Thomas Höft

Komische Oper, Berlin, 1993; musikalische Leitung: Michail Jurowski, Libretto, Choreographie und Inszenierung: Arila Siegert, Bühne: Hans Dieter Schaal, Kostüme: Jutta Harnisch, Dramaturgie: Karin Schmidt-Feister

Das Ballett schildert eines der zahlreichen Abenteuer, die Odysseus auf seiner zehnjährigen Heimfahrt von Troja nach Ithaka erlebt.

Eines Tages landet er in Begleitung seiner Soldaten auf einer einsamen Insel, wo die Zauberin Circe mit ihrem kleinen Volk lebt. Odysseus verliebt sich in die schöne Frau. Aber das Glück ist nicht von Dauer. Er zieht weiter, und Circe bleibt allein zurück.

»Die Irrfahrt von Troja nach Ithaka ist der Weg des leibhaft gegenüber der Naturgewalt unendlich schwachen und im Selbstbewußtsein erst sich bildenden Selbst durch die Mythen. ... Die Abenteuer, die Odysseus besteht, sind allesamt gefahrvolle Lockungen, die das Selbst aus der Bahn seiner Logik herausziehen.« (Max Horkheimer und Theodor Adorno)

Die Bühne stellt sich als geheimnisvoller Ort dar, halb Schiffsdeck, halb Insel mit gewölbtem, schwankendem Boden.

Wer dieses weiße Landschaftsdeck betritt, wird von einem hellen, in der Erde steckenden Gebäude angelockt, in dessen Frontwand eine Türöffnung leuchtet. Hier wird Circe mit ihrem kleinen Heer von Verführerinnen erscheinen. Die Verstrickungen beginnen. »Zwischen einsamen Feldern ging er an einem Haus vorbei. Sie spähte durch die halbgeöffnete Tür. Sie lächelte. Und dieses Lächeln war von solcher Kraft, daß die ewigen Geste des Lebens ins Schwanken gerieten. Die Erde neigte sich. Die Bäume, das Gras, alles drängte Odysseus zu jenem Tor, das sich leise öffnete. Er trat ein. Drinnen war es kühl und dunkel, es duftete wie zerschnittene, saftige Früchte. Der dünne Faden einer Quelle plätscherte leise. Die Frau hieß Circe.« (Jean Giono, *Die Geburt der Odyssee*)

Gehen und Bleiben. Gehen und Bleiben. Gehen und Bleiben. Zunächst ein Ort des Fahrens und Segelns. Fließen im Fluß. Es gibt kein Entrinnen, alles wird mitgespült, Körper, Arme, Köpfe, Gedanken, Musik und Sehnsüchte. Vergangenheiten tauchen auf, rätselhafte Erinnerungen. Das verwitterte Bild einer Steinfigur. Blicke irren ab, suchen nach unten, an den Wänden entlang, suchen nach oben. Trümmer am Boden: Sind es Stücke vom eigenen Körper, sind es herausgebrochene Gedanken? Das Wasser zittert ringsum und glitzert vielversprechend.

Gehen und Bleiben. Dann diese Tür, die sich langsam öffnet, dieses Landen, dieses Ankommen, dieses Erobern und Erforschen einer Insel. Die Lockungen nehmen zu. Die Verführung beginnt. Die jetzt enstehende Landschaft ist Schiffsdeck, Berg, Welle, Haus und Dachterrasse in einem. In der Mitte die Mulde, der Eingang in das Haus, in die Erde, in den Mutterleib.

Gehen und Bleiben. Der Traum vom Anfang steigt auf, von einer Zeit ohne Unterschied zwischen Baum und Mensch, zwischen Stein und Hand, zwischen Vogel und Mund. Langsam bewegen sich die Gedanken im Wind. In der Ferne schaukelt die Zeit über dem Meer. Die fremde Welt ist erobert und hat die Eindringlinge verschluckt. Mann und Frau prallen aufeinander. Die Wunde der Geschlechtlichkeit blutet. Innen und außen. Natur. Erlebnis als Explosion. Die ganze Schöpfung zieht vorbei. Danach wird das Paradies ein Zoo sein, werden in den Wohnmulden die Kissen geschüttelt, werden die Kataloge der möglichen Reisen durchblättert und wird das mythologische Meer in den Bildschirmen flimmern. Gehen und Bleiben. Gehen und Bleiben. Gehen und Bleiben.

Odysseus sucht das Abenteuer, will immer unterwegs sein. Circe dagegen ist die Seßhafte, die mit dem Boden verwurzelte Zauberin. Für eine Weile dämpft ihre erotische Kraft die Unruhe des Mannes. Aber er ist für Heim und Herd und die gemütliche Wohnmulde nicht geschaffen.

Der Horizont lockt. Das Meer ruft.

»Es gibt ..., vielleicht stammt der Satz von Borges, nur zwei Geschichten, die von dem Mann am Kreuz und die von dem Mann, der nach Hause kam, ohne anzukommen. Die Odyssee der Frauen hat erst begonnen.« (Annette Meyhöfer)

Les Troyens

The Conquest of Troy (La prise de Troie)
The Trojans in Carthage (Les Troyens à Carthage)
Grand opera in five acts by Hector Berlioz based on Vergil's Aeneid

Städtische Bühnen Frankfurt am Main, 1983; conductor: Michael Gielen, director: Ruth Berghaus, sets: Hans Dieter Schaal (with Max von Vecquel), costumes: Nina Ritter, dramaturgy: Klaus Zehelein

The opera begins with the fall of the city of Troy and ends with the vision of the foundation of Rome. There is destruction and there is reconstruction, and in between we see tragedies, visions, love stories, wars and adventures. Here too the theme is going and staying. Aeneas, the brother of Odysseus, is a man of action who was not born to a narrow existence in the arms of Dido.

Two locations are defined and depicted on the stage in Frankfurt: Troy and Carthage. Rome remains a vision. The Carthage scene occupies most of the stage.

Troy has walls like land that has been dug over. A few years after Berlioz composed his piece, Heinrich Schliemann was to excavate to find Troy and did in fact find traces of an ancient civilization. Mythology and history permeate each other.

The Trojans appear, carefully feeling their way around the dark courtyard of a fortress. They have ten years of war, fear, privation and captivity behind them.

Cassandra has crawled into a crude, simple tent.

In Carthage, the achievements of seven years of peace and reconstruction are being celebrated. Dido has created a place where it would be possible to settle comfortably. But the periphery is open, paths lead down to the sea, the desert and the African jungle. The stage turns further, presenting views of parts of the landscape, then warehouses, harbour-side situations and fragments of gardens. More building is taking place everywhere.

The end is played on an enormous slope. Garden, deck, runway, place of longing and transition. Here Dido ends her life fully in the public eye. The place becomes a floating garden tomb on the edge of the world. There is a tangle of paths in the background.

Her final vision is of the coming cosmopolitan city of Rome. She has a premonition that Carthage will fall like Troy before it and that Rome will dominate the new world.

Her beloved, Aeneas has indeed left her behind in her despair, but she knows that he will found this city of Rome. He is the coming hero, and she must sacrifice herself.

Die Trojaner (Les Troyens)

Die Eroberung von Troja (La prise de Troie)
Die Trojaner in Karthago (Les Troyens à Carthage)
Große Oper in fünf Akten von Hector Berlioz nach Vergils Aeneis

Städtische Bühnen Frankfurt am Main, 1983; musikalische Leitung: Michael Gielen, Inszenierung: Ruth Berghaus, Bühne: Hans Dieter Schaal (mit Max von Vecquel), Kostüme: Nina Ritter, Dramaturgie: Klaus Zehelein

Die Oper beginnt mit dem Untergang der Stadt Troja und endet mit der Vision der Gründung Roms. Es wird zerstört und aufgebaut, dazwischen ereignen sich die Tragödien, die Visionen, die Liebesgeschichten, die Kriege und Abenteuer. Auch hier ist das Thema: Gehen und Bleiben. Äneas, Bruder des Odysseus, ist ein Mann der Tat, der nicht zum spießigen Dasein in den Armen der Dido geboren ist.

Auf der Bühne in Frankfurt werden zwei Orte definiert und dargestellt: Troja und Karthago. Rom bleibt eine Vision. Das Bild Karthagos nimmt den größten Teil der Bühne ein.

Troja hat Wände wie Spatenstiche. Einige Jahre nach Berlioz' Komposition wird Heinrich Schliemann nach Troja graben und tatsächlich Spuren einer alten Zivilisation finden. Mythologie und Geschichte durchdringen einander.

Die Trojaner erscheinen vorsichtig tastend in einem dunklen Burghof. Zehn Jahre Krieg, Angst, Entbehrung und Gefangensein liegen hinter ihnen.

Kassandra hat sich in einem groben, einfachen Zelt verkrochen.

In Karthago wird nach sieben Jahren Frieden und Aufbau das Erreichte gefeiert. Dido hat einen Ort geschaffen, an dem man es sich wohnlich einrichten könnte. Aber die Ränder sind offen, Wege führen hinaus zum Meer hin, in die Wüste, in den afrikanischen Urwald. Die Bühne dreht sich weiter, gibt Landschaftsteile dem Blick frei, dann Lagerräume, Situationen am Hafen und Fragmente von Gärten. Überall wird weiter gebaut.

Das Ende spielt auf einer riesigen Schräge. Garten, Deck, Landebahn, Ort der Sehnsucht und des Übergangs. Hier beendet Dido ihr Leben in aller Öffentlichkeit. Der Ort wird zum schwimmenden Gartengrab am Rande der Welt. Ein Wegknäuel im Hintergrund.

Ihre Schluß-Vision gilt der kommenden Weltstadt Rom. Sie ahnt, daß Karthago wie Troja untergehen und Rom die neue Welt beherrschen wird.

Der Geliebte Äneas hat sie zwar allein in ihrer Verzweiflung zurückgelassen, aber sie weiß, daß er dieses Rom gründen wird. Er ist der kommende Held, und sie muß sich opfern.

Part 1: The Conquest of Troy

The Trojans are surprised by the sudden departure of the Greeks and search their abandoned camp. Only a large wooden horse remains. Cassandra issues a warning but no one listens to her, no one understands her. After the horse has been taken into the city, the disaster takes its course. Troy is destroyed, and many Trojans are killed. When the Greeks get into the palace, all the remaining Trojan women stab themselves to death to avoid captivity, including Cassandra. Aeneas and his retinue set sail across the sea.

The stage locations: »The Conquest of Troy. 1. The Greek army's abandoned camp outside the city gates. 2. A chamber in Aeneas's palace, illuminated only weakly by a lamp. 3. A room inside Priam's palace.«

Teil 1: Die Eroberung von Troja

Die Trojaner wundern sich über den plötzlichen Abzug der Griechen und durchsuchen deren verlassenes Lager. Nur ein großes hölzernes Pferd ist zurückgeblieben. Kassandra warnt, aber niemand hört auf sie, niemand versteht sie. Nachdem man das Pferd in die Stadt gezogen hat, nimmt das Unheil seinen Lauf. Troja wird zerstört, viele Trojaner finden den Tod. Als die Griechen in den Palast eindringen, erdolchen sich alle zurückgebliebenen trojanischen Frauen, um der Gefangenschaft zu entgehen, auch Kassandra. Äneas zieht mit einigen Gefolgsleuten hinaus auf das Meer.

Die Bühnenbild-Orte: »Die Eroberung von Troja. 1. Das von den Griechen verlassene Heerlager vor den Toren der Stadt. 2. Ein Gemach im Palast von Äneas, das nur schwach von einer Lampe erhellt wird. 3. Ein Raum im Inneren des Palastes von Priamus.«

Part 2: The Trojans in Carthage

Dido is the Queen of Carthage. When Aeneas
lands there, she is being threatened by a strange
army. Aeneas helps her to defeat her enemies.
Then Dido and Aeneas fall in love. But the hero
cannot stay. One morning he is found to have left
Carthage for Italy. He is destined to found Rome.
Dido burns all the mementoes of her lover and
stabs herself to death.

    The stage locations: »The Trojans in Carthage.
1. The scene is a wide, open garden-room in
Dido's palace in Carthage. 2. Royal hunt. The
scene is an African forest in the morning. 3. Dido's
gardens by the seashore. 4. Seashore with many
Trojan tents. 5. Dido's chamber in the morning.
6. Ritual of the dead. Part of Dido's garden by the
sea.«

Teil 2: Die Trojaner in Karthago

Dido ist die Königin von Karthago. Als Äneas dort
landet, wird sie von einem fremden Heer bedroht.
Äneas hilft ihr, die Feinde zu besiegen. Dann verlieben sich Dido und Äneas ineinander. Aber der
Held kann nicht bleiben. Eines Morgens hat er
Karthago in Richtung Italien verlassen. Seine Bestimmung ist es, Rom zu gründen. Dido verbrennt
alle Erinnerungen an den Geliebten und erdolcht
sich.

    Die Bühnenbild-Orte: »Die Trojaner in Karthago.
1. Die Szene zeigt einen weiten offenen Gartensaal
im Palast Didos in Karthago. 2. Königliche Jagd.
Die Szene stellt einen afrikanischen Wald am Morgen dar. 3. Die Gärten der Dido am Meeresufer. 4.
Meeresufer mit vielen Zelten der Trojaner. 5. Wohn-
gemach der Dido am Morgen. 6. Totenritual. Ein
Teil von Didos Garten am Meer.«

The Ring of the Nibelung – The Rhinegold, The Valkyrie, Siegfried, The Twilight of the Gods

With *Orpheus and Eurydice*, *Circe and Odysseus* and *Les Troyens* we have so far been in the world of the Greek myths.

Their topography includes the enormous area of water that is the Mediterranean, its coasts and shores, cities and islands, sun and heat.

But Wagner's operas are set in the gloomy, misty and always somewhat rainy realm of Nordic mythology. He wanted his world of collage to set an icy Nordic narrative mountain against the Greek flood of images and stories. It is not the sea that is the linking topos, but the Rhine. This mighty river with its many tributaries forms the backbone of the body of narrative.

In ancient times, when there were neither roads nor firm paths, the great river arteries became convenient links between settled areas. The power-hungry, mighty tribes settled on their banks, wreaking havoc in the known world with their ambushes, blackmail, intrigues and war.

Biologically speaking, all life comes from water, and civilization starts by the water. It is only logical that Richard Wagner should start his *Rhinegold* in the river Rhine.

»On the bottom of the Rhine. Greenish twilight, lighter towards the top and darker towards the bottom. The full height of the stage is filled with surging water, flowing restlessly from the right to the left …« (Stage direction: Richard Wagner)

The song of the almost naked Rhine Maidens who swim through the water at the beginning of the opera sounds archaic, like something from early childhood or Dada: »Wagalaweia! Wallala weiala weia …«

This is a situation as in paradise. The Rhine Maidens are creatures of nature, nymphs, water fairies. Mythological archetypes of a pre-Christian period.

As long as they are alone together, the world is still in order and in full harmony. But these creatures are not children any longer. When a man appears – the Nibelung Alberich – they are transformed into sexual beings who tempt and flirt. Circes of the underwater world. Actually their task is to guard the gold at the bottom of the Rhine. But their seductive power is not equal to this. Alberich does not allow himself to be beguiled; he steals the gold, and after this the disaster takes its course. It is a kind of fall in reverse, the Biblical one was sexual in its nature; Adam allows himself to be seduced be Eve, and all future human beings will be descended from this primal couple. Alberich actually wanted to start some love-play with the Rhine Maidens, but they do not take him seriously, they tease and despise him because he is so ugly. Perhaps he steals the gold only to take his revenge, and through unrequited love. If they had yielded to him the world would not have lost its equilibrium.

All that Alberich, who comes from the underworld, now wants to do is to exploit the treasure he has stolen in the sense that he wants to rule the world, he wants to wrest power from the gods, who are entitled to it. But Wotan is weak and not much better than Alberich. He too works with intrigues, murder and manslaughter. No one will be the victor at the end of the *Ring*. The gods are doomed to fall, and Alberich's world, the realm of the Nibelungs, goes up in flames. The Rhine Maidens, along with the men and women of the Gibichung race will be the only ones to survive. They seize the ring in the midst of the inferno and swim to the bottom of the Rhine, back where they came from.

Anyone who mines the earth and rips out its resources throws it out of balance, destroys its harmony. Neither the gods nor the Nibelungs can do anything about this. The programme was fatal from the outset. Is the incarnation, the development of power and the emergence of civilization a false development for humanity?

Wagner's pessimistic interpretation of history carries even more weight if we remember that the great world catastrophes of the 20th century were all in the future when he was writing and composing his *Ring*.

Any interpretation is conceivable today: the *Ring* could be set in outer space, in a submarine at the bottom of the sea, in Arctic ice, in burned-out oil-fields in the Gulf, in the jungle, on a skyscraper in central Manhattan, in a bourgeois living room, in a swimming bath, on the Obersalzberg, in an empty theatre, in a gymnasium or in a bombed parliament building. And any one of these would coincide with one of Wagner's narrative planes. Faced with this helplessness, we comply with his instructions, read his stage directions very carefully and take them seriously. As we know, he was highly resistant to the superficial Makart-style lushness of his day. He loved extremes, icy caves, Neuschwanstein and the invisible. Sometimes he had a vision of an invisible theatre. We do not know whether he would have enjoyed a Hollywood film or would have preferred a white square on a white ground. At odds with himself as he was, he would perhaps have accepted both. In any case he was able to imagine that his *Ring* might only be performed once, at best on the banks of the Rhine. The sets, theatre and score were then to be burned.

In Mannheim there was a framing device that ran through all the parts of the work: a concrete myth-space between the orchestra pit and the stage, a kind of waiting-room for the gods and the other mythical figures. Here is was comfortable and securely fortified, both at the same time. An enormous concrete wall served as the curtain, it rose or fell as needed. Associations with fortresses, bunkers and dam walls could be evoked.

After this, all the locations appear as defined by Wagner: the caves of Nibelheim, the mountain heights for the gods, the wild mountain landscapes, the mighty ash tree in Hunding's hut, the forest and hall of the Gibichings. And above all there was the Valkyries' rock. As this image recurs, it became a kind of visual leitmotif.

To make the Rhine visible, the flowing waters of the Rhine were projected on to the great concrete wall, and as Wagner had requested, it flowed from right to left.

Der Ring des Nibelungen – Rheingold, Walküre, Siegfried, Götterdämmerung

Mit *Orpheus und Eurydike*, *Circe und Odysseus* und *Die Trojaner* befanden wir uns bisher in der griechischen Mythologie.

Zu ihrer Topographie gehören die riesige Wasserfläche des Mittelmeeres, die Küsten- und Uferzonen, Städte und Inseln, die Sonne und die Wärme.

Wagners Opern hingegen spielen im düsteren, nebeligen und immer etwas verregneten Reich der nordischen Mythologie. Mit seiner Collagenwelt wollte er der griechischen Bilder- und Geschichtenflut ein nordisch-vereistes Erzähl-Gebirge entgegenstellen. Nicht das Meer ist der verbindende Topos, sondern der Rhein. Dieser gewaltige Fluß mit seinen diversen Nebenarmen bildet das Rückgrat des Erzählkörpers.

In archaischen Zeiten, als es weder Straßen noch befestigte Wege gab, wurden die großen Flußadern zu bequemen Verbindungen zwischen den besiedelten Gebieten. An den Ufern setzten sich die machthungrigen, starken Geschlechter fest, die mit ihren Überfällen, Erpressungen, Intrigen und Kriegen Unheil über die damalige Welt brachten.

Aus dem Wasser ist biologisch alles Leben entstanden, und am Wasser nimmt die Zivilisation ihren Anfang. Es ist nur folgerichtig, daß Richard Wagner sein *Rheingold* im Rhein beginnen läßt.

»Auf dem Grund des Rheins. Grünliche Dämmerung, nach oben zu lichter, nach unten zu dunkler. Die Höhe ist von wogendem Gewässer erfüllt, das rastlos von rechts nach links zu strömt ...« (Szenenanweisung: Richard Wagner)

Der Gesang der nahezu nackten Rheintöchter, die zu Beginn der Oper durch das Wasser schwimmen, hört sich archaisch, frühkindlich-dadaistisch an: »Wagalaweia! Wallala weiala weia ...«

Es herrscht ein paradiesischer Zustand. Die Rheintöchter sind Naturwesen, Nymphen, Wasserfeen. Mythologische Archetypen einer vorchristlichen Zeit.

Solange sie untereinander sind und miteinander spielen, ist die Welt noch in Ordnung und in voller Harmonie. Diese Geschöpfe sind jedoch keine Kinder mehr. Taucht ein Mann auf – der Nibelung Alberich – verwandeln sie sich in sexuelle Wesen, die locken und flirten. Circen der Unterwasserwelt. Eigentlich ist es ihre Aufgabe, das Gold am Grunde des Rheins zu bewachen. Dazu reicht ihre verführerische Kraft jedoch nicht aus. Alberich läßt sich nicht umgarnen; er raubt das Gold, womit das Unheil seinen Lauf nimmt. Es ist eine Art umgekehrter Sündenfall, der biblische war sexueller Natur; Adam läßt sich von Eva verführen, und alle zukünftigen Menschen werden von diesem Urpaar abstammen. Alberich wollte eigentlich ein Liebesspiel mit den Rheintöchtern beginnen, aber sie nehmen ihn nicht ernst, sie necken und verachten ihn wegen seiner Häßlichkeit. Vielleicht raubt er das Gold nur aus Rache und verschmähter Liebe. Hätten sie ihn erhört, wäre die Welt nicht aus dem Gleichgewicht geraten.

Alberich, der Unterweltler, hat jetzt nur noch die Vermehrung seines geraubten Schatzes im Sinn, er will die Weltmacht, will sie den Göttern entreißen, denen sie eigentlich zusteht. Aber Wotan ist schwach und nicht viel besser als Alberich, auch er arbeitet mit Intrigen, Mord und Totschlag. Am Ende des *Rings* wird keiner siegen. Die Götter sind zum Untergang bestimmt, und die Welt Alberichs, das Nibelungenreich, geht in Flammen auf. Die Rheintöchter werden neben den Männern und Frauen von Gibichungen die einzigen sein, die überleben. Sie holen sich mitten im Inferno den Ring und schwimmen auf den Grund des Rheins, dorthin, woher sie gekommen sind.

Wer die Erde abbaut, ihr die Schätze entreißt, bringt sie aus dem Gleichgewicht, zerstört ihre Harmonie. Weder die Götter noch die Nibelungen können an diesem Verlauf etwas ändern. Das Programm war von Anfang an tödlich. Ist die Menschwerdung, die Entfaltung von Macht und die Entstehung der Zivilisation eine Fehlentwicklung der Evolution?

Wagners pessimistische Deutung der Mythologie erhält noch mehr Gewicht, wenn man bedenkt, daß die großen Weltkatastrophen des 20. Jahrhunderts Zukunft waren, als er an seinem *Ring* schrieb und komponierte.

Jede Interpretation ist heute denkbar: Man kann den *Ring* im Weltall spielen lassen, in einem U-Boot am Meeresgrund, im arktischen Eis, auf verbrannten Ölfeldern am Golf, im Urwald, auf einem Wolkenkratzer mitten in Manhattan, in einem spießigen Wohnzimmer, in einer Badeanstalt, auf dem Obersalzberg, in einem leeren Theater, in einer Turnhalle oder in einem zerbombten Parlament. Und immer würde man eine Erzählebene Wagners treffen. In dieser Hilflosigkeit halten wir uns an ihn, lesen seine Anweisungen ganz genau und nehmen sie ernst. Wie wir wissen, hatte er eine große Abneigung gegen den oberflächlichen Makart-Pomp seiner Zeit. Er liebte das Extreme, die Eishöhle, Neuschwanstein und das Unsichtbare. Manchmal hatte er die Vision eines unsichtbaren Theaters. Ob er an einem Hollywoodfilm oder eher an einem weißen Quadrat auf weißer Fläche seine Freude gehabt hätte, wissen wir nicht. Zerrissen wie er war, hätte er vielleicht beides akzeptiert. Jedenfalls konnte er sich vorstellen, daß sein *Ring* nur einmal aufgeführt wird, am besten am Rhein. Anschließend sollten Bühnenbild, Theater und Partitur verbrannt werden.

In Mannheim gab es einen Rahmen, der sich als Bild durch alle Stücke zog: einen Beton-Mythenraum zwischen Orchestergraben und Bühne, eine Art Wartesaal der Götter und der anderen mythischen Figuren. Hier war es gemütlich und wehrhaft, beides zugleich. Eine riesige Betonwand diente als Vorhang. Je nach Bedarf senkte oder hob sie sich. Assoziationen an Burg, Bunker und Staudamm konnten sich einstellen.

Danach kommen alle Orte vor, wie von Wagner bestimmt: die Höhlen Nibelheims, die Bergeshöhen für die Götter, die wilden Berglandschaften, die mächtige Esche in Hundings Hütte, der Wald und die Gibichungenhalle. Vor allem gibt es den Walkürenfels. Da dieses Bild immer wieder auftaucht, ist es zu einer Art bildnerischem Leitmotiv geworden.

Um den Rhein sichtbar zu machen, wurde auf die große Betonwand fließendes Rheinwasser projiziert, das, wie von Wagner gefordert, von rechts nach links floß.

The Rhinegold

Opera in four scenes by Richard Wagner. Preliminary evening to the stage festival play *The Ring of the Nibelung*

Nationaltheater Mannheim, 1999/2000; conductor: Jun Märkl, director: Martin Schüler, sets: Hans Dieter Schaal, costumes and properties: Marie-Luise Strandt, projections: Hans Peter Böffgen, dramaturgy: Christian Carlstedt and Dietmar Schwarz

The settings: »1. At the bottom of the Rhine. 2. An open area on the mountain-tops. 3. Underground chasm. Nibelheim. 4. Back to the open area on the mountain-tops, as in 2.«

The first set in Mannheim is constructed like a view into the Rhine from the bowels of the earth. The surface of the water can be seen from below.

In the second scene the mountain-tops appear, with a view of Valhalla, a white, cold, snowy landscape. The gods are cold. Valhalla glows in the background as a projection: skyscrapers, passing clouds. What is real, what is just fiction? Giants built Valhalla. Now they come to Wotan to ask for their wages. He had promised them his wife's sister. Then they all hear about Alberich's theft of the gold. Wotan extorts the gold from him by a trick and pays the giants with it to purchase his wife's sister's freedom. Erda appears and gives her warning (»Mother Earth«).

The third scene shows Nibelheim. The audience sees an underground machine shop. Neon lighting. Sulphurous vapour is streaming out of all the cracks.

In the final scene the gods gather to cross the rainbow bridge to Valhalla, whose image can be seen in the distance, pale and misty, as in a fog. In Mannheim the bridge consisted of a rainbow-coloured carpet that led to a gangway – the gods as space travellers in the dream realm of myth.

Das Rheingold

Oper in vier Szenen von Richard Wagner. Vorabend zu dem Bühnenfestspiel *Der Ring des Nibelungen*

Nationaltheater Mannheim, 1999/2000; musikalische Leitung: Jun Märkl, Inszenierung: Martin Schüler, Bühne: Hans Dieter Schaal, Kostüme und Requisiten: Marie-Luise Strandt, Projektionen: Hans Peter Böffgen, Dramaturgie: Christian Carlstedt und Dietmar Schwarz

Die Bühnenbild-Orte: »1. Auf dem Grund des Rheins. 2. Freie Gegend auf Bergeshöhen 3. Unterirdische Kluft. Nibelheim. 4. Wieder freie Gegend auf Bergeshöhen wie 2.«

Das erste Bild in Mannheim ist wie ein Blick aus dem Erdinneren heraus in den Rhein gebaut. Man sieht die Wasserfläche von unten.

Im zweiten Bild erscheinen die Bergeshöhen mit Blick auf Walhall, eine weiße kalte Schneelandschaft. Die Götter frieren. Walhall leuchtet im Hintergrund als Projektion: Wolkenkratzer, vorbeiziehende Wolken. Was ist wirklich, was nur fiktiv? Riesen haben Walhall erbaut. Nun finden sie sich bei Wotan ein, um ihren Lohn zu fordern. Er hatte ihnen die Schwester seiner Frau versprochen. Dann hören alle vom Goldraub Alberichs. Mit einem Trick erpreßt Wotan das Gold und bezahlt damit die Riesen, um die Schwester seiner Frau freizukaufen. Erda erscheint und mahnt (»Mutter Erde«).

Das dritte Bild zeigt Nibelheim. Man sieht eine unterirdische Maschinenhalle. Neonlicht. Schwefeldampf strömt aus allen Ritzen.

Im letzten Bild versammeln sich die Götter zum Gang über die Regenbogenbrücke. In der Ferne ist das Bild von Walhall zu erkennen, blaß und dunstig wie im Nebel. Die Brücke bestand in Mannheim aus einem regenbogenfarbenen Teppich, der zu einer Gangway führte – die Götter als Raumfahrer im Traumreich der Mythen.

The Valkyrie

Opera in three acts, first day of the stage festival play The Ring of the Nibelung

Nationaltheater Mannheim, 1999/2000; conductor: Jun Märkl, director: Martin Schüler, sets: Hans Dieter Schaal, costumes and properties: Marie-Luise Strandt, projections: Hans Peter Böffgen, dramaturgy: Christian Carlstedt and Dietmar Schwarz

The settings: »1. A room in Hunding's hut. 2. A wild, rocky place, with a thrusting rock and a gorge. 3. The summit of the rocky mountain, the Valkyries' rock.«

The Valkyrie begins with Hunding's famous room with a tree growing through it: Wagner's description says: »The interior of a living room. In the centre is the trunk of a mighty ash tree whose strongly raised roots are lost deep in the ground; the tree is separated from its top by a timbered roof that is cut through in such a way that the trunk and the branches, which stretch out on all sides, can go out through precisely corresponding openings; it is assumed that the leafy top of the tree spreads out over this roof. A timbered room has now been constructed around the trunk of the tree, as a centre point …«

A surreal space. Most of the locations in the *Ring* are derived from a romantic, romanticized Germanic world that also alluded to something that was contemporary at the time on a second plane. Why is this massive ash tree in the middle of the room? Hunding could just as well have built his house at the side of it. Of course this is not just any tree, but the world ash tree, a kind of primal tree, perhaps. And there is something special in its trunk: the sword that was once thrust in there by »an old man in a blue robe«, with a hat pulled deep over his eyes, and that so far no one has been able to pull out. Hunding is thus guarding a mythical place that represents something like a fortress prison for the ash tree and the sword.

In Mannheim this mighty tree did actually grow through Hunding's house. There was a real fire burning in the hearth, and there were stuffed birds on the cornices. Only the night outside the great window was artificial, made up of foil, projections and stage painting.

In this room Siegmund and Sieglinde, a long separated brother and sister, meet. Sieglinde lives here with Hunding. The brother and sister fall in love with each other, and their son Siegfried is conceived during the first night they spend together.

Second scene of *The Valkyrie*: the wild rocky place is formed by a sloping diagonal surface that takes up the whole width of the stage. Stylized rocks are lying around on the right and left and a rounded mountaintop curves upwards in the background. The gorge is represented by an incision in the sloping surface.

This bleak and inhospitable landscape is given a romantic aspect by a surreal doorway in the middle of the mountain: when the door is open, it reveals a view of a transfigured mountain panorama with snowy peaks and the setting sun.

Which path shall we choose? Do we go out into the distant landscape and the universe or inside, into our own past?

Siegmund and Hunding come to fight in the wild landscape. Finally Siegmund is killed, and Sieglinde flees into Fafner's forest, where she will bring Siegfried into the world, to be brought up by Mime.

The third scene of *The Valkyrie*: a rocky mountaintop, the Valkyries' rock. »The Valkyries, Wotan's daughters, are no longer fulfilling their original, archaic function. It was they who laid the heroes down on the battlefields, bringing them their peace in a sheltering, maternal gesture. Now they are recruiting heroes for Wotan's final army, building a protective wall around the anxious fantasies of their father, who is at the same time admitting his fear by doing this and at the same time demanding unconditional obedience. He makes the women into his instruments and builds them into the context of his world theatre as an auxiliary troop. By robbing them of their maternal aspect, denying them the opportunity to lay down their son, he is causing the struggle between male and female to crystallize: the male god functionalizes dying for the purposes of war – a fantasy of armed fighting forces intended to defend a god who wants to die.« (Juliane Votteler)

In Mannheim the Valkyries' rock was sunk in a black cave on the summit: it is possible to see the sky through a huge, oval hole. Snow is falling. It is icy cold up here.

Inside the remnants of war can be seen, cannons, bunkers, ruins, rubble. The world of heroes is slow to be transfigured. Hundreds of thousands, millions of the dead are rotting and stinking. The vultures are circling. And the gateway to immortality is a hole in the sky. The Valkyries too stare out into the infinity of the black universe; there must be a meaning, the heroic death cannot have been in vain.

At the end of *The Valkyrie* Wotan lays Brünnhilde down here and surrounds her with a massive ring of fire. Only the boldest hero will be able to walk through it.

Wotan now sinks further and further into depression. None of his infidelities, intrigues and power games can take him any further.

Die Walküre

Oper in drei Aufzügen, erster Tag des Bühnenfestspiels *Der Ring des Nibelungen*

Nationaltheater Mannheim, 1999/2000; musikalische Leitung: Jun Märkl, Inszenierung: Martin Schüler, Bühne: Hans Dieter Schaal, Kostüme und Requisiten: Marie-Luise Strandt, Projektionen: Hans Peter Böffgen, Dramaturgie: Christian Carlstedt und Dietmar Schwarz

Die Bühnenbild-Orte: »1. Wohnraum, Hundings Hütte. 2. Wildes Felsengebirge, mit Felsjoch und Schlucht. 3. Gipfel des Felsberges, Walkürenfels.«

Die Walküre beginnt mit dem berühmten Raum Hundings, der von einem Baum durchwachsen wird: In Wagners Beschreibung heißt es: »Das Innere eines Wohnraums. In der Mitte steht der Stamm einer mächtigen Esche, dessen stark erhabene Wurzeln sich weithin in den Erdboden verlieren; von seinem Wipfel ist der Baum durch ein gezimmertes Dach geschieden, welches so durchschnitten ist, daß der Stamm und die nach allen Seiten hin ausstreckenden Äste durch genau entsprechende Öffnungen hindurch gehen; von dem belaubten Gipfel wird angenommen, daß er sich über dieses Dach ausbreite. Um den Eschenstamm, als Mittelpunkt, ist nun ein Saal gezimmert ...«

Ein surrealer Raum. Die meisten Orte im *Ring* entstammen einer romantischen, romantisierten Germanenwelt, die in einer zweiten Bedeutungsebene auch damals Zeitgenössisches meinte. Warum gibt es mitten im Zimmer diese gewaltige Esche? Hunding hätte sein Haus ebenso auch neben sie bauen können. Freilich handelt es sich nicht um irgendeinen Baum, sondern um die Weltesche, eine Art Urbaum vielleicht. In seinem Stamm steckt etwas Besonderes: das Schwert, das einst »ein Greis in blauem Gewand« mit tiefhängendem Hut in ihn hineingestoßen hat und das bisher keiner herausziehen konnte. Hunding bewacht demnach einen mythischen Ort, der für Esche und Schwert so etwas wie ein Burggefängnis darstellt.

In Mannheim wurde das Haus Hundings tatsächlich von diesem gewaltigen Baum durchwachsen. Im Kamin brannte richtiges Feuer, und auf den Simsen standen ausgestopfte Vögel. Nur die Nacht vor dem großen Fenster war künstlich, ein Produkt aus Folien, Projektion und Theatermalerei.

In diesem Raum begegnen sich Siegmund und Sieglinde, das lang getrennte Geschwisterpaar. Sieglinde lebt hier mit Hunding. Das Geschwisterpaar verliebt sich ineinander, und in der ersten Nacht, die sie gemeinsam verbringen, wird ihr Sohn Siegfried gezeugt.

Zweites Walküren-Bild: Eine die ganze Bühnenbreite einnehmende schräge Diagonalfläche formt das wilde Felsengebirge. Links und rechts liegen stilisierte Felsbrocken, im Hintergrund wölbt sich ein abgerundeter Bergrücken. Die Schlucht ist mit einem Einschnitt in die Schräge dargestellt.

Die kahle unwirtliche Landschaft erhält durch eine surreale Türöffnung mitten im Berg ihren romantischen Ausblick: Ist die Tür geöffnet, sieht man hinaus auf ein verklärtes Gebirgspanorama mit Schneegipfeln und Sonnenuntergang.

Welchen Weg wählen wir? Gehen wir in die Ferne der Landschaft und des Weltalls hinaus oder nach innen, hinein in unsere eigene Vergangenheit?

Hier in dieser wilden Landschaft kommt es zum Zweikampf zwischen Hunding und Siegmund. Schließlich fällt Siegmund, und Sieglinde flieht in den Wald Fafners, wo sie Siegfried zur Welt bringt, den Mime aufziehen wird.

Drittes Walküren-Bild: Gipfel des Felsberges, Walkürenfels. »Die Walküren, Wotans Töchter, sind nicht mehr in ihrer ursprünglichen, archaischen Funktion tätig. Sie waren es, die die Helden auf den Schlachtfeldern niederlegten, sie in einer mütterlichen, bergenden Geste zur Ruhe betteten. Nun sammeln sie die Helden zur Rekrutierung für Wotans Endheer, bauen den Schutzwall um die Angstphantasien des Vaters, der seine Furcht damit offen eingesteht und gleichzeitig unbedingten Gehorsam fordert. Er instrumentalisiert die Frauen und baut sie in den Kontext seines Welttheaters als Hilfstruppe ein. Indem er sie um den Aspekt der Mütterlichkeit beraubt, ihnen die Möglichkeit, den Sohn niederzulegen verweigert, kristallisiert sich der Kampf des Männlichen mit dem Weiblichen: der männliche Gott funktionalisiert das Sterben für den Krieg – Phantasie einer bewehrten Schutzmacht, die einen Gott, der sterben will, verteidigen soll.« (Juliane Votteler)

In Mannheim wurde der Walkürenfels in eine schwarze Gipfelhöhle eingesenkt: Durch ein riesiges, ovales Loch kann man den Himmel sehen. Schnee fällt herab. Es ist eiskalt hier oben.

Im Inneren Kriegsreste, Kanonen, Bunker, Trümmer, Schutt. Die Welt der Helden verklärt sich nur mühsam. Hunderttausende, Millionen von Toten verwesen stinkend. Die Aasgeier kreisen. Und das Tor zur Unsterblichkeit ist ein Loch im Himmel. Auch die Walküren starren hinaus in die Unendlichkeit des schwarzen Alls; es muß einen Sinn geben, der Heldentod kann nicht umsonst gewesen sein.

Am Ende der *Walküre* legt Wotan hier Brünnhilde nieder und umgibt sie mit einem gewaltigen Feuerkreis. Nur der kühnste Held wird ihn durchschreiten.

Wotan wird jetzt zunehmend depressiver. Alle Seitensprünge, Intrigen, Machtspiele führen ihn nicht weiter.

Siegfried

Opera in three acts, second day of the stage festival play *The Ring of the Nibelung*

Nationaltheater Mannheim, 1999/2000; conductor: Jun Märkl, director: Martin Schüler, sets: Hans Dieter Schaal, costumes and properties: Marie-Luise Strandt, projections: Hans Peter Böffgen, dramaturgy: Christian Carlstedt and Dietmar Schwarz

The settings for the action: »1. Forest. Rocky cave and forge. 2. Deep forest with Fafner's cave. 3. Wild area. 4. The Valkyries' rock.«

In Mannheim, the first three scenes are dominated by a gigantic mound of sawn-off tree trunks piled on top of each other. Mime has established himself in a wild ruined property in front of the almost vertical wall consisting of discs cut from tree-trunks: the forge with the fire and hearth is in the middle, the work benches to the right and left, and he lives in a parked railway carriage.

Mime's foster-child Siegfried moves freely and naturally in these surroundings. He is utterly uncomplicated and untouched by civilization. A real child of nature in the manner of Rousseau.

He succeeds effortlessly in reforging the sword »Nothung«, which had been broken in the fight between Siegmund and Hunding. Mime had been trying in vain to do this for a long time.

For the second scene, the railway carriage was taken out and the pile of wood split down the middle. As it broke apart it slowly revealed Fafner's cave: a black hole with a wall of gold bars built up in front of it that the dragon used as a hiding-place.

Now everyone wants the ring that is in the dragon's cave. Siegfried begins to provoke the sleeping monster. But all it does is boom in its bass voice from the cave. »I lie and possess: let me sleep!« But finally it does appear. A giant pair of eyes appears above the wall of gold bars and Siegfried plunges his newly forged sword deep into its heart.

When Mime tries to kill Siegfried with a poisoned drink the hero strikes for a second time and murders him as well. Suddenly Siegfried understands the song of a woodbird, who tells him about Brünnhilde and the Valkyries' rock. He sets off to see it, filled with curiosity.

The fourth scene shows the Valkyries' rock again, with the large, oval hole showing the sky. Wotan is sitting at the entrance to the cave, as the wanderer. When Siegfried appears, he stands in his way. Siegfried smashes Wotan's spear impatiently and rushes in to wake Brünnhilde. She wakes up, and embraces the hero, delirious with love.

Siegfried

Oper in drei Aufzügen, zweiter Tag des Bühnenfestspiels *Der Ring des Nibelungen*

Nationaltheater Mannheim, 1999/2000; musikalische Leitung: Jun Märkl, Inszenierung: Martin Schüler, Bühne: Hans Dieter Schaal, Kostüme und Requisiten: Marie-Luise Strandt, Projektionen: Hans Peter Böffgen, Dramaturgie: Christian Carlstedt und Dietmar Schwarz

Die Bühnenbild-Orte der Handlung: »1. Wald. Felsenhöhle und Schmiede. 2. Tiefer Wald mit Fafner-Höhle. 3. Wilde Gegend. 4. Walkürenfels.«

In Mannheim bestimmt ein riesiger Berg aus übereinandergestapelten, abgesägten Baumstämmen die ersten drei Bilder. Vor der fast senkrechten, aus Baumscheiben bestehenden Wand hat sich Mime in einem verwilderten Ruinenanwesen eingerichtet: die Schmiede mit dem Feuer und dem Kamin in der Mitte, die Werkbänke rechts und links, sein Wohnbereich in einem abgestellten Zugwaggon.

Mimes Zögling Siegfried bewegt sich in dieser Umgebung frei und natürlich. Er ist vollkommen unkompliziert und von der Zivilisation unberührt. Ein echtes Naturkind im Rousseauschen Sinne.

Mühelos gelingt es ihm, das Schwert »Nothung«, das im Kampf zwischen Hunding und Siegmund zertrümmert worden war, wieder zusammenzufügen. Mime hatte sich darum lange Zeit vergeblich bemüht.

Für das zweite Bild wurde der Eisenbahnwaggon hinausgefahren, und der Holzstapelberg spaltete sich in der Mitte. Beim Auseinanderbrechen gab er langsam den Blick auf Fafners Höhle frei: ein schwarzes Loch, vor dem eine Goldbarrenwand aufgebaut war, die dem Drachen als Versteck diente.

Alle wollen nun den Ring, der in der Höhle des Drachen liegt. Siegfried beginnt das schlafende Ungeheuer zu reizen. Aber es dröhnt nur mit seiner Baßstimme aus der Höhlentiefe. »Ich lieg und besitz: Laßt mich schlafen!« Schließlich erscheint es doch. Über der Goldbarrenwand taucht sein riesiges Augenpaar auf, und Siegfried stößt ihm das neu geschmiedete Schwert mitten ins Herz.

Als Mime Siegfried mit einem Gifttrank töten will, stößt der Held ein zweites Mal zu und ermordet auch ihn. Plötzlich versteht Siegfried den Gesang eines Waldvogels, der von Brünnhilde und dem Walkürenfels erzählt. Neugierig macht er sich dorthin auf den Weg.

Das vierte Bild zeigt wieder den Walkürenfels mit dem großen ovalen Himmelsloch. Wotan sitzt als Wanderer am Eingang der Höhle. Als Siegfried erscheint, stellt er sich ihm in den Weg. Ungeduldig zerschlägt Siegfried den Speer Wotans und stürzt in den Raum, um Brünnhilde zu wecken. Sie erwacht und umarmt liebestrunken den Helden.

The Twilight of the Gods

Opera in a prelude and three acts, third day of the stage festival play *The Ring of the Nibelung*

Nationaltheater Mannheim, 1999/2000; conductor: Jun Märkl, director: Martin Schüler, sets: Hans Dieter Schaal, costumes and properties: Marie-Luise Strandt, projections: Hans Peter Böffgen, dramaturgy: Christian Carlstedt and Dietmar Schwarz

The settings for the action: »1. The Valkyries' rock. 2. The Gibichungs' hall on the Rhine. 3. The Valkyries' rock. 4. On the banks of the river, outside the Gibichungs' hall. 5. Wild wooded and rocky valley by the Rhine. 6. The Gibichungs' hall.«

The Twilight of the Gods has brought us to civilization. The Gibichungs' marble hall seems large and showy. The only thing that is now needed for absolute power is the ring that Siegfried is wearing on his finger. Hagen manages to kill Siegfried's by using false promises, magic potions, lies and intrigues. Siegfried's burial is celebrated with the most stupendous funeral march in the history of opera.

Then Brünnhilde, the betrayed woman, has a massive funeral pyre erected. Her suicide is intended to free the world from the curse of the ring. But the Gibichungs are not the only ones who are to burn. Valhalla goes up in flames as well, and the Rhine bursts its banks in a flash flood. The Rhine Maidens pull Hagen and the ring down into the depths.

What is left? Wagner's last stage direction says: »The men and women watch the events and the phenomenon, speechless with shock. The curtain falls.«

The people survive. We are still alive. Only the gods and the Nibelungen have gone down. But have they really?

At the beginning of *The Twilight of the Gods* we see the three Norns who – like divine spiders – are spinning golden ropes and commenting on past events as they do so. Suddenly the rope breaks. They give up in resignation and go down to the Erda, the Earth Mother.

In Mannheim this scene is not played on the Valkyries' rock, as prescribed, but in the Rhine Maiden's oval Rhine aquarium, which has now been tilted, and has the trunks of trees growing through it.

Then comes the Gibichungs' gigantic marble hall on the Rhine. In the background is a large window with a view of the river bank.

Large stone armchairs and tables with living-room lamps are reminiscent of a hotel lobby or a large waiting room.

Shortly before the end of the opera the view through the window changes: skyscrapers emerge from the Rhine landscape, at an alarming angle, as if after an earthquake. We have unmistakably arrived at the present day, having emerged from the myth at the speed of a lift. Perhaps we have been watching the story from here all the time.

Götterdämmerung

Oper in einem Vorspiel und drei Aufzügen, dritter Tag des Bühnenfestspiels *Der Ring des Nibelungen*

Nationaltheater Mannheim, 1999/2000; musikalische Leitung: Jun Märkl, Inszenierung: Martin Schüler, Bühne: Hans Dieter Schaal, Kostüme und Requisiten: Marie-Luise Strandt, Projektionen: Hans Peter Böffgen, Dramaturgie: Christian Carlstedt und Dietmar Schwarz

Die Bühnenbild-Orte der Handlung: »1. Der Walkürenfels. 2. Halle der Gibichungen am Rhein. 3. Walkürenfels. 4. Uferraum, vor der Halle der Gibichungen. 5. Wildes Wald- und Felsental am Rhein. 6. Die Halle der Gibichungen.«

Mit der *Götterdämmerung* sind wir in der Zivilisation angekommen. Die marmorne Halle der Gibichungen erscheint groß und protzig. Das einzige, was jetzt noch zur absoluten Macht fehlt, ist der Ring, den Siegfried am Finger trägt. Durch falsche Versprechungen, Zaubertränke, Lügen und Intrigen gelingt es Hagen, Siegfried zu töten. Mit dem gewaltigsten Trauermarsch der Operngeschichte wird Siegfrieds Beerdigung zelebriert.

Dann läßt Brünnhilde, die Betrogene, einen gewaltigen Scheiterhaufen errichten. Ihr Selbstmord soll die Welt vom Fluch des Rings befreien. Aber es bleibt nicht beim Brand von Gibichungen. Auch Walhall geht in Flammen auf, und der Rhein tritt mit einer Springflut über die Ufer. Die Rheintöchter ziehen Hagen und den Ring mit in die Tiefe.

Was bleibt? Wagners letzte Regieanweisung lautet: »Die Männer und Frauen schauen in sprachloser Erschütterung dem Vorgange und der Erscheinung zu. Der Vorhang fällt.«

Das Volk überlebt. Wir leben noch. Nur die Götter und Nibelungen sind untergegangen. Sind sie es wirklich?

Zu Beginn der *Götterdämmerung* sehen wir drei Nornen, die – wie göttliche Spinnen – goldene Seile spinnen und dabei die vergangenen Ereignisse kommentieren. Plötzlich reißt das Seil, resigniert geben sie auf und steigen hinab zur Urmutter Erda.

In Mannheim spielt die Szene nicht im Walkürenfels, wie vorgeschrieben, sondern in dem ovalen Rhein-Aquarium der Rheintöchter. Inzwischen ist es schräg und wild durchwachsen von Baumstämmen.

Dann folgt die riesige Marmorhalle der Gibichungen am Rhein. Im Hintergrund ein großes Fenster mit Blick zum Ufer des Flusses.

Große Steinsessel und Tische mit Wohnzimmerlampen erinnern an eine Hotelhalle oder an einen großen Wartesaal.

Kurz vor dem Ende der Oper ändert sich der Blick aus dem Fenster: Aus der Rheinlandschaft tauchen Wolkenkratzer auf, in bedenklicher Schräglage, wie nach einem Erdbeben. Wir sind eindeutig im Heute angekommen, aufgestiegen aus dem Mythos im Aufzugstempo. Von hier aus haben wir vielleicht die ganze Zeit die Geschichte betrachtet.

Patmos

Azione musicale by Wolfgang von Schweinitz after the Book of Revelation, text by Martin Luther and D. E. Sattler
Congress hall of the Deutsches Museum as a co-production for the Munich Biennale with the Staatstheater Kassel, 1990; direction and choreography: Ruth Berghaus, conductor: Adam Fischer, sets: Hans Dieter Schaal, costumes and properties: Marie-Luise Strandt

The composer calls this work an Azione musicale in 7 acts with Introitus. It is not an opera in the traditional sense, nor is it a Passion, but Christian ecclesiastical music with the sounds of the 20th century on a Biblical search. No composer had previously set this tremendous text.

There are two Johns in Christian teaching: John the Baptist, who baptized Jesus in the Jordan, and John the disciple, who probably went to Ephesus after his master was crucified. From here he was banished to the island of Patmos for spreading the Christian doctrine.

Here John wrote the Book of Revelation in a cave. He gives an account of the end of the world in mysterious, often surreal images, then – after the defeat of Satan and the Anti-Christ – the building of the divine Jerusalem on earth.

The concept of revelation, uncovering, a literal translation of the Greek word apocalypse, presumes that the world or the truth were previously concealed. It is only when the letters are written and the seven seals broken that the disaster can be seen: earthquakes, drought, hunger, war, sickness and death. The horsemen of the apo-calypse bring ruin and extinction. After this the Kingdom of God shines forth, and the New Jerusalem descends. First come the threats, and then the promises of heaven. The enemies were clearly defined: the anti-Christian, Roman occupying forces. In his letters to the seven Christian communities in Asia Minor, John is using a kind of secret language. Subversive messages from prison.

While I was looking for clues on Patmos, a tourist plane crashed into the highest mountain on the island of Samos. The pall of smoke could be seen in the distance from the ship. Forty people are killed. Later I look at the piece of rock on which John is said to have rested his head to sleep. From here you can see only a chink of the sky. Birds pass through the image from time to time.

We are coming closer to today's stories. As tourists, we dig into strangers' pasts with curious eyes. The camera records what we have seen. Realities overlap. A story is constructed in which archaeology is mixed with the present. Mental architecture. Pictorial archaeology.

The stage setting for the action: in the libretto it says only »on the island«, nothing more. In Munich and Kassel the site of an archaeological dig is shown.

Figures come up out of square holes, revived ideas, near and far at the same time. With them, things that were missing come back to the light of day: letters, books, typewriters, crosses, model churches, shards, stones, words, notes, images, fragments of figures, skulls, bones, buckets, hoses, tubes, basins, tubs, faces, blinded faces.

The incision in the flesh of the earth becomes an incision in our consciousness. Prophets' voices. Scientists' voices. Mixtures. Images burn and fall apart into ash.

The occupying forces create order violently, they suppress the new religion. The early Christians are still living camouflaged and dig their catacombs under ancient Rome. Sometime or other they come up into the daylight, build churches and bury their dead in cemeteries.

The text of Revelation in Braille: about the intelligibility of the world, demystifying it, decoding it. Detective work, research work. Natural sciences, enlightenment. Set against this, those who blur issues, the false prophets, the storytellers who lay false trails – the religions.

The archaeological digs become the trenches of warfare. War. Conflict.

Opposing world views. Throwing stones at each other, texts and ideas. Throwing mud and bombs at each other. Throwing rooms and news at each other. Throwing images at each other and drowning in the flood.

The opera *Patmos* depicts the condition of the world before it ends. The catastrophes are described as events that lie ahead. We look back from the point of view of today. Gigantic fields of corpses have inserted themselves between the visions of the past and the present day, the earth is steeped in the blood of countless battles. The catastrophes of the two world wars, the Holocaust, Hiroshima and Nagasaki thrust into the image like charred memorials.

If the prophecies of Revelation are right, then six of the seven seals have already been opened. Perhaps it is only a small step to opening the seventh.

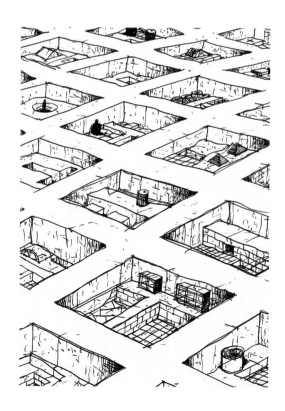

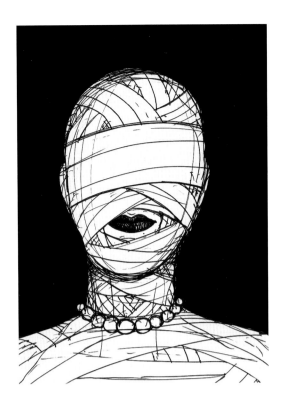

Patmos

Azione musicale von Wolfgang von Schweinitz
nach der Apokalypse des Johannes, Text von Martin Luther und D. E. Sattler

Kongreßsaal des Deutschen Museums als Koproduktion der Münchner Biennale mit dem Staatstheater Kassel, 1990; Inszenierung und Choreographie: Ruth Berghaus, musikalische Leitung: Adam Fischer, Bühne: Hans Dieter Schaal, Kostüme und Requisiten: Marie-Luise Strandt

Der Komponist nennt dieses Werk eine Azione musicale in 7 Akten mit Introitus. Es ist keine Oper im herkömmlichen Sinne, auch keine Passion, sondern christliche Kirchenmusik mit den Klängen des 20. Jahrhunderts auf biblischer Spurensuche. Den gewaltigen Text hatte bisher noch kein Komponist vollständig vertont.

In der christlichen Lehre gibt es zwei Johannesfiguren: Johannes, den Täufer, der Jesus im Jordan getauft hat, und Johannes, den Jünger, welcher nach der Kreuzigung seines Meisters wahrscheinlich nach Ephesus ging. Von dort verbannte ihn die römische Besatzungsmacht wegen der Verbreitung christlicher Lehren auf die Insel Patmos.

Hier schrieb Johannes in einer Höhle die Apokalypse nieder. In rätselhaften, oft surrealen Bildern schildert sie das Ende der Welt und – nach der Überwindung des Satans und des Antichrist – die Errichtung des himmlischen Jerusalem auf Erden.

Der Begriff Offenbarung oder Enthüllung, die wörtliche Übersetzung des griechischen Wortes Apokalypse, setzt voraus, daß die Welt oder die Wahrheit vorher verborgen waren. Erst wenn die Briefe geschrieben und die sieben Siegel zerbrochen sind, gibt sich das Unheil zu erkennen: Erdbeben, Dürre, Hunger, Krieg, Krankheiten und Tod. Die apokalyptischen Reiter bringen Verderben und Auslöschung. Danach leuchtet das Reich Gottes, und das himmlische Jerusalem kommt herab. Erst die Drohungen, dann die himmlischen Versprechungen. Die Feinde waren klar definiert, es sind die antichristlichen, römischen Besatzer. In seinen Briefen an die sieben christlichen Gemeinden Kleinasiens verwendet Johannes eine Art Geheimsprache. Subversive Kassiber.

Während ich auf Patmos Spuren suche, prallt auf Samos ein Touristenflugzeug gegen den höchsten Berg der Insel. Vom Schiff aus sieht man in der Ferne den Qualm. Vierzig Menschen finden den Tod. Später betrachte ich den Felsblock, auf den Johannes seinen Kopf zum Schlafen niedergelegt haben soll. Von hier aus sieht man den Himmel nur einen Spalt breit. Ab und zu kreuzen Vögel das Bild.

Wir nähern uns den Geschichten von heute. Als Touristen graben wir mit neugierigen Blicken in fremden Vergangenheiten. Der Photoapparat dokumentiert das Gesehene. Realitäten überlagern sich. Es entsteht eine Geschichtskonstruktion, in der sich Archäologisches mit Gegenwärtigem mischt. Gedanken-Architektur. Bild-Archäologie.

Bühnenbild-Ort der Handlung: Im Libretto steht nur »auf der Insel«, sonst nichts. In München und Kassel sieht man ein Ausgrabungsfeld.

Aus quadratischen Löchern tauchen Figuren auf, wiederbelebte Gedanken, nah und fern zugleich. Mit ihnen kommen verschollene Dinge ans Tageslicht: Briefe, Bücher, Schreibmaschinen, Kreuze, Kirchenmodelle, Scherben, Steine, Worte, Töne, Bilder, Figurenfragmente, Schädel, Knochen, Eimer, Schläuche, Rohre, Becken, Wannen, Gesichter, verblendete Gesichter.

Der Schnitt ins Fleisch der Erde wird zum Schnitt durch unser Bewußtsein. Stimmen der Propheten. Stimmen der Wissenschaftler. Vermischungen. Bilder brennen und zerfallen zu Asche.

Die Besatzer schaffen gewaltsam Ordnung, sie unterdrücken die neue Religion. Noch leben die frühen Christen getarnt und untergraben mit ihren Katakomben das antike Rom. Irgendwann kommen sie nach oben ans Tageslicht, errichten Kirchen und begraben ihre Toten auf Friedhöfen.

Der Text der Apokalypse in Blindenschrift: Von der Lesbarkeit der Welt, ihrer Enträtselung, ihrer Entschlüsselung. Detektivarbeit, Forscherarbeit. Naturwissenschaften, Aufklärung. Dagegen die Einnebler, die falschen Propheten, die Geschichtenerzähler, die falsche Spuren legen – die Religionen.

Die archäologischen Gräben werden zu Schützengräben. Krieg. Kampf.

Weltanschauungen gegeneinander. Sich mit Steinen bewerfen, mit Texten und Gedanken. Sich mit Schlamm bewerfen und mit Bomben. Sich mit Räumen bewerfen und mit Nachrichten. Sich mit Bildern bewerfen und in der Bilderflut ertrinken.

Die Oper Patmos schildert den Zustand der Welt, bevor sie untergeht. Die Katastrophen werden als bevorstehende Ereignisse beschrieben. Wir blicken von heute aus zurück. Zwischen die damaligen Visionen und heute haben sich riesige Leichenfelder geschoben, die Erde ist getränkt mit dem Blut unzähliger Schlachten. Die Katastrophen der beiden Weltkriege, des Holocaust, Hiroshimas und Nagasakis ragen ins Bild wie verkohlte Mahnmale.

Wenn die Vorhersagen der Apokalypse stimmen, dann sind sechs der sieben Siegel bereits geöffnet. Vielleicht ist es wirklich nur noch ein kleiner Schritt zur Öffnung des siebten.

Moses und Aron

Opera in three acts (incomplete) by Arnold Schön-
berg, libretto by the composer based on Exodus
and Leviticus

Deutsche Staatsoper Berlin, 1987; conductor:
Friedrich Goldmann, director: Ruth Berghaus,
sets: Hans Dieter Schaal, costumes: Marie-Luise
Strandt, dramaturgy: Sigrid Neef

»Thou shalt not make to thyself any graven image« is the key sentence in the opera. Moses
proclaims this to his people, whom he has led
out of their Egyptian captivity into the desert.
»Only, eternal, omnipresent, invisible and unimag-
inable God …!« Moses, the radical, resists any
image of God since his return from Mount Sinai,
on which he has spent forty days alone. He be-
lieves only in the invisible power and the words of
the ten commandments that he received from
God on the mountain.

During his absence the people have relapsed
into idolatry, and spurred on by Moses' brother
Aaron they are celebrating with orgies around the
Golden Calf. Moses is angry and has his brother
arrested. He sacrifices his brother and condemns
him to death in order to have his teaching accepted.

The basic discussion that is being conducted
here is about worshipping or forbidding images.
The Jewish religion still forbids the worship of images. But the Christian church has developed
into a religion of images.

»Sigrid Neef: Could we not say that the opera
Moses und Aron is a perfect example, absolutely
demanding that a »new dimension« should be invented, that the central thought, the central image, God, is absent present and this absence
produces movement?

Ruth Berghaus: It would be possible to use
dancers to capture this principle that gains its
power from absence, this abstract thought that
seems active. They are always around people,
calming, touching, influencing, dance as a per-
manent movement, constantly interrupting and
preventing hardening, order, regularity, repose.
So that a longing is created for these moving
beings when they are not present on stage.

Heiner Müller: That is very important. No performance can be created without the category
of absence. This has been completely forgotten.
Covering the world completely with images is a
habit of television programmes and films. The
ban on images, one of the themes of *Moses und
Aron*, is enormously interesting here. One result
of Postmodernism is the notion of onward! – to
the latest design. The world can be replaced by
reproduction. Photography is the end of the
world, photography is becoming a substitute
for reality.

People only go to India so that they can show
the slides at home. That is quite trivial, but it is
associated with this ban on images. God's absence is his power.

Ruth Berghaus: Now there really is an absence of things that can be experienced of that
kind in the world.

Heiner Müller: Moses, Marx, Freud, Einstein –
those are four pioneers of absence. Moses –
God's absence because of the ban on images,
Marx – the absence of a final social condition because of the Utopia of Communism, Freud – the

absence of the essential, the sub-conscious, the
suppressed and Einstein – the theory of relativity,
the absence of the actual space-time relation.
These are four formulations of the ban on images. The fact that it was impossible to finish the
opera is linked with this. It would have given it
a frame, it would have become an image. Even
Schönberg is inhibited about the image as something that buries reality and any sense of process. It is possible to see this resistance to the
image, above all to the frame, in Picasso's work
as well.

What is expected of you is that you should
give the thing a frame so that everyone knows
what he or she has to think about it. But that is
precisely what can't be done.

Ruth Berghaus: You'd have to go mad with
the resources available.

Heiner Müller: Yes, you can avoid the frame if
you start to design an image and before it is really seen you bring in the next one, painted over
it, so that any particular image is never really con-
cluded by being given a frame. That's what you
mean by inflating the resources. The model for
that – and this doesn't come from me now,
clever people have found this out with reference
to this idea – is »picture description«. That's why
the term is used. An image is started and then
another one comes along that resolves the first
one or questions it. An image that you could actually take home with you is never created.

Sigrid Neef: But that's precisely what you expect, being able to take it home with you.

Heiner Müller: Yes, that is the fingerprints and
photographs treatment of art, that's the expecta-
tion. It has something to do with effect. Success
means people leaning back and saying: we've
found something out now, we know what was
meant now, and it was beautiful.

Sigrid Neef: So this staging in various layers
is an interpretation of the ban on images.

Heiner Müller: Yes, an image is always something that suppresses other images, covers up
the other ones. Why do I have the right to
choose precisely this image and thus to cover
other ones up?

It has something to do with selection as well.
The persecution of the Jews is a counter-move-
ment to the ban on images. Auschwitz would
not have been possible without an image of the
Jews. You have to have an image of something
before you can destroy it.

Ruth Berghaus: Yes, an image can be destroyed.

Heiner Müller: Music is not an image, music
is thinking about images.«
(Extract from a conversation between Sigrid
Neef, Ruth Berghaus and Heiner Müller on 4 October 1987)

The stage set for the Berlin *Moses und Aron*
translates the Biblical locations into the architectural language of today. The desert becomes an
enormous steel chamber with hints of lockers.
There is a suggestion of the Wailing Wall in Jerusalem and the bank vaults in which the Nazis
kept the treasures that had been stolen from the
Jews.

The actual state of things is kept hidden. The
people that has been delivered from captivity
has arrived in the next prison. Moses offers the
Promised Land, the earthly paradise that he says

lies beyond the desert on the far horizon. It is
flowing with milk and honey. There they will find
peace and freedom.

Moses becomes a Faustian explorer, a scientific seeker who wants to get to the absolute, to
the very core. And when he has reached that
core he splits the uranium atom and thus cata-
pults the world into the greatest possible catastrophe: the globe as a whole can be destroyed.

In front of the steel wall with its hints of lockers
is a replica of the table with the apparatus used
by Otto Hahn (with Fritz Strassmann) in 1938 to
demonstrate the first splitting of the atom. The
original table is in the department of scientific
chemistry in the Deutsches Museum, Munich.

In this opera, God represents the invisible
force that brings all life into being and causes it
to pass away again. Moses is a radical eradicator
and desert fanatic. Not even the name of God is
to be spoken. He is an inhuman God of emptiness, of nothing and of central power.

Life could be beautiful, filled with images,
colourful, full of music and dance, if Aaron had
his way.

Each individual with his own delusions. A
dream monastery that in reality is a prison and a
penitentiary. Prayer and torture take place by adjacent walls.

The stepped pyramid as a monastery of
thought. Doors open and close. When they are
opened, images are revealed, when they are
closed they disappear again. Revealing and concealing. Thinking in images. Thinking abstractly.
Fine art against mathematics. The theory of relativity consists half of the written word, the other
half is mathematical formulae. It contains no illus-
trations. Why do we have both eyes and mind?
Why do we see and think? Should every image
really be a lie, a one-sided statement, a way of
playing things down? What do we think when we
see the mountains of corpses in the concentration camps when they were opened at the end of
the Second World War, in photographs and on
film?

Rooms transform themselves into other
rooms. People transform themselves into other
people. Behind every door there is another reality,
another image.

The end: Moses has won. Aaron is dead.

The promises came to nothing. No New
Jerusalem and no land flowing with milk and
honey, but holy wars, civil wars, murder and
manslaughter, the earth strewn with the dead,
an invisible God who is silent, as he was at the
beginning. His invisibility could be coped with,
but it is hard to accept his silence.

Moses und Aron

Oper in drei Akten (unvollendet) von Arnold Schönberg, Text vom Komponisten nach dem 2. und 3. Buch Mose

Deutsche Staatsoper Berlin, 1987; musikalische Leitung: Friedrich Goldmann, Inszenierung: Ruth Berghaus, Bühne: Hans Dieter Schaal, Kostüme: Marie-Luise Strandt, Dramaturgie: Sigrid Neef

»Du sollst dir kein Bildnis machen«, lautet der Schlüsselsatz der Oper. Moses verkündet ihn seinem Volk, das er aus der ägyptischen Gefangenschaft heraus in die Wüste geführt hat. »Einziger, ewiger, allgegenwärtiger, unsichtbarer und unvorstellbarer Gott ...!« Moses, der Radikale, bekämpft seit seiner Rückkehr vom Berg Sinai, auf dem er allein vierzig Tage verbracht hat, jedes Abbild Gottes. Er glaubt nur an die unsichtbare Kraft und an den Text der zehn Gebote, die er auf dem Berg von Gott empfangen hat.

Während seiner Abwesenheit ist das Volk wieder in die Götzenverehrung zurückgefallen, und angestachelt von Aron, dem Bruder Moses, feiert es Orgien um das Goldene Kalb. Moses ist zornig und läßt seinen Bruder verhaften. Um seine Lehre durchzusetzen, opfert er den Bruder und verurteilt ihn zum Tode.

Es ist die Grunddiskussion um die Verehrung oder das Verbot der Bilder, die hier geführt wird. Bis heute lehnt die jüdische Religion die Bilderverehrung ab. Die christliche Kirche dagegen hat sich zu einer reinen Religion der Bilder entwickelt.

»Sigrid Neef: Erscheint die Oper *Moses und Aron* nicht als ein exemplarisches Beispiel, fordert sie nicht geradezu auf, eine »neue Dimension« zu erfinden, daß der zentrale Gedanke, das zentrale Bild, Gott, abwesend anwesend ist und diese Abwesenheit Bewegung hervorbringt?

Ruth Berghaus: Dieses durch Abwesenheit mächtige Prinzip zu fassen, diese abstrakten, aber tätig wirkenden Gedanken, das könnte mit Tänzern gelingen. Sie sind immer um die Leute herum, beruhigen, berühren, beeinflussen, Tanz als eine dauernde Bewegung, die Verfestigung, Ordnung, Gleichmaß, Ruhe ständig stört und verhindert. So daß eine Sehnsucht entsteht nach diesen Wesen in Bewegung, daß sie dadurch auch dann anwesend sind, wenn sie auf der Bühne nicht präsent sind.

Heiner Müller: Das ist ganz wichtig. Es läßt sich keine Aufführung herstellen ohne die Kategorie der Abwesenheit. Das ist völlig in Vergessenheit geraten. Die vollständige Abdeckung der Welt mit Bildern ist eine Gewöhnung von Fernsehsendungen und Filmen. Das Bilderverbot, ein Thema von *Moses und Aron*, ist hier ungeheuer interessant. Ein Ergebnis von Postmoderne ist: Vorwärts zum letzten Design. Die Welt wird ersetzbar durch Abbildung. Die Photographie ist das Ende der Welt, Photographie wird ein Ersatz für Wirklichkeit.

Man fährt nur nach Indien, um zu Hause die Dias zu zeigen. Das ist ganz trivial, aber es hat mit diesem Bilderverbot zu tun. Die Abwesenheit Gottes ist seine Macht.

Ruth Berghaus: Nun ist eine solche Abwesenheit von Erfahrbarem wirklich in der Welt vorhanden.

Heiner Müller: Moses, Marx, Freud, Einstein – das sind vier Pioniere der Abwesenheit. Moses – die Abwesenheit Gottes durch das Bilderverbot, Marx – die Abwesenheit eines gesellschaftlichen Endzustandes durch die Utopie des Kommunismus, Freud – die Abwesenheit des Wesentlichen, des Unbewußten, des Verdrängten und Einstein – die Relativitätstheorie, die Abwesenheit der eigentlichen Raum-Zeit-Relation. Das sind vier Formulierungen des Bilderverbots. Damit hängt es zusammen, daß es unmöglich war, die Oper zu vollenden. Sie hätte dann einen Rahmen bekommen, wäre zum Bild geworden. Auch bei Schönberg gibt es diese Hemmung vor dem Bild als Beerdigung von Wirklichkeit und Prozeßhaftem. Auch bei Picasso ist dieser Widerstand gegen das Bild, vor allem gegen den Rahmen zu beobachten.

Was man von dir erwartet, ist, daß du der Sache einen Rahmen gibst, damit jeder weiß, was er davon zu halten hat. Aber das genau das geht nicht.

Ruth Berghaus: Man müßte mit den Mitteln wuchern.

Heiner Müller: Ja, du kannst den Rahmen vermeiden, wenn du anfängst, ein Bild zu entwerfen, und bevor das wirklich gesehen wird, bringst du das nächste, als Übermalung, so kommt nie ein Bild zu Ende, das einen Rahmen bekommt. Das meinst du doch mit Inflation der Mittel. Das Modell dafür – das ist jetzt nicht von mir, das haben kluge Leute darüber befunden – ist »Bildbeschreibung«. Deswegen heißt es auch so. Da wird immer ein Bild angefangen und dann kommt ein anderes, was das alte auflöst oder in Frage stellt. Es kommt nie ein Bild zustande, das du wirklich mit nach Hause nehmen kannst.

Sigrid Neef: Aber das ist genau die Erwartung, es mit nach Hause nehmen zu können.

Heiner Müller: Ja, das ist die erkennungsdienstliche Behandlung von Kunst, das ist die Erwartung. Es hat etwas mit Wirkung zu tun. Erfolg ist, wenn die Leute sich zurücklehnen und sagen: Jetzt haben wir etwas erfahren, jetzt wissen wir, was gemeint war, und es war schön.

Sigrid Neef: Dieses Inszenieren in mehreren Schichten ist dann die Übersetzung des Bilderverbotes.

Heiner Müller: Ja, ein Bild ist auch immer eine Verdrängung von anderen Bildern, ein Zudecken der anderen. Wieso habe ich das Recht, gerade dieses Bild auszuwählen und damit anderes zuzudecken?

Das hat auch etwas mit Selektion zu tun. Die Judenverfolgung ist die Gegenbewegung zum Bilderverbot. Auschwitz wäre nicht möglich, ohne ein Bild vom Juden. Man muß ein Bild von etwas haben, bevor man es zerstören kann.

Ruth Berghaus: Ja, ein Bild ist zerstörbar.

Heiner Müller: Musik ist kein Bild, Musik ist Denken über Bilder.«

(Ausschnitt aus einem Gespräch zwischen Sigrid Neef, Ruth Berghaus und Heiner Müller, das am 4. Oktober 1987 stattfand)

Das Bühnenbild zu *Moses und Aron* in Berlin übersetzt die biblischen Orte in eine heutige Architektursprache. Die Wüste wird zu einer riesigen Stahlkammer mit angedeuteten Schließfächern. Die Jerusalemer Klagemauer klingt an und die Banktresore, in denen die Nazis die den Juden geraubten Schätze aufbewahrt haben.

Das Eigentliche bleibt verborgen. Das aus der Gefangenschaft befreite Volk ist im nächsten Gefängnis angekommen. Moses verspricht das gelobte Land, das irdische Paradies, das sich hinter der Wüste am fernen Horizont befände. Dort fließe Milch und Honig. Dort herrsche Frieden und Freiheit.

Moses wird zum faustischen Forscher, zum wissenschaftlichen Sucher, der ins Absolute, in den Kern vorstoßen will. Im Innersten angekommen spaltet er das Uran-Atom und stürzt die Welt damit in die größtmögliche Katastrophe: Der Globus als Gesamtheit ist zerstörbar.

Vor der Stahlschließwand steht eine Nachbildung des Tisches mit der Apparatur, durch die 1938 von Otto Hahn (zusammen mit Fritz Strassmann) die erste Atomkernspaltung nachgewiesen wurde. Das Original des Tisches befindet sich in der Abteilung für wissenschaftliche Chemie im Deutschen Museum, München.

Gott stellt in dieser Oper die unsichtbare Kraft dar, die alles Leben entstehen und vergehen läßt. Moses ist ein radikaler Auslöscher und Wüstenfanatiker. Nicht einmal den Namen Gottes darf man aussprechen. Es ist ein unmenschlicher Gott der Leere, des Nichts und der zentralen Kraft.

Schön könnte das Leben sein, mit Bildern angefüllt, bunt, voller Musik und Tanz, wenn Aron sich durchgesetzt hätte.

Jeder enzelne in seinem Wahn. Ein Traumkloster, das in Wirklichkeit ein Gefängnis und Zuchthaus ist. Beten und Foltern geschehen Wand an Wand.

Die Stufen-Pyramide als Denkkloster. Türen öffnen und schließen sich. Beim Öffnen werden Bilder sichtbar, beim Schließen verschwinden sie wieder. Zeigen und verbergen. In Bildern denken. Abstrakt denken. Bildende Kunst gegen Mathematik. Die Relativitätstheorie besteht zur einen Hälfte aus Text, zur anderen aus mathematischen Formeln. Keine Abbildung ist in ihr enthalten. Warum haben wir beides: Augen und Geist? Warum sehen und denken wir? Sollte wirklich jedes Bild eine Lüge sein, eine einseitige Festlegung, eine Verharmlosung? Was denken wir, wenn wir die Leichenberge der am Ende des Zweiten Weltkrieges geöffneten Konzentrationslager auf Photos und in Filmen sehen?

Räume verwandeln sich in andere Räume. Menschen verwandeln sich in andere Menschen. Hinter jeder Tür befindet sich eine andere Realität, ein anderes Bild.

Das Ende: Moses hat gesiegt. Aron ist tot.

Die Versprechungen führten ins Leere. Kein himmlisches Jerusalem und kein Land, in dem Milch und Honig fließen, sondern heilige Kriege, Bürgerkriege, Mord und Totschlag, die Erde übersät mit Toten, ein unsichtbarer Gott, der schweigt wie am Anfang. Seine Unsichtbarkeit wäre verkraftbar, aber sein Schweigen kaum.

Divara – Wasser und Blut (»Divara – Water and Blood«)
Opera by Azio Corghi with a libretto by José Samarago
    Teatro Nacional De São Carlos, Lisbon, July 2000; conductor: Will Humburg, director: Christof Nel, sets: Hans Dieter Schaal

Divara is an opera about the Anabaptists in Münster. It describes an almost clinical case of mass hysteria based on fanatical religious fervour. The story is set in the Westphalian town of Münster in the early 16th century. After Martin Luther nailed his 95 theses about indulgences to the door of the Schlosskirche in Wittenberg on 31.10.1517 the idea of the Reformation spread like wildfire through northern Europe. Luther was followed by numerous other reformers like Calvin or Zwingli, for example and by other religious movements. One of these was the Anabaptists, who rejected the baptism of children and argued for adult baptism. The Catholic Church fought them with particular fervour. They were cruelly persecuted wherever they appeared. From 1534 onwards many of them – the majority from Holland – gathered in Münster, where the city authorities were liberal and anti-clerical. Something that started on a small and harmless scale gradually became more and more challenging and demanding. Finally the movement peaked in a city revolution.

    This is where the action of the opera begins. The clerical gentlemen are taken prisoner and after a short time the Anabaptists set up their own power structure in the city. In the early stages their thinking is shaped by basic Christian ideals. Seen from today's perspective, we can find some socialist and Communist ideas among them: first property is abolished, then money. Ultimately the institution of marriage is abandoned and polygamy is introduced. All these decisions are preceded by interminable discussions.

    When the Anabaptists' leader, Jan van Leyden, is proclaimed king and surrounds himself with the trappings of kingship, the inhabitants of Münster become sceptical. But now it is too late. The city gates have long been closed. The first murders of people who think otherwise begin. A reign of terror waits for God to name the city of Münster as his New Jerusalem. Signs are sought, nothing happens, but life in the city becomes increasingly intolerable and cruel. Only Divara, the wife of Jan van Leyden, and thus the queen, argues for a new approach. But fate has long decided against her. For months the city has been in a state of siege; it has been surrounded by royal and princely armies.

    After it is recaptured in 1535 the invading soldiers murder almost all the inhabitants. The leaders of the Anabaptists were cruelly tortured and murdered at a public meeting of the people in the market-place. Their corpses were hung in iron cages from the tower of the town church. The cages are still hanging there to this day.

Divara – Wasser und Blut
Oper von Azio Corghi nach einem Text von José Samarago
    Teatro Nacional De São Carlos, Lissabon, Juli 2000; musikalische Leitung: Will Humburg, Inszenierung: Christof Nel, Bühne: Hans Dieter Schaal

Divara ist eine Oper über die Wiedertäufer in Münster. Sie beschreibt einen fast klinischen Fall von Massenhysterie, dem eine fanatische Religiosiät zu Grunde liegt. Die Geschichte spielt zu Beginn des 16. Jahrhunderts in der westfälischen Stadt Münster. Nachdem Martin Luther am 31.10.1517 an der Schloßkirche zu Wittenberg seine 95 Thesen über den Ablaß angeschlagen hatte, verbreitete sich der Reformationsgedanke wie ein Lauffeuer durch das nördliche Europa. Neben Luther gab es in dessen Nachfolge zahlreiche andere Reformatoren wie etwa Calvin oder Zwingli und auch religiöse Bewegungen. Eine war die der Wiedertäufer, welche die Kindertaufe ablehnten und sich für die Erwachsenentaufe einsetzten. Von der katholischen Kirche wurden gerade sie besonders hart bekämpft. Überall dort, wo sie auftauchten, verfolgte man sie grausam. Von 1534 an versammelten sich viele von ihnen – meist kamen sie aus Holland – in Münster, wo die Stadtverwaltung liberal und antiklerikal eingestellt war. Was ganz klein und harmlos begann, wurde nach und nach immer ernster und fordernder. Schließlich gipfelte die Bewegung in einer Stadtrevolution.

    Hier setzt die Opernhandlung ein. Die geistlichen Herren werden gefangengenommen, und nach kurzer Zeit errichten die Wiedertäufer in der Stadt eine eigene Machtstruktur. Am Anfang sind die Gedanken mit urchristlichen Idealen durchsetzt. Von heute aus gesehen, können wir darin sozialistisch-kommunistische Ideen entdecken: Zuerst wird das Eigentum abgeschafft, dann das Geld. Schließlich gibt man auch die Institution der Ehe preis und führt die Vielehe ein. Allen Entscheidungen gehen endlose Diskussionen voraus.

    Als sich der Anführer, Jan van Leyden, zum König ausruft und sich mit königlichen Attributen umgibt, werden die Bewohner von Münster skeptisch. Aber jetzt ist es zu spät. Längst sind die Stadttore geschlossen. Es kommt zu ersten Morden an Andersdenkenden. Ein Terrorregime wartet darauf, daß Gott die Stadt Münster zu seinem himmlischen Jerusalem ernennt. Man forscht nach Zeichen, nichts geschieht, aber das Leben in der Stadt wird immer unerträglicher und grausamer. Einzig Divara, die Frau Jan van Leydens und damit die Königin, setzt sich für eine mildere Gangart ein. Das Schicksal hat jedoch längst gegen sie entschieden. Seit Monaten befindet sich die Stadt in einem Belagerungszustand; königliche und fürstliche Armeen halten sie umstellt.

    Nach ihrer Rückeroberung, 1535, ermordeten die eindringenden Soldaten fast alle Einwohner. Bei einer öffentlichen Volksveranstaltung auf dem Marktplatz wurden die Anführer der Wiedertäufer grausam gefoltert und hingerichtet. Ihre Kadaver hängte man in Eisenkäfigen am Turm der Stadtkirche auf. Die Käfige befinden sich dort noch heute.

A white, light, labyrinthine space was created for the Lisbon performance: all that can be seen are corridors and openings that lead to other spaces, walled up and secret doors, mysterious wall fragments and letter-boxes, behind which the watchers lurk. Everyone is watching everyone else. Badly built, surreal, absurd architecture. Equipment glides in noiselessly on rails, X-ray altars, confessionals and instruments of torture.

    Glimpses of lost souls. The concept of truth is terroristically narrowed down until it allows no room for manoeuvre any more. At the end everyone is in the same prison. The only way out is death.

    Light comes from above, and from a long way away. Nobody notices that there are no windows, nobody looks up, nobody knocks down the walls. The inmates of the room are too concerned with their own psyche, their own inner world.

Für die Aufführung in Lissabon entstand ein weißer, heller, labyrinthischer Raum: Es gibt nur Durchgänge und Öffnungen, die in andere Raum-Bereiche führen, vermauerte und geheime Türen, rätselhafte Wandfragmete und Briefschlitze, hinter denen die Beobachter lauern. Jeder bewacht jeden. Eine verbaute, surreale, absurde Architektur. Auf Schienen fahren Geräte lautlos herein, Röntgenaltäre, Beichtstühle und Folterwerkzeuge.

    Blicke in verirrte Seelen. Der Begriff der Wahrheit wird terroristisch eingeengt, bis er keine Bewegungsfreiheit mehr zuläßt. Am Ende sitzen alle in einem Gefängnis. Der einzige Ausweg ist der Tod.

    Das Licht fällt von oben herab, kommt von weit her. Niemand bemerkt, daß es kein Fenster gibt, niemand blickt nach oben, niemand zerschlägt die Wände. Zu sehr sind die Insassen des Raums mit ihrer eigenen Psyche, ihrer eigenen Innenwelt beschäftigt.

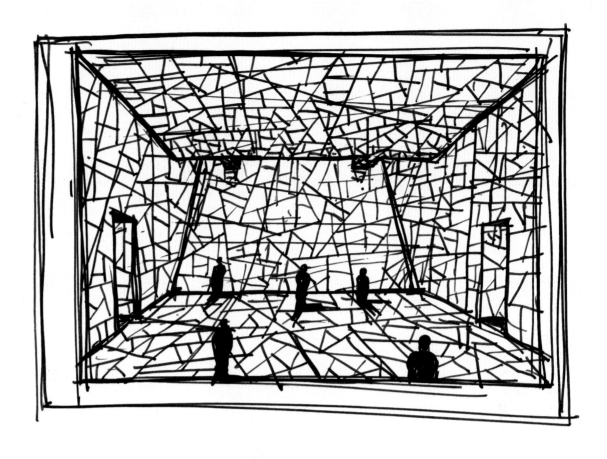

Saint François d'Assise

Opera by Olivier Messiaen, eight Franciscan
scenes (Scènes Franciscaines) in three acts,
libretto by the composer

San Francisco Opera House, 2002; conductor:
Donald Runnicles, director: Nicolas Brieger, sets:
Hans Dieter Schaal, costumes: Andrea Schmidt-
Futterer, dramaturgy: Wolfgang Willascheck

Saint François d'Assise is Olivier Messiaen's only
opera, which he wrote and composed from 1975
to 1983 for Rolf Liebermann for the Opéra Garnier in Paris.

Actually the composer walls planning an opera
about Christ, but when he established that a
piece of work of this kind would not be possible
for him, he chose a human successor of the Son
of God, St. Francis of Assisi. St. Francis was
born in 1182, the son of a rich merchant in Assisi.
It was not until the age of 26 that he recognized
his true vocation and went about the country as
a poor wanderer and preacher of repentance. He
is said to have been of a cheerful and simple dis-
position, filled with a love of nature. He was also
quite selfless, and ready to make sacrifices. As
»God's troubadour« he not only preached to human beings, but also to the birds and the rocks.
In the mountains of the Averno near Arezzo the
wounds of Christ appeared on his body after a
long period of solitary meditation. Francis was
canonized by the Pope just two years after his
death in Assisi.

Messiaen could identify with the saint because
Francis was an ordinary man who lived out the
gospel in a very radical way. For the composer,
all the themes that were important to him were to
be found in the figure of St. Francis: a profound
feeling for the Catholic religion, the wish to live
his life in the way of Christ, a worship of nature
and a sense of mysticism.

Saint François d'Assise is a work that is so uncompromising in its religion and so radical that it
stands up to functional, consumption-crazed reality like a massive monolith. St. Francis
preached precisely the opposite of everything
that we feel worthy of adoration: a return to simplicity, to poverty, to life in simple woodland cells,
to nature and to humble prayer. Not the pursuit
of knowledge and power, not scientific enlightenment is the aim, but patience in the face of riddles, recognition of miracles, the secret of stig-
matization, religious mysticism. Messiaen's music
is prayer. It does not know how to search. It simply admires. The music describes the universe as
an audible cosmos, in musical turns and towering accumulations that are always the same, like
the work of Bruckner, for example, that have the
character of invocations. The leaves rustle, time
flows by, the birds sing.

The opera starts with the statement: »I am
afraid.« This is not spoken by Francis, but by one
of his confrères. This sentence is repeated a few
times in the course of the plot. And then revul-
sion has to be overcome. Francis wants to kiss
the leper. After an inner struggle, he succeeds,
and ultimately the sick man is healed as well.
Francis can work miracles!

Anyone who hears this opera is stepping into
an artistic space. Outside the traffic is roaring,
dealers are shouting figures into their mobiles,
competitors are being delivered to hospital in

ambulances, injured. The everyday war is going
on, and here in this space religion is unfolding
like a Romantic dream of mystical ecstasy. A trip
through space for the soul. A tumult of fantasy
images. Devotion. A pilgrimage to a possible paradise. The music proclaims this. Birds and angels
are its messengers. Messiaen is the medium.

Actually, like *Moses und Aron* and *Patmos*,
this opera declines to be illustrated. These works
are all placed on the fringes of what can be represented. Their force arises – as Heiner Müller
said in the conversation about *Moses und Aron* –
from »absence«. The actual event is the music.
It sounds, intones, towers up, falls apart, flows
away, without ever becoming visible. But we
need images so as not to get lost in the desert
and on the endless ocean. So we search the
horizon with the naked eye or with binoculars,
latch on to any object that appears, whether it
is a cloud, a bird or a block of ice. Everyone
dreams of arriving. Of the port. Of the land beyond the horizon. Of the world beyond the world.
And sometimes we have attacks of longing, fantasies of sloughing the skin. Away with the surface! Images beyond images. Images beyond the
images beyond the images!

The stage locations: »First scene: the cross.
A road. Steps in the middle of the stage. To the
right and left of the steps are two rows of dense,
towering, dark-green cypresses. The steps rise
to a considerable height, where a large black
cross stands out against the sky. Second scene:
Lauds. Inside a small, fairly gloomy monastery
church with three adjacent vaults. In the middle
of the stage, a red light, indicating the presence
of the sacrament, is glowing in the background
in front of a small altar. Third scene: Saint Francis
kisses the leper. In the hospital of San Salvatore
near Assisi. A low room in the leprosy ward. A
bench, two stools. On the right in the background is a window looking out into a gloomy alleyway. Fourth scene: the itinerant angel. On the
Verna mountain. On the left is a small, very plain
hall in the monastery, closed off by a great gate.
In the centre is a path leading into the wood.
Beeches, pines, some fissured rocks, beyond
this, shimmering blue mountains. On the right is
a small grotto. The gate to the monastery hall is
open. Fifth scene: the angel making music. Set
as four. Sixth scene: preaching to the birds. In
the hermitage of the Carceri. A road flooded with
sunlight leads over a little bridge and is continued
like a terrace above a little gorge. An enormous
oak tree thrusts up out of the gorge with its
broad, black mossy branches, high above the
road; its narrow leaves, growing in tufts, seem to
glow in the sunshine. The first slopes of Monte
Subasio and the mountain of San Rufino rise up
at the top, almost covering up the blue sky. The
foothills are covered with a green carpet of oak
trees. Part of the road is patterned with the play
of light and shade from the great green oak tree.
Seventh scene: the stigmata. In the Verna. A
bizarre and higgledy-piggledy chaos of rocks. A
kind of cave under a rocky promontory. On the
left, a flight of steps leads down into the cave. On
the right: a very narrow path, with no way out,
leading to the wall of rock. A large, pointed fragment of rock hangs as though forced in between
the walls surrounding the narrow path. This is the
»Sasso spicco«. The whole rock is covered with

black and green moss, everything is fissured, fur-
rowed and jagged. It is night. An area of black
sky is visible above the rock. Eighth scene: death
and a new life. Inside the little Porziuncola church
in Santa Maria degli Angeli. Black vaults, the floor
is paved with stone slabs. The undecorated walls
are made of rough, clumsy stones, some of them
fitted together imperfectly. Late evening light …
St. Francis lies on the floor, dying.«

The San Fransciso opera house is one of the
largest in the world. The auditorium seats almost
4000 people. The set responds to this problem
of size with clear, simple forms. In the centre is a
curving path that rises to three metres above the
level of the stage. To the left and right of this are
the façades of buildings; these can be moved,
and extend or restrict the overall space available.
In the background there is a view of a town that
has been half destroyed, burnt black and lurching diagonally to one side. In front of this is a
three metre high town wall with a lot of doors.

The stations of the plot take place on the path,
on the edge of it, and in the urban landscape
around it. For the long sermon to the birds – the
central part of the opera – huge white leaves float
down from above.

This image presents a view of a final condition.
The earth has been destroyed and sealed with
metal. Francis preaches against this destruction.
At the end we are left with the dream of the
weightlessness of the birds and of music. The
sunlight becomes brighter and brighter, until it
dissolves and extinguishes the visible world.

Religious and musical mysticism is a profound,
ancient way of reconciling the internal and external worlds. Secure in the tremendous harmony of
the creation, there is no more fear. The aim is not
to explain, nor to enlighten – simply to transfig-
ure.

Der heilige Franziskus von Assisi (Saint François d'Assise)

Oper von Olivier Messiaen, acht franziskanische Szenen (Scènes Franciscaines) in 3 Akten, Text vom Komponisten

San Francisco Opera House, 2002; musikalische Leitung: Donald Runnicles, Inszenierung: Nicolas Brieger, Bühne: Hans Dieter Schaal, Kostüme: Andrea Schmidt-Futterer, Dramaturgie: Wolfgang Willascheck

Saint François d'Assise ist die einzige Oper von Olivier Messiaen, an der er von 1975 bis 1983 im Auftrag von Rolf Liebermann für die Pariser Opéra Garnier geschrieben und komponiert hat.

Eigentlich plante der Komponist eine Christusoper, aber als er feststellte, daß eine solche Arbeit für ihn nicht zu leisten war, wählte er einen menschlichen Nachfolger des Gottessohnes, den heiligen Franziskus. Dieser wurde 1182 als Sohn eines reichen Kaufmanns in Assisi geboren. Erst im Alter von 26 Jahren erkannte er seine wahre Berufung und zog als armer Wander- und Bußprediger durch die Lande. Er soll ein fröhliches und einfaches Wesen gehabt haben, von der Liebe zur Natur erfüllt und von großer Selbstlosigkeit und Opferbereitschaft gewesen sein. Als »Troubadour Gottes« predigte er nicht nur den Menschen, sondern auch den Vögeln und Steinen. In den Averner Bergen bei Arezzo zeigten sich nach langer Meditation in Einsamkeit die Wundmale Christi an seinem Körper. Bereits zwei Jahre nach seinem Tod in Assisi ist Franziskus vom Papst heilig gesprochen worden.

Messiaen konnte sich mit dem Heiligen identifizieren, weil dieser ein normaler Mensch war, der das Evangelium in großer Radikalität nachlebte. Für den Komponisten klangen alle Themen, die ihm wichtig waren, in der Figur des Franziskus an: die tiefe katholische Religiosität, das Bemühen, sein Leben in der Nachfolge Christi zu entfalten, die Naturverehrung und die Mystik.

Saint François d'Assise ist ein Werk, das sich heute in seiner religiösen Unbedingtheit und Radikalität wie ein gewaltiger Block gegen die funktionstüchtige und komsumberauschte Realität stellt. Der heilige Franz predigte genau das Gegenteil von dem, was uns als anbetungswürdig erscheint: zurück zur Einfachheit, zur Armut, zum Leben in einfachen Waldklausen, zur Natur und zum demütigen Gebet. Nicht die Vermehrung von Wissen und Macht, nicht die wissenschaftliche Aufklärung ist das Ziel, sondern das Ausharren vor dem Rätsel, das Anerkennen des Wunders, das Geheimnis der Stigmatisierung, die religiöse Mystik. Messiaens Musik ist Gebet. Sie kennt die Suche nicht. Sie bewundert nur. In immer gleichen musikalischen Wendungen und Auftürmungen, wie beispielsweise auch bei Bruckner, die den Charakter von Anrufungen haben, beschreibt die Musik das Universum als hörbaren Kosmos. Die Blätter rauschen, die Zeit strömt, die Vögel singen.

Die Oper beginnt mit dem Satz: »Ich habe Angst.« Nicht Franziskus, sondern sein Mitbruder spricht ihn aus. Dieser Satz wiederholt sich im Laufe der Handlung einige Male. Und dann die Überwindung des Ekels: Franziskus will den Aussätzigen küssen. Nach innerem Kampf gelingt es ihm, und am Ende ist der Kranke sogar geheilt. Franziskus kann Wunder vollbringen!

Wer diese Oper hört, betritt einen Kunstraum. Draußen tobt der Verkehr, die Händler rufen ihre Zahlen über Handys, die Konkurrenten werden verletzt in Krankenhäuser eingeliefert. Der alltägliche Krieg ereignet sich, und hier in diesem Raum entfaltet sich die Religion wie ein romantischer Traum als mystische Ekstase. Raumfahrt der Seele. Phantasiebildertaumel. Andacht. Wallfahrt in ein mögliches Paradies. Die Musik kündet davon. Vögel und Engel sind ihre Botschafter. Messiaen das Medium.

Eigentlich entzieht sich die Oper jeder Bebilderung wie *Moses und Aron* und wie *Patmos*. Diese Werke sind alle am Rande des Darstellbaren angesiedelt. Ihre Kraft entsteht – wie Heiner Müller in dem Gespräch über *Moses und Aron* gesagt hat – aus der »Abwesenheit«. Das eigentliche Ereignis ist die Musik. Sie klingt, tönt, türmt sich auf, zerfällt, fließt dahin, ohne je sichtbar zu werden. Man könnte sich die Augen verbinden und nur zuhören. Aber wir brauchen die Bilder, um nicht verloren zu gehen in der Wüste und auf dem unendlichen Meer. So suchen wir den Horizont ab mit bloßen Augen oder mit Ferngläsern, klammern uns an jeden auftauchenden Gegenstand, sei es eine Wolke, ein Vogel oder ein Eisblock. Jeder träumt vom Ankommen. Vom Hafen. Vom Land hinter dem Horizont. Von der Welt hinter der Welt. Und manchmal kommt es zu Anfällen von Sehnsucht, zu Häutungsphantasien. Fort mit der Oberfläche! Bilder hinter den Bildern. Bilder hinter den Bildern hinter den Bildern!

Die Bühnenbild-Orte: »Erstes Bild: das Kreuz. Eine Straße. Eine Stiege in der Mitte der Bühne. Rechts und links von der Stiege zwei Reihen von dichten, hochragenden dunkelgrünen Zypressen. Die Stiege führt weit in die Höhe, wo sich ein großes, schwarzes Kreuz vom Himmel abhebt. Zweites Bild: die Laudes. Im Inneren einer kleinen ziemlich düsteren Klosterkirche mit drei aneinander anschließenden Gewölben. In der Mitte der Bühne leuchtet im Hintergrund vor einem kleinen Altar ein rotes Licht, das die Gegenwart des Allerheiligsten anzeigt. Drittes Bild: der heilige Franziskus küßt den Aussätzigen. Im Hospital San Salvatore bei Assisi. Niedriger Raum in der Leprastation. Eine Bank, zwei Schemel. Rechts im Hintergrund ein auf ein finsteres Gäßchen gehendes Fenster. Viertes Bild: der wandernde Engel. Auf dem Berg der Verna. Links ein kleiner, sehr schlichter Saal des Klosters, von einem großen Tor abgeschlossen. In der Mitte ein Pfad, der in den Wald führt. Buchen, Pinien, einige zerklüftete Felsen, dahinter blauschimmernde Berge. Rechts: eine kleine Grotte. Die Pforte zum Klostersaal ist geöffnet. Fünftes Bild: der musizierende Engel. Bild wie vier. Sechstes Bild: die Vogelpredigt. In der Klause der Carceri. Eine von Sonnenlicht überflutete Straße führt über eine kleine Brücke und setzt sich terrassenartig über einem kleinen Abgrund fort. Aus dem Abgrund ragt eine riesige Eiche mit ihren weiten, schwarzen und bemoosten Ästen weit über die Straße empor; ihre schmalen, in Büscheln wachsenden Blätter scheinen im Sonnenlicht zu glänzen. In der Höhe, den blauen Himmel fast verdeckend, erheben sich die ersten Anhöhen des Monte Subasio und des Berges von San Rufino, die von einem grünen Eichenteppich völlig überzogen sind. Spiele von Licht und Schatten werfen auf einen Abschnitt der Straße das Abbild der Äste und Blätter der großen grünen Eiche. Siebtes Bild: die Stigmata. In der Verna. Durcheinander von bizarr ineinander verschachtelten Felsen. Eine Art Höhle unter einem Felsvorsprung. Links führt eine kleine Treppe in die Höhle herab. Rechts: ein sehr schmaler Pfad ohne Ausgang, der zur Felswand führt. Ein großer spitzer Felsbrocken hängt wie eingezwängt zwischen den Wänden, die den schmalen Pfad umgeben. Es ist der »Sasso spicco«. Der ganze Felsen ist von schwarzgrünem Moos bedeckt, alles ist zerklüftet, zerfurcht und gezackt. Es ist Nacht. Über den Felsen ist ein Stück schwarzen Himmels sichtbar. Achtes Bild: der Tod und das neue Leben. Im Inneren der kleinen Porziuncola-Kirche in Santa Maria degli Angeli. Schwarzes Gewölbe, der Boden ist mit Steinplatten belegt. Die schmucklosen Mauern sind aus unbehauenen, unbeholfen und zum Teil schief übereinandergefügten Steinen gebaut. Späte Abenddämmerung ... Der heilige Franz liegt sterbend am Boden.«

Das Opernhaus von San Francisco gehört zu den größten der Welt. Der Zuschauerraum faßt nahezu 4000 Menschen. Das Bühnenbild beantwortet dieses Größenproblem mit klaren, einfachen Formen. Im Zentrum liegt ein geschwungener Weg, der vom Bühnenniveau bis auf drei Meter ansteigt. Links und rechts davon stehen Hausfassaden, die verfahrbar sind und den Gesamtraum verengen oder erweitern können. Im Hintergrund sieht man auf eine halbzerstörte Stadt, schwarz verbrannt und schräg gekippt. Davor eine drei Meter hohe Stadtmauer mit vielen Türen.

Die Stationen der Handlung ereignen sich auf dem Weg, an seinem Rand und in der Stadtlandschaft um ihn herum. Für die lange Vogelpredigt – den zentralen Teil der Oper – schweben riesige weiße Blätter von oben herab.

Das Bild zeigt einen Endzustand. Die Erde ist zerstört und mit Metall versiegelt. Franziskus predigt gegen die Zerstörung an. Am Ende bleibt der Traum von der Schwerelosigkeit der Vögel und der Musik. Das Licht der Sonne wird immer heller, bis es die sichtbare Welt überblendet und auslöscht.

Die religiöse und musikalische Mystik ist eine tiefe, uralte Möglichkeit, die Innenwelt mit der Außenwelt zu versöhnen. Alles ist außen, alles ist innen. Aufgehoben in der gewaltigen Harmonie der Schöpfung, gibt es keine Angst mehr. Nicht die Klärung, auch nicht die Aufklärung, sondern nur noch die Verklärung ist das Ziel.

Titus (La clemenza di Tito)

Opera seria in two acts by Wolfgang Amadeus Mozart, libretto by Caterino Mazzolà after Pietro Metastasio

Ulmer Theater, 2000; conductor: Thomas Mandl, direction and choreography: Arila Siegert, sets: Hans Dieter Schaal, costumes: Marie-Luise Strandt, dramaturgy: Bettina Bartz

It was not only architects who turned to the formal language and stylization of Greece and Rome after 1500, painters, sculptors, writers, poets, librettists and composers were fascinated by the stories of antiquity as well. They liked to make comparisons. Adam and Eve, Jesus and Mary moved into the background and even the angels were increasingly pushed out by lascivious female bodies, now called Venus, Aphrodite or Cleopatra and Vitellia. Art had to dress up in mythological or ancient costumes. Penetrating the genuine, naked realms of the soul had to be done gradually.

Mozart lived and worked between two ages. He depended on his noble patrons, who insisted on ancient and mythological material, and he hated them – the nobility and the stories – because inside he was already a modern artist looking for subjective expression, who wanted to create his works freely and independently. In the last year of his life, 1791, he composed *La clemenza di Tito* as a commission for the nobility, reluctantly, and above all for the money. *The Magic Flute* was written at almost the same time: a German Singspiel for Vienna's popular Vorstadttheater. Perhaps the fact that he was torn between two worlds and two ages was one of the reasons for his early death.

Titus is a historical figure who lived in ancient Rome from AD 39 to 81. He took over supreme command from his father in the war against the Jews. In AD 70 he destroyed Jerusalem and the temple in the city. After his return to Rome he became one of the peace-loving emperors, who looked after the needs of his subjects for eleven years.

The title of the opera means Titus's mercy. The action takes place in AD 79. Thus Titus is 40 years old and has two more years to live. Of course the plots turns around love, death, jealousy and hatred, as in most operas. The trigger is Titus's Hebrew mistress Berenice, whom he has brought back from the Holy Land. Vitellia, an ambitious Roman noblewoman, resists her rival. She wants to be Empress, and hatches a plot, but she loses her grip on it. All the characters are changed radically in the whirlpool of the struggle for power. Ultimately Titus pardons the guilty parties, including Vitellia. This dream of the good, paternal ruler is repeated in many of Mozart's operas. In reality Mozart would have been pleased to do without anyone who wielded power. He was steeped in the ideas of the French Revolution. But he was not born to be a revolutionary.

The settings for the plot: »In Vitellia's house. Part of the Forum Romanum, adorned with magnificent triumphal arches, obelisks and trophies; in the background is the Capitol, with a boulevard leading to it. A welcoming chamber in the imperial palace on the Palatine hill. Large hall for public audiences. The throne, a chair and a table. Magnificent square in front of a large amphitheatre, whose interior can be glimpsed through an arch. The conspirators have already appeared in the arena, condemned to fight the wild beasts.«

When reading these descriptions of locations and architecture by the librettist one is reminded of Rome as it is today, of Baroque paintings and – with horror – of monumental Hollywood films in the fifties. It is these naïvely mendacious and overloaded film images above all that intrude most on our imagination. Nothing against the Rome of the Fellini films, in which the city proliferates into a wild collage of ruins, Via Veneto, spaghetti and crazy individuals, and also nothing against the current view from a hotel window of the noisy, smelly city that seems like an open wound. But does this have anything to do with Titus? Perhaps an austerely reduced classical eye is called for. Minimalism creates tension.

There was no realism in Ulm. The only historical allusions were in front of the proscenium arch: two ancient columns. Otherwise there was nothing on the stage but two marble buildings with three sides that were almost closed and looking into a large, white staircase on the fourth side. Stagehands who were part of the action moved the buildings after each scene. Sometimes the walls made narrow alleyways, then a great square would open up again.

Stylized city architecture that was part of the action, involving itself in it. Geometrically reduced, between threat and protection, lurching between prestige and ridicule. A ballet with buildings. An architectural dance. The staircase waltz.

Anyone who went into the buildings was safe from the eyes of strangers, who had no access. But anyone outside is in public, unprotected and exposed to every eye.

Titus (La clemenza di Tito)

Opera seria in zwei Akten von Wolfgang Amadeus Mozart, Libretto von Caterino Mazzolà nach Pietro Metastasio

Ulmer Theater, 2000; musikalische Leitung: Thomas Mandl, Inszenierung und Choreographie: Arila Siegert, Bühne: Hans Dieter Schaal, Kostüme Marie-Luise Strandt, Dramaturgie: Bettina Bartz

Nicht nur die Architekten bedienten sich nach 1500 der griechischen und römischen Formensprache und Stilisierung, auch die Maler, Bildhauer, Schriftsteller, Dichter, Librettisten und Komponisten waren fasziniert von den antiken Geschichten. Man zog gern Vergleiche. Adam und Eva, Jesus und Maria traten in den Hintergrund, und auch die Engel wurden zunehmend von lasziven Frauenkörpern verdrängt, die man jetzt Venus, Aphrodite oder Kleopatra und Vitellia nannte. Kunst hatte sich mythologisch oder antik zu kostümieren. Nur ganz allmählich konnte man in den unverstellten, nackten Seelenbereich vordringen.

Mozart lebte und arbeitete zwischen den Zeiten: Er war abhängig von seinen adligen Auftraggebern, die antik-mythologische Stoffe forderten, und er haßte sie – Adel wie Geschichten – weil er innerlich bereits der nach subjektivem Ausdruck suchende moderne Künstler war, der seine Werke frei und unabhängig schaffen wollte. In seinem letzten Lebensjahr, 1791, komponierte er *Titus* als Auftragswerk für den Adel, widerwillig und vor allem des Geldes wegen. Fast gleichzeitig entstand *Die Zauberflöte*, ein deutsches Singspiel für das volkstümliche Vorstadttheater Wiens. Vielleicht war die Zerrissenheit zwischen den Welten und den Zeiten ein Grund für seinen frühen Tod.

Titus ist eine historische Figur, er hat im antiken Rom wirklich gelebt, von 39 bis 81 nach Christus. Als Feldherr übernahm er von seinem Vater den Oberbefehl über den Krieg gegen die Juden. 70 nach Christus zerstörte er Jerusalem und den Tempel in der Stadt. Nach seiner Rückkehr wurde er zu dem friedliebenden römischen Kaiser, der sich elf Jahre lang für die Bedürfnisse seiner Untertanen einsetzte.

Die Oper heißt *La clemenza di Tito* (Die Milde des Titus). Die Handlung setzt im Jahre 79 n. Chr. ein. Titus ist demnach 40 Jahre alt und hat noch zwei Jahre zu leben. Natürlich kreist die Geschichte wie in den meisten Opern um Liebe, Tod, Eifersucht und Haß. Auslöser ist die hebräische Geliebte Berenice, die Titus aus dem Heiligen Land mitgebracht hat. Vitellia, eine ehrgeizige Frau aus dem römischen Hochadel, bekämpft die Widersacherin. Sie will Kaiserin werden und zettelt eine Verschwörung an, die ihr jedoch entgleitet. Im Strudel des Machtkampfs werden alle Personen deformiert. Am Ende begnadigt Titus die Schuldigen, auch Vitellia. Dieser Traum vom gütigen, väterlichen Herrscher wiederholt sich in vielen Mozartopern. In Wirklichkeit hätte Mozart gern auf alle Machthabenden verzichtet. Die Gedanken der Französischen Revolution arbeiteten in ihm. Zum Revolutionär war er jedoch nicht geboren.

Die Bühnenbild-Orte der Handlung: »Im Hause Vitellias. Ein Teil des Forum Romanum, prächtig mit Triumphbögen, Obelisken und Trophäen geschmückt; im Hintergrund das Kapitol, zu dem eine Prachtstraße führt. Freundliches Gemach im kaiserlichen Palast auf dem Palatin. Großer Saal für öffentliche Audienzen. Der Thron, ein Sessel und ein Tisch. Prächtiger Platz vor einem großen Amphitheater, dessen Inneres man durch offene Bögen erblickt. In der Arena sieht man bereits die Verschwörer, die zum Kampf mit den wilden Tieren verurteilt sind.«

Wenn man diese Architekur- und Ortsangaben des Librettisten liest, denkt man an das heutige Rom, an barocke Gemälde und – mit Erschrecken – an die Monumentalfilme der fünfziger Jahre aus Hollywood. Diese naiv-verlogenen und überfrachteten Filmbilder sind es vor allem, die sich in der Vorstellung querlegen. Nichts gegen das Rom der Fellini-Filme, in denen die Stadt zu einer wilden Collage aus Ruinen, Via Veneto, Spaghetti und verrückten Typen auswuchert, auch nichts gegen den heutigen Blick aus dem Hotelzimmerfenster auf die lärmende und stinkende Stadt, die wie eine offene Wunde wirkt. Aber hat das alles etwas mit Titus zu tun? Vielleicht ist doch eher der streng reduzierte, klassische Blick gemeint. Minimalismus erzeugt Spannung.

Es gab in Ulm keinen Realismus. Die einzigen historischen Andeutungen lagen vor dem Bühnenportal: zwei antike Säulen. Ansonsten standen auf der Bühne nur zwei mobile Marmorhäuser, die drei fast ganz geschlossene Seiten hatten und von der vierten Seite den Einblick in ein großes, weißes Treppenhaus freigaben. Mitwirkende Bühnenarbeiter verschoben die Häuser nach jeder Szene. Manchmal verengten sich die Wände zu schmalen Gassen, dann wieder öffneten sich größere Platzsituationen.

Eine mitspielende, sich einmischende, stilisierte Stadtarchitektur. Geometrisch reduziert, zwischen Bedrohung und Schutz, zwischen Repräsentation und Verhöhnung schwankend. Haus-Ballett. Architektur-Tanz. Treppenwalzer.

Wer sich in die Häuser zurückzieht, ist vor Blicken und fremdem Zugriff geschützt. Wer jedoch außerhalb steht, ist öffentlich, ungeschützt, allen Blicken ausgeliefert.

The Magic Flute

A German opera in two acts by Wolfgang Amadeus Mozart, libretto by Emanuel Schikaneder

Hessisches Staatstheater, Wiesbaden, 1996; conductor: Toshiyuki Kamioka, director: Dominik Neuner, sets: Hans Dieter Schaal, costumes: Ute Frühling, dramaturgy: Norbert Abels

With *The Magic Flute*, Mozart had perhaps arrived where he had always wanted to be: in the suburban theatre, which was closer to the circus and the fair than to the powder and wigs of the court theatre. Mozart liked to express himself in course, anal language, as his letters show. Here we find »the duchess arse (»bömerl«), countess pisslover«, and then the »princess smellherway with her 2 daughters, though they are already married to 2 princes mustbelly of pigcock«. Again and again we have an impression that Mozart remained an anarchic child throughout his life, always inclined towards pranks and all sorts of magic tricks.

The Magic Flute tells the story of Prince Tamino and his counterpart Papageno, the birdcatcher, a child of nature. Both of them are young; they are pubescent and experience this period as a confusing muddle between a fairy-tale forest and the austere architecture of adulthood. The opera opens in a rocky place that could also be a labyrinth. Tamino's first words: »Help, help, or I am lost!« He is being pursued by a serpent, does not know where he is or who he is. Papageno appears and claims to be able to save him. He too cannot distinguish between fiction and reality.

And then a fairy-tale sequence of events begins of which it is scarcely possible to say whether they are taking place, being read, heard or dreamed in the young men's fantasy world, or whether they are really happening.

The Queen of the Night commissions the two of them to rescue her daughter from the hands of the evil priest of the sun temple. They allow themselves to be involved in the adventure, and so discover love and with it sexuality. They are subjected to numerous tests and strange rituals, and are finally able to enter the adult world, now no longer so wicked, as one of a couple in each case. The night is condemned as a negative place and Sarastro, the High Priest, sings: »The rays of the sun drive out the night, destroying the power arrogated by hypocrites!« We are reminded of enlightenment and better, brighter times determined by reason. Actually the story is of a rite of initiation, the introduction of two young men into the adult world. Childhood and puberty are glorified here as a fairy-tale, fanciful but baffling period – close to paradise. An abbreviated fall – with the serpent as a quotation – is the start of it all, and leads to their being driven out of the dream world. Life begins, and the questions, dangers and fears start to increase. What will lie beyond the forest? This is where, as we shall see, the adult world has set itself up, with all its hollow chaos of rites and rules. The young men realize only gradually that there is also a higher meaning within the marble of the law: dignity and humanity.

The anarchic individual faces the state, the ego faces the institution.

Once more we see that Mozart and his librettist were no revolutionaries: ultimately their opera is about conforming to and recognizing the adults' laws, and not destroying them. The dreamy days of childhood and the turbulence of puberty are now to be followed by the longest period in life, ritualized and cemented by law. It is only death that will redeem the adults from their »civil service posts for life«.

The Magic Flute quotes many archetypes of the theatrical and operatic worlds: Adam and Eve, the above-mentioned fall of man in paradise, the contrast between the worlds of day and night and thus between good and evil, the Orpheus motif: anyone who plays the magic flute (reminiscent of the pipes of Pan), has power over human beings and animals; Papageno, the birdcatcher, who is himself half bird, reminds us of man's ambiguous nature, half animal, half intellectual and cultural being.

How can a work like this be directed and staged today? Can and should one try to put oneself back into a time when there were only painted and drawn pictures and portraits, in which childhood took place among home-made dolls' houses, images of the saints and the everyday pre-industrial magic of the city and the fair?

When reading we think of comics, computer games and fantasy films. Childhood has changed its rooms and its images, but at its core it is still the same story as it has always been.

One thinks of a child's attic room, in a terraced house, somewhere in a suburb, the model railway under the comic-strewn bed, in the aquarium on top of the cupboard is a small, dimly lit jungle, there are erotic photographs on the inside of the cupboard door, and the stuffed animals of the past behind the cushions on the bed.

Intoxicated fantasies of freedom, flight and breaking out come crowding in, then at night there are nightmares, and finally flight into the nocturnal municipal park, the surge of fear, further away, always further away. Living outside, without a roof over one's head.

When reading Schikaneder's stage directions they are more reminiscent of a film than a stage play or an opera. One place constantly turns into another. A theatre of transformation. Magic theatre.

»A rocky place, with trees here and there. A lavishly furnished room in Sarastro's palace; an ottoman in the foreground. Three temples are standing in a grove: reason, nature, wisdom. A palm forest. Short temple forecourt. Garden in full moonlight, in the middle is a grove in which Pamina is sleeping. The theatre is transformed into a hall. There are two benches at the front. The theatre represents an interior; it is half in darkness. Eighteen priests in sixes, forming a triangle. The theatre is transformed into a garden. The theatre is transformed; it can show a waterfall and a mountain spewing fire. The theatre is transformed back into the previous garden. Transformation: rocky place; it is night. Transformation: thunder, lightning and storm: the whole theatre is immediately transformed into a sun.«

Mozart composed most of *The Magic Flute* in a little summerhouse in Vienna that Schikaneder had made available to him. Schikaneder also laid on good food and amusing company. Today the »Magic Flute Summerhouse« is in the garden behind the Mozarteum. It suggested the idea of treating the piece as a meditation on architecture.

The Magic Flute draws its life from the contrast between nature and built architecture. As architecture always requires a settled way of life and an ordered society it is a matter for adults. Tents and temporary accommodation are for young people.

At the beginning we have the little birdcage that Papageno carries on his back. Birds are supposed to live in this house, and buildings like this crop up increasingly as the plot develops. They join in the action, fall in love with each other, move together, have their own desires, dreams, quarrels, and then reconcile themselves with each other. In the course of history, larger and larger buildings start to appear. Of course the adults' temples are the biggest. These buildings are noble and proud. Many buildings make a village, even more make a town and a society. All the buildings have the basic motif of the entrance hole and a bar to land on, as found in birdcages. The dream of living in and with nature does not die. Ultimately the couples will move into these houses, have their love children and become part of a larger community.

Die Zauberflöte

Eine deutsche Oper in zwei Akten von Wolfgang Amadeus Mozart, Text von Emanuel Schikaneder
Hessisches Staatstheater, Wiesbaden, 1996; musikalische Leitung: Toshiyuki Kamioka, Inszenierung: Dominik Neuner, Bühne: Hans Dieter Schaal, Kostüme: Ute Frühling, Dramaturgie: Norbert Abels

Mit der *Zauberflöte* war Mozart dort angekommen, wo er vielleicht immer hingewollt hatte: im Vorstadttheater, das dem Zirkus und dem Jahrmarkt näher war als die gepuderten und perückenverzierten höfischen Theater. Mozart drückte sich, wie seine Briefe belegen, gern in derber Analsprache aus. Da gab es »die Ducheße arschbömerl, die gräfin brunzgern«, und dann »die fürstin riechzumtreck mit ihren 2 Töchtern, die aber schon an 2 Prinzen Mußbauch von Sauschwanz verheyratet sind«. Immer wieder hat man den Eindruck, Mozart sei Zeit seines Lebens ein anarchistisches Kind geblieben, stets zu Späßen und allerlei Zauberkunststücken aufgelegt.

Die *Zauberflöte* erzählt die Geschichte des Prinzen Tamino und seines naturburschigen Gegenspielers, des Vogelfängers Papageno. Beide sind jung; sie befinden sich in der Pubertät und erleben diese Zeit als Verwirrspiel zwischen Märchenwald und strenger Erwachsenen-Architektur. Die Oper beginnt in einer felsigen Gegend, die auch ein Labyrinth sein könnte. Taminos erste Worte: »Zu Hilfe! Zu Hilfe! Sonst bin ich verloren!« Er wird von einer Schlange verfolgt, weiß nicht, wo er ist und wer er ist. Papageno taucht auf und gibt sich als Retter aus. Auch er kann nicht zwischen Fiktion und Realität unterscheiden.

Dann setzen die märchenhaften Vorgänge ein, von denen man kaum sagen kann, ob sie in der Phantasiewelt der jungen Männer spielen, angelesen, gehört und geträumt werden oder sich wirklich ereignen.

Die Königin der Nacht gibt beiden den Auftrag, ihre Tochter aus den Händen der bösen Priester des Sonnentempels zu befreien. Sie lassen sich auf das Abenteuer ein, entdecken dabei die Liebe und mit ihr die Sexualität, werden zahlreichen Prüfungen und merkwürdigen Ritualen unterzogen, um am Schluß als Paare in die Welt der nicht mehr so bösen Erwachsenen einzutreten. Die Nacht wird als Ort des Negativen verdammt und Sarastro, der Oberpriester singt: »Die Strahlen der Sonne vertreiben die Nacht, zernichten der Heuchler erschlichene Macht!« Man denkt an Aufklärung und bessere, vernunftbestimmte, hellere Zeiten. Eigentlich erzählt die Geschichte von einem Initiationsritus, von der Einweihung zweier junger Männer in die Erwachsenenwelt. Kindheit und Pubertät werden dabei als märchenhafte, verspielte aber undurchschaubare Zeit verherrlicht – dem Paradies nahe. Ein verkürzter Sündenfall – die Schlange als Zitat – steht am Anfang und führt zur Vertreibung aus der Traumwelt. Das Leben beginnt, und damit nehmen die Fragen, die Gefahren und Ängste zu. Was wird hinter dem Wald liegen? Dort hat sich, wie man sehen wird, die Erwachsenenwelt mit ihrem hohlen Brimborium von Riten und Gesetzen aufgebaut. Erst allmählich sollen die jungen Männer erkennen, daß in den marmornen Gesetzen auch ein höherer Sinn liegt: Würde und Humanität.

Das anarchische Individuum steht dem Staat gegenüber, das Ich der Institution.

Wieder sieht man, daß Mozart und sein Librettist keine Revolutionäre waren: Am Ende geht es um die Anpassung und die Anerkennung der Gesetze der Erwachsenen, nicht etwa um deren Zerstörung. Nach der Traumzeit der Kindheit und der turbulenten Zeit der Pubertät soll jetzt die längste Zeit des Lebens folgen, gesetzlich ritualisiert und zementiert. Erst der Tod wird die Erwachsenen aus ihrem »Lebensbeamtentum« erlösen.

In der *Zauberflöte* werden viele Archetypen der Theater- und Opernwelt zitiert: Adam und Eva, der bereits erwähnte Sündenfall im Paradies, der Gegensatz zwischen Tag- und Nachtwelt und damit zwischen Gut und Böse, das Orpheus-Motiv: Wer die Zauberflöte spielt (Erinnerung an die Panflöte), hat Macht über Menschen und Tiere; Papageno, der Vogelfänger, der schon selbst ein halber Vogel ist, erinnert an die Zwitternatur des Menschen, halb Tier, halb geistig-kulturelles Wesen.

Wie läßt sich heute so ein Werk inszenieren und auf die Bühne bringen? Kann und soll man sich zurückversetzen in eine Zeit, in der es nur gemalte und gezeichnete Bilder und Abbilder gab, in der sich die Kindheit noch zwischen selbstgebastelten Puppenstuben, Heiligenbildern und vorindustriellem Stadt- Alltags- und Jahrmarktszauber abspielte?

Beim Lesen denken wir an Comics, Computerspiele und Fantasy-Filme. Die Kindheit hat ihre Räume und Bilder gewechselt, im Kern ist sie jedoch die gleiche Geschichte wie zu allen Zeiten geblieben.

Man denkt an Kinderzimmer unter der Mansarde, in einem Reihenhaus, irgendwo in einem Vorort, unter dem mit Comics übersäten Bett die Modelleisenbahn, im Aquarium auf dem Schrank ein kleiner fahl beleuchteter Urwald, auf der Innenseite der Schrankwände erotische Photos und hinter den Kissen auf dem Bett die Stofftiere der Vergangenheit.

Rauschartige Anfälle von Freiheits-, Flucht- und Ausbruchsphantasien, nachts dann die Alpträume, schließlich die Flucht in den nächtlichen Stadtpark, die aufkommende Angst, weiter fort, immer weiter fort. Draußen leben, ohne Dach über dem Kopf.

Wenn man Schikaneders Angaben zum Bühnenbild liest, denkt man eher an einen Film als an ein Theaterstück oder eine Oper. Ständig verwandelt sich ein Ort in einen anderen. Verwandlungstheater. Zaubertheater.

»Eine felsige Gegend, hie und da Bäume. Reich ausgestattetes Zimmer in Sarastros Palast; vorne eine Ottomane. In einem Hain stehen die drei Tempel: der Vernunft, der Natur, der Weisheit. Ein Palmenwald. Kurzer Vorhof des Tempels. Garten im Vollmondschein, in der Mitte eine Laube, in der Pamina schläft. Das Theater verwandelt sich in eine Halle. Vorne sind zwei Bänke. Das Theater stellt einen Innenraum dar; es ist halbdunkel. Achtzehn Priester in Form eines Dreiecks zu je sechs aufgestellt. Das Theater verwandelt sich in einen Garten. Das Theater verwandelt sich; es kann einen Wasserfall und einen feuerspeienden Berg zeigen. Das Theater verwandelt sich wieder in den vorigen Garten. Verwandlung: Felsgegend; es ist Nacht. Verwandlung: Donner, Blitz und Sturm: Sogleich verwandelt sich das ganze Theater in eine Sonne.«

Mozart komponierte den größten Teil der *Zauberflöte* in einem kleinen Wiener Gartenhäuschen, das ihm Schikaneder zur Verfügung gestellt hatte. Schikaneder sorgte auch für gutes Essen und lustige Gesellschaft. Heute steht das »Zauberflöten-Häuschen« im Garten hinter dem Mozarteum. Es gab den Anstoß für die Idee, das Stück auch als Meditation über Architektur zu interpretieren.

Die Zauberflöte lebt vom Gegensatz zwischen Natur und gebauter Architektur. Da Architektur immer Seßhaftigkeit und eine geordnete Gesellschaft voraussetzt, ist sie eine Angelegenheit der Erwachsenen. Zum Jugendlichen paßt das Zelt, die flüchtige Behausung.

Am Anfang steht das kleine Vogelhaus, das Papageno auf dem Rücken trägt. Darin sollen die Vögel wohnen. Diese Häuser vermehren sich im Laufe der Handlung. Sie spielen mit, verlieben sich, rücken zusammen, haben Sehnsüchte, träumen, streiten, versöhnen sich. Im Laufe der Geschichte tauchen immer größere Häuser auf. Die Tempel der Erwachsenen sind natürlich am größten. Diese Häuser sind erhaben und stolz. Viele Häuser bilden ein Dorf, noch mehr Häuser eine Stadt und eine Gesellschaft. Alle Häuser behalten als Grundmotiv das Einflugloch und die Landestange wie Vogelhäuser. Der Traum vom Leben in und mit der Natur stirbt nicht. Die Paare werden am Ende in diese Häuser einziehen, Kinder der Liebe zeugen und Teil einer großen Gemeinschaft sein.

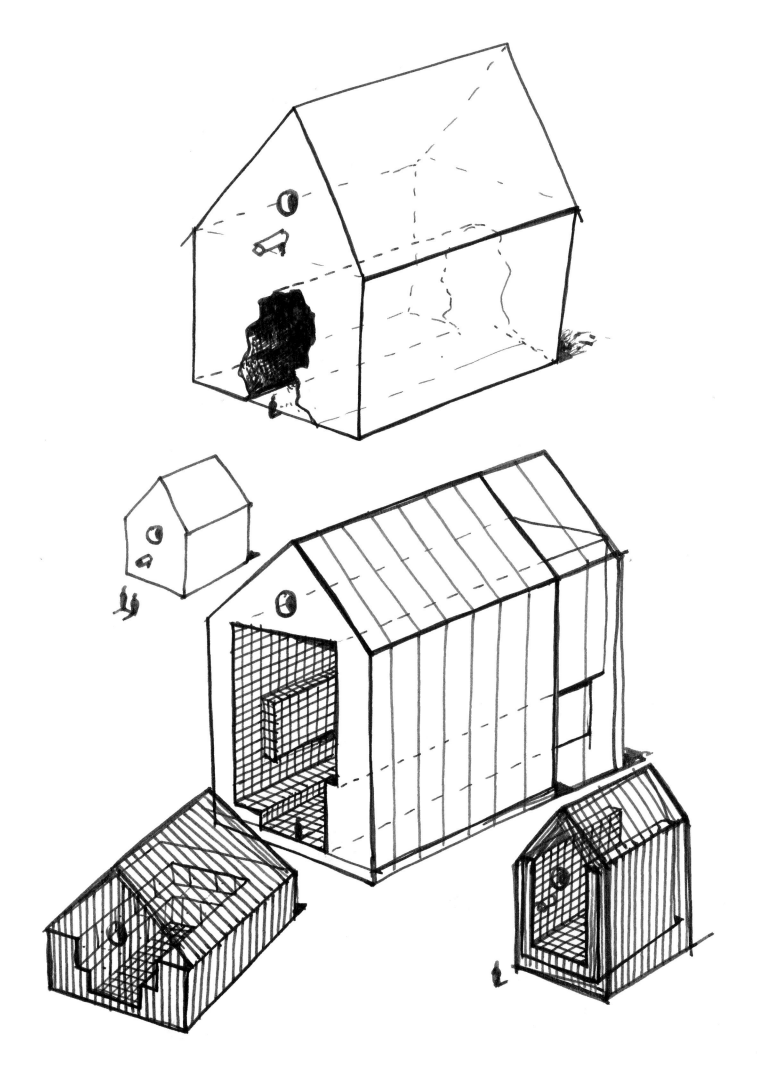

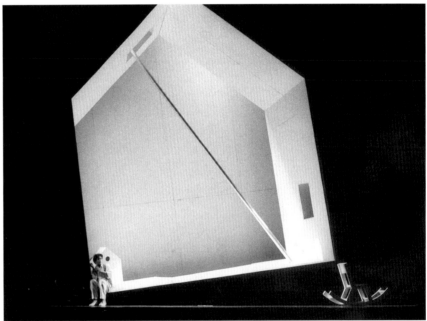

Der Prinz von Homburg

Opera by Hans Werner Henze, libretto based on a play by Heinrich von Kleist, arranged for music by Ingeborg Bachmann

Hessisches Staatstheater, Wiesbaden, 1997; conductor: Hilary Griffiths, director: Dominik Neuner, sets: Hans Dieter Schaal, costumes: Ute Frühling, dramaturgy: Norbert Abels

Here too we are shown a young man who is to move from the dream world of puberty into the urban landscape of adults. Admittedly the prince is somewhat older than Tamino and Papageno, and the events that happen around him are considerably more dangerous and brutal than they are in the fairy-tale wood of *The Magic Flute*.

The Prince of Homburg was born into a militaristic world. His initiation can only take the form of a victory on the battlefield. But at the very beginning of the play he day-dreams his way through the crucial briefing. He is playing with the laurel wreath he longs for and dreaming of love. Then he goes into battle without waiting for orders from his father, the Elector. His operation leads to victory, but he is condemned to death for disobedience by the court martial, whose overlord is his father. He is pardoned only when he accepts that he behaved incorrectly and no longer resists his father's authority.

At heart the prince is an artist by nature. He is interested only in fulfilling himself, and sees war as an artistic campaign that will bring him immortality and a hero's fame. As a dreamer he denies reality and is almost destroyed by it. His victory is pure chance, his survival is an act of education by his father. Society will tolerate only the conforming citizen, soldier or artist.

Kleist himself did not succeed in conforming. He travelled through Europe like a man possessed, and wrote his works. He did not see a single one of his plays on stage. The theatre did not discover the power of his poetry until a hundred years after his death.

When Henze composed his opera *Der Prinz von Homburg*, he identified himself with the protagonist as an outsider. The generation of his fathers had caused the greatest catastrophe in world history in the form of the Second World War. Over fifty million people died on the battlefields, in the cities and concentration camps. Did the prince have a better dream? His rebellion was only half-hearted, he was not against war, he was just against being oppressed by his father. Kleist loved extreme situations. He could not be helped.

The stage settings: »The garden of the Palace of Fehrbellin. In the palace. The battlefield at Fehrbellin. Prison. The Electress's room. The Elector's room. Prison. The Elector's room. The garden of the Palace of Fehrbellin.«

In Wiesbaden all the locations were brought together within a single space: the father's world has closed in to become a bunker prison from which there is only one escape route: victory in the coming battle. A slit provides a glimpse of a landscape that is a battlefield in reality. The gardens of Fehrbellin can be seen in the foreground. The ground is sandy, a place that invites dreaming.

Der Prinz von Homburg

Oper von Hans Werner Henze, Text nach einem Schauspiel von Heinrich von Kleist, für Musik eingerichtet von Ingeborg Bachmann

Hessisches Staatstheater, Wiesbaden, 1997; musikalische Leitung: Hilary Griffiths, Inszenierung: Dominik Neuner, Bühne: Hans Dieter Schaal, Kostüme: Ute Frühling, Dramaturgie: Norbert Abels

Auch hier wird ein junger Mann beschrieben, der aus der Traumwelt der Pubertät in die Stadtlandschaft der Erwachsenen eintreten soll. Freilich ist der Prinz etwas älter als Tamino und Papageno es sind, und die Vorgänge, die sich um ihn herum ereignen, sind wesentlich gefährlicher und brutaler als im Märchenwald der *Zauberflöte*.

Der Prinz von Homburg ist in eine militaristische Welt hineingeboren worden. Seine Initiation kann nur mit einem Sieg auf dem Schlachtfeld erfolgen. Doch bereits zu Beginn des Stückes verträumt er die entscheidende Lagebesprechung. Er spielt mit dem ersehnten Lorbeerkranz und träumt von der Liebe. Dann zieht er in die Schlacht, ohne die Befehle seines Vaters, des Kurfürsten, abzuwarten. Zwar ist das Unternehmen siegreich, aber wegen seines Ungehorsams verurteilt ihn das Kriegsgericht, dessen oberster Herr sein Vater ist, zum Tode. Erst als er sein falsches Verhalten einsieht und sich nicht mehr gegen die väterliche Macht auflehnt, wird er begnadigt.

Im Innersten ist der Prinz eine Künstlernatur. Er will nur sich selbst verwirklichen und sieht im Sieg eine Kunstaktion, die ihm Unsterblichkeit und Heldentum verspricht. Als Träumer verkennt er die Wirklichkeit und wird von ihr fast vernichtet. Sein Sieg ist purer Zufall, sein Überleben eine Erziehungstat des Vaters. Nur der Angepaßte wird von der Gesellschaft geduldet.

Kleist selbst ist die Anpassung nicht gelungen. Wie ein Gejagter reiste er durch Europa und schrieb seine Werke. Nicht eines seiner Dramen hat er auf der Bühne gesehen. Erst hundert Jahre nach seinem Tod entdeckten die Theater die Kraft seiner Dichtung.

Als Henze die Oper *Der Prinz von Homburg* komponierte, identifizierte er sich als Außenseiter mit der Hauptfigur. Die Generation seiner Väter hatte mit dem Zweiten Weltkrieg die größte Katastrophe der Menschheitsgeschichte verursacht. Über fünfzig Millionen Menschen starben auf den Schlachtfeldern, in den Städten und Konzentrationslagern. Hatte der Prinz den besseren Traum? Seine Rebellion war nur halbherzig, er war nicht gegen den Krieg, er war nur gegen die Unterdrückung durch seinen Vater. Kleist liebte Extremsituationen. Man konnte ihm nicht helfen.

Die Bühnenbild-Orte der Handlung: »Der Garten des Schlosses von Fehrbellin. Im Schloß. Schlachtfeld von Fehrbellin. Gefängnis. Zimmer der Kurfürstin. Zimmer des Kurfürsten. Gefängnis. Zimmer des Kurfürsten. Der Garten des Schlosses zu Fehrbellin.«

In Wiesbaden wurden alle Orte in einem Raum zusammengefaßt: Die väterliche Welt hat sich zu einem Bunkergefängnis geschlossen, aus dem es nur ein Entkommen gibt, den Sieg in der bevorstehenden Schlacht. Ein Schlitz läßt den Blick auf eine Landschaft frei, die in Wirklichkeit ein Schlachtfeld ist. Im Vordergrund sieht man den Garten von Fehrbellin. Der Boden ist sandig, ein Ort, der zum Träumen einlädt.

»The Prince of Homburg, our brave cousin, the sleepwalking young man, one who speaks in fiery tongues, a German Hamlet, playing with life and with death – that is the hero of my new opera … But the tension between the individual being and reasons of State, questions of disregard for law and order, a man trembling before the force of the powers that be, the courage to resist these powers – all that could happen today, or could have happened a thousand or two thousand years ago …« (Hans Werner Henze)

»Der Prinz von Homburg, unser tapferer Vetter, der traumwandelnde junge Herr, ein mit feurigen Zungen Redender, ein deutscher Hamlet, mit dem Leben wie mit dem Tode spielend – das ist der Held meiner neuen Oper … Doch die Spannung zwischen dem Sein des einzelnen und der Staatsraison, Fragen der Mißachtung von Gesetz und Ordnung, das Zittern eines Menschen vor der Gewalt der herrschenden Macht, der Mut, sich solcher Macht zu widersetzen – all das könnte auch heute geschehen oder hätte vor tausend oder zweitausend Jahren sein können …« (Hans Werner Henze)

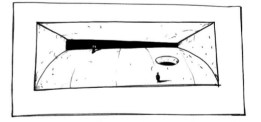

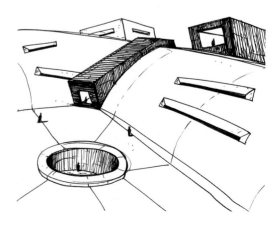

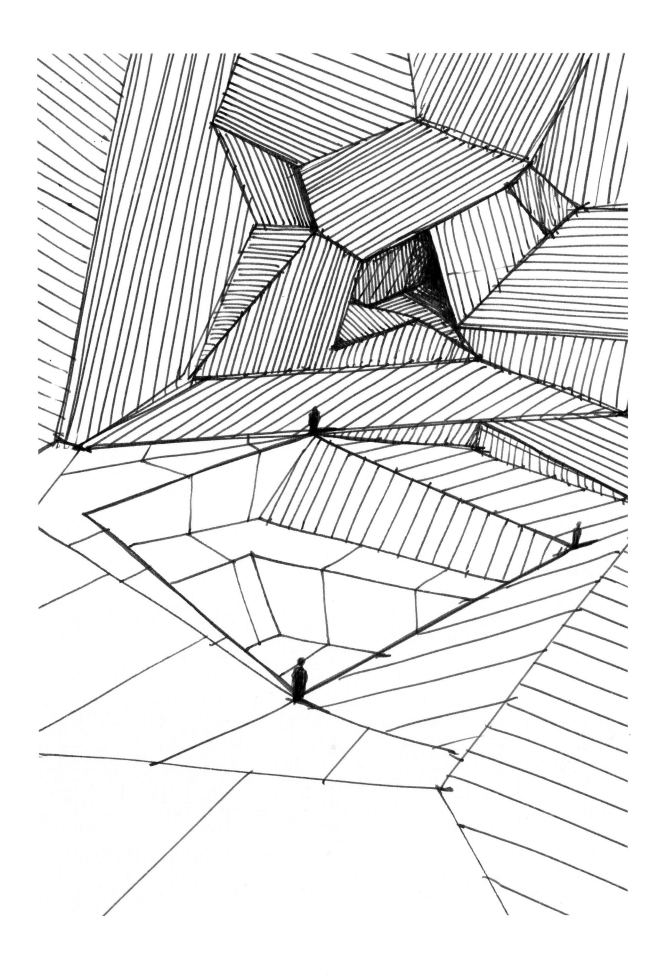

Nacht, Mutter des Tages (»Night, Mother of Day«)

Stage play by Lars Norén
  Akademietheater, Vienna, 1991; director: Guy Joosten, sets: Hans Dieter Schaal, costumes: Karin Seydtle, dramaturgy: Jutta Ferbers

Lars Norén was born in Stockholm in 1944. His plays are in the gloomy tradition of Strindberg, Ibsen and Ingmar Bergman.

He wrote this play in 1982. The text has strongly autobiographical elements. The scene is a large kitchen in a hotel, and the date is 9 May 1956. Norén's parents managed a hotel. And as in the play, his father was an alcoholic.

A family is described – father, mother and two sons. The family as the germ cell of violence and war. The ego is an indefinable prison made up of perception and desires. Other people break into this world. No warmth is possible The sexual act is the greatest humiliation, love is unmasked as a transfigured carnality here. Submission and murder. The cry of orgasm is the death cry.

Then there are the children of these actions. No one has chosen this world, this family, this house, people are thrown into them by an alien violence, and move about in them as if in an alien hell. Trapped in the body, trapped in ideas and desires, trapped in relationships, trapped in a cold shell. Doors and windows offer the possibility of escaping, but the prison will not release anyone. We always carry this place within us. For this reason we are left only with violence against other people, against our father, our mother, our brother. If someone were the strongest, the system would perhaps function in spite of everything. But the former centre, the father, collapses. Alcohol is the abyss, the infinite well-hole at the bottom of which archaic primal myths give off their vapours.

The stage space defines the situation precisely. It is a cold, almost clinical place with kitchen units and a corner with a dining table in it. A battlefield of hatred where there should be love. In the background is a large square window with the father's office behind it. Sometime during the play he will smash the glass in a fit of rage. Above it is a little dovecote (a little arched window) and under it a door leading out into the yard.

As the play proceeds, the kitchen section moves imperceptibly from left to right. The kitchen space becomes smaller and more cramped. Finally the living-room furniture is crushed and lying in the chink of space that remains. A second room then opens up on the left, which turns out to be the parents' bedroom towards the end of the piece: a double bed comes out of the wall. This is where everything began, here the two sons were conceived in fits of feeling that both father and mother took to be love.

Nacht, Mutter des Tages

Theaterstück von Lars Norén
  Akademietheater, Wien, 1991; Inszenierung: Guy Joosten, Bühne: Hans Dieter Schaal, Kostüme: Karin Seydtle, Dramaturgie: Jutta Ferbers

Lars Norén wurde 1944 in Stockholm geboren. Er steht mit seinen Stücken in der düsteren Tradition von Strindberg, Ibsen und Ingmar Bergman.

Das Theaterstück schrieb er 1982. Der Text trägt stark autobiographische Züge. Ort der Handlung ist eine große Küche in einem Hotel, die Zeit der 9. Mai 1956. Auch die Eltern Noréns hatten ein Hotel gepachtet. Und wie im Stück war auch sein Vater Alkoholiker.

Beschrieben wird eine Familie – Vater, Mutter und zwei Söhne. Die Familie als Urzelle von Gewalt und Krieg. Das Ich ist ein undefinierbares Gefängnis aus Wahrnehmung und Sehnsüchten. Die andern brechen in diese Welt ein. Wärme ist nicht möglich. Der Geschlechtsakt ist die größte Erniedrigung, hier wird der als Liebe verklärte Trieb entlarvt. Unterwerfung und Ermordung. Der Orgasmusschrei ist der Todesschrei.

Dann die Kinder dieser Aktionen. Niemand hat sich diese Welt, diese Familie, dieses Haus ausgewählt, man ist von fremder Gewalt hineingeworfen, geht darin herum wie in einer fremden Hölle. Gefangen im Körper, gefangen in den Vorstellungen und Wünschen, gefangen in den Beziehungen, gefangen in einem kalten Gehäuse. Die Türen und Fenster bieten die Möglichkeit zu entkommen, aber das Gefängnis gibt niemanden frei. Man trägt diesen Ort für immer in sich. Deswegen bleibt nur die Gewalt gegen die anderen, den Vater, die Mutter, den Bruder. Wäre jemand der stärkste, würde das System vielleicht dennoch funktionieren. Aber die ehemalige Mitte, der Vater, zerfällt. Alkohol ist der Abgrund, das endlose Brunnenloch, auf dessen Grund archaische Urmythen dampfen.

Der Bühnenbild-Raum beschreibt die Situation genau. Es ist ein kalter, fast klinischer Ort mit Küchenelementen und Eßtischecke. Schlachttraum des Hasses, wo eigentlich Liebe sein sollte. Im Hintergrund ein großes quadratisches Fenster, hinter dem das Büro des Vaters liegt. Irgendwann im Laufe des Stücks wird er in einem Wutanfall die Scheiben zertrümmern. Darüber ein kleiner Taubenschlag (kleines Fenster mit Bogen) und darunter eine Tür, die hinaus in den Hof führt.

Im Laufe der Aufführung schiebt sich unmerklich langsam das Küchenelement von links nach rechts. Der Küchenraum wird immer kleiner und enger. Zum Schluß sind die Wohnmöbel zerquetscht und liegen im verbliebenen Raumspalt. Links öffnet sich dann ein zweiter Raum, der sich gegen Ende des Stücks als Schlafzimmer der Eltern herausstellt: Ein Doppelbett fährt aus der Wand. Hier nahm alles seinen Anfang, hier wurden diese Söhne in Anfällen von Gefühl gezeugt, die beide, Vater und Mutter, für Liebe hielten.

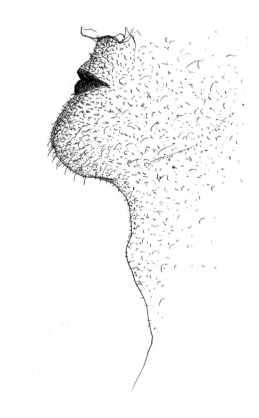

Fierrabras

Opera by Franz Schubert, libretto by Joseph Kupelwieser

Theater an der Wien (Wiener Festwochen), 1988, from 1990 at the Staatsoper, Vienna; conductor: Claudio Abbado, director: Ruth Berghaus, sets: Hans Dieter Schaal, costumes: Marie-Luise Strandt

Fierrabras is a typical product of Biedermeier Romanticism. Young men dream of friendship, love, happiness and peace in a war-like environment. The action is set at the time of Charlemagne. The Europeans are fighting the Moors during the Saracen wars, the Christians against the heathen.

Fierrabras, the son of the Moorish prince, falls in love with Charlemagne's daughter after being captured by the emperor's knights. A delegation sent by Charlemagne to the Moors are taken by the enemy and condemned to death. But the story does end in goodwill. The loving couples – there are several of them – are able to come together. Only Fierrabras, the noble hero, comes away empty-handed.

This opera may have been a memorial to his circle of friends, without whom Franz Schubert would scarcely have survived in Vienna. He never had a home of his own. He always dreamed of wandering, of travelling around, of great journeys and strange countries. While spending the last months of his life sick in his brother's home in Kettenbrückengasse in Vienna he read Cooper's *Lederstrumpf* (»Leatherstocking« tales) and was already in the New World in his imagination. If he had survived the illness he would perhaps have emigrated.

At the centre of the staging idea is a tower that has been cut open. This is the location for the circle of friends and for the women. Emotions circle around, and are embroidered on to fabrics and cushions by the women, and carried outside by the men, as a conflict. Bodies, armour, castles. Romanticism transfigured in the evening light, colliding with thick walls of rock, against metal fortresses, and in the distance the Blue Flower can be seen glowing.

The Romantic warriors appear, their feelings are frozen into ice. Then they start hitting out at each other, and swarms of black crows fly up into the air. Later the crows will settle on the corpses and pick out the warriors' romantic eyes.

Friendships, power games, treachery. The adult world knows only the architecture of power, battle, victory and defeat. What remains are the artists' dreams.

We are reminded of a picture by Goya: a group of fanciful, Romantic rococo figures are wandering through flowery landscapes in idle dalliance. The sun is shining, and they think they can hear the twittering of birds. Suddenly a wind gets up, clouds blot out the sun, the temperature shoots down, it begins to snow and heavily armed troops appear on the horizon. War has broken out. The first dead fall to the ground, their faces are torn to pieces. The Siberian winter slowly covers them up.

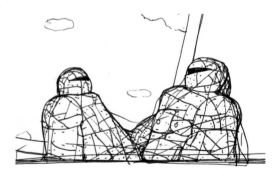

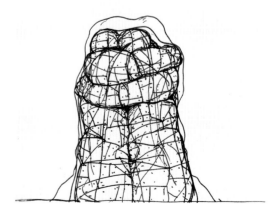

Fierrabras

Oper von Franz Schubert, Libretto von Joseph Kupelwieser

Theater an der Wien (Wiener Festwochen), 1988, ab 1990 an der Staatsoper, Wien; musikalische Leitung: Claudio Abbado, Inszenierung: Ruth Berghaus, Bühne: Hans Dieter Schaal, Kostüme: Marie-Luise Strandt

Fierrabras ist ein typisches Werk der biedermeierlichen Romantik. Inmitten einer kriegerischen Umgebung träumen junge Männer von Freundschaft, Liebe, Glück und Frieden. Die Handlung spielt zur Zeit Karls des Großen. Während der Sarazenenkriege kämpfen die Europäer gegen die Mauren, die Christen gegen die Heiden.

Fierrabras, der Sohn des Maurenfürsten, verliebt sich in die Tochter Karls, nachdem er von dessen Rittern festgenommen wurde. Eine Abordnung Karls, die ins Maurenland geschickt worden ist, wird dort vom Feind verhaftet und zum Tode verurteilt. Dennoch löst sich die Geschichte in Wohlgefallen auf. Die verliebten Paare – es gibt deren mehrere – bekommen einander. Nur Fierrabras, der edle Held, geht leer aus.

Für Franz Schubert stellt diese Oper vielleicht auch ein Denkmal für seinen Freundeskreis dar, ohne den er in Wien kaum überlebt hätte. Er hat niemals eine eigene Wohnung besessen. Immer träumte er vom Wandern, vom Umherfahren, von großen Reisen und fernen Ländern. Als er in der Wiener Kettenbrückengasse bei seinem Bruder krank die letzten Monate seines Lebens verbrachte, las er Coopers *Lederstrumpf* und lebte in seiner Phantasie bereits in der neuen Welt. Hätte er die Krankheit überlebt, wäre er vielleicht ausgewandert.

Im Zentrum der Bühnenbildidee steht ein aufgeschnittener Turm. Ort des Freundeskreises und der Frauen. Die Gefühle kreisen, werden von den Frauen in Stoffe und Kissen eingestickt, von den Männern als Kampf nach draußen getragen. Körper, Rüstungen, Burgen. Die Romantik verklärt sich im Abendlicht, prallt gegen dicke Felswände, gegen Metallburgen, und in der Ferne leuchtet die Blaue Blume.

Die romantischen Kämpfer tauchen auf, ihre Gefühle erstarren zu Eis. Dann schlagen sie aufeinander los, und schwarze Krähenschwärme fliegen auf. Später werden die Vögel sich auf die Kadaver setzen und die romantischen Augen der Kämpfer auspicken.

Freundschaften, Machtspiele, Verrat. Die Erwachsenenwelt kennt nur die Architektur der Macht, den Kampf, den Sieg und die Niederlage. Was bleibt, ist der Traum der Künstler.

Man denkt an ein Bild Goyas: Eine Gruppe verspielter, romantischer Rokoko-Gestalten wandert tändelnd durch blühende Landschaften. Die Sonne scheint, und man glaubt, Vogelgezwitscher zu hören. Plötzlich kommt Wind auf, Wolken verdunkeln die Sonne, die Temperatur stürzt ab, es beginnt zu schneien, und schwerbewaffnete Truppen zeigen sich am Horizont. Es herrscht Krieg. Die ersten Toten fallen zu Boden, ihre Gesichter sind zerrissen. Langsam deckt der sibirische Winter sie zu.

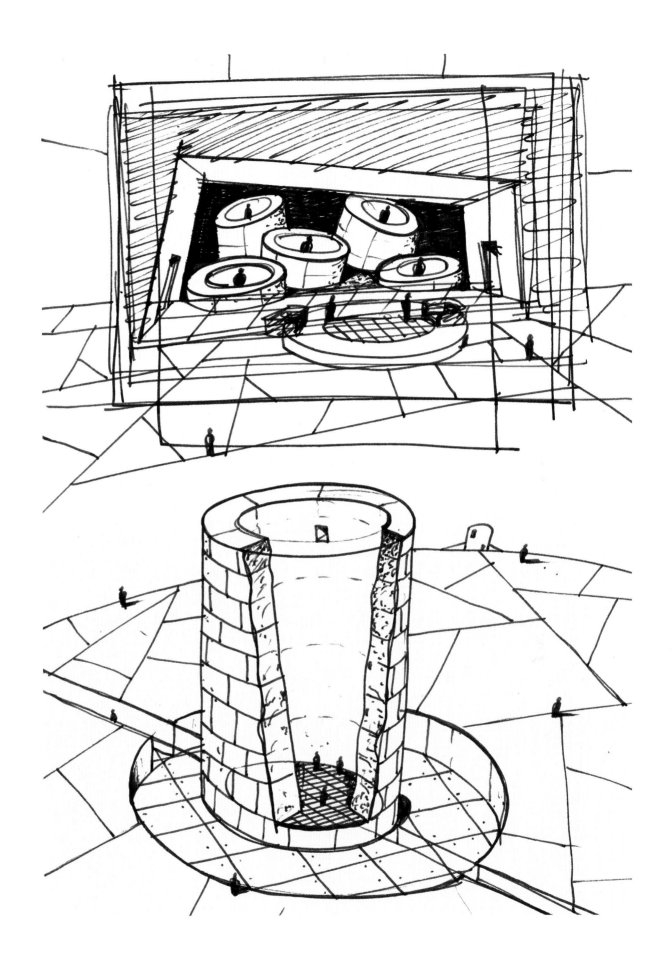

A Masked Ball

Melodrama in three acts by Giuseppe Verdi to a libretto by Antonio Somma based on Eugène Scribe's libretto *Gustave III* ou *Le bal masqué*

Oper Nürnberg, 1995; conductor: Eberhard Kloke, director: Jürgen Tamchina, sets: Hans Dieter Schaal, costumes: Beate Tamchina, dramaturgy: Wolfgang Hofer

This opera by Giuseppe Verdi takes us into the work of the greatest master of melodrama in the history of music. Without his work we would not know how fate sounds, how jealousy wails and mourning laments. Almost all his libretti deal with individuals whose great emotions take them into the machinery of political events. Censorship required that material should be historical, and well away from the events of the day. But every spectator in those days was aware of the real position. Verdi's political emotions were tied up with the unification of Italy. He fought against the foreign intruders, France and Austria, with his own resources. Italy was to be free and unoccupied, and it was to be able to assert itself in the world as a great nation.

Verdi is actually counterpart to Wagner. But while Wagner wallowed in the mythological primordial soup, Verdi remained more on the surface. He was interested in sufferers, lovers, people who were ill, outsiders and villains with their emotions and political involvements.

The plot of *Un Ballo in Maschera* is based on historical events that took place in Stockholm. King Gustav III was murdered there in 1792 by his Captain Anckarström during a masked ball. Verdi had a libretto written by Antonio Somma in response to a commission from the Teatro San Carlo in Naples. When the opera was complete, it was banned by the censor. The plot was to be shifted to a more distant country. So the story was finally placed in Boston, and is now set in the late 17th century.

The Governor of Boston is in love with his best friend's wife. When the friend finds out about this, he joins a conspiracy that is already under way against the governor. In the end the friend stabs the governor to death during a masked ball.

The stage set located the story in a high hall. There was a view through a large window into a snowy vista. An open fire was burning in the middle of the hall. Doorways and openings suggested the surrounding rooms. Palace hall and waiting room, ballroom and lobby in a large hotel.

The individual rooms were created by closing and opening up a whole variety of spaces. Spaces as locations where emotions take place.

Ein Maskenball

Melodrama in drei Akten von Giuseppe Verdi nach einem Libretto von Antonio Somma nach dem Libretto *Gustave III* ou *Le bal masqué* von Eugène Scribe

Oper Nürnberg, 1995; musikalische Leitung: Eberhard Kloke, Inszenierung: Jürgen Tamchina, Bühne: Hans Dieter Schaal, Kostüme: Beate Tamchina, Dramaturgie: Wolfgang Hofer

Mit dieser Oper von Giuseppe Verdi treten wir in das Werk des größten Melodramatikers der Musikgeschichte ein. Ohne seine Werke wüßten wir nicht, wie das Schicksal klingt, wie die Eifersucht jammert und die Trauer klagt. Fast alle seine Libretti handeln von Individuen, die mit ihren großen Gefühlen in das Räderwerk politischer Vorgänge geraten. Die Zensur forderte, daß die Stoffe historisch, weit weg von der Gegenwart anzusiedeln seien. Jeder Zuschauer damals erkannte jedoch die aktuellen Bezüge. Verdis politisches Pathos galt der Einigung Italiens. Mit seinen Mitteln bekämpfte er die fremden Eindringlinge: Frankreich und Österreich. Italien sollte frei und unbesetzt sein, es sollte sich in der Welt als große Nation behaupten können.

Verdi ist der eigentliche Gegenspieler Wagners. Doch während Wagner in der mythologischen Ursuppe wühlte, blieb Verdi mehr an der Oberfläche. Ihn interessierten die Leidenden, die Liebenden, die Kranken, die Außenseiter, die Bösewichte mit ihren Emotionen und politischen Verstrickungen.

Die Handlung des *Maskenball* beruht auf historischen Ereignissen, die sich in Stockholm zugetragen haben. Dort wurde 1792 König Gustav III. während eines Maskenballs von seinem Hauptmann Anckarström ermordet. Verdi ließ sich im Auftrag des Teatro San Carlo von Neapel ein Libretto von Antonio Somma schreiben. Als die Oper komponiert war, wurde sie von der Zensur verboten. Man verlangte eine Verlegung der Handlung ins ferne Ausland. So landete die Geschichte schließlich in Boston und spielt nun Ende des 17. Jahrhunderts.

Der Gouverneur von Boston liebt die Frau seines besten Freundes. Als dieser das Geheimnis entdeckt, schließt er sich einer Verschwörung an, die gegen den Gouverneur gerichtet ist. Am Ende ersticht der Freund den Gouverneur während eines Maskenballs.

Das Bühnenbild siedelte die Geschichte in einer hohen Halle an. Durch das große Fenster sah man hinaus auf verschneite Landschaften. In der Mitte der Halle brannte ein offenes Kaminfeuer. Türen und Öffnungen ließen die Räume ringsum ahnen. Palastraum und Wartesaal, Festsaal und Eingangshalle in einem großen Hotel.

Durch das Verschließen und Öffnen einzelner Fenster und Türöffnungen ließen sich die unterschiedlichsten Räume erzeugen. Räume als Ereignisort von Emotionen.

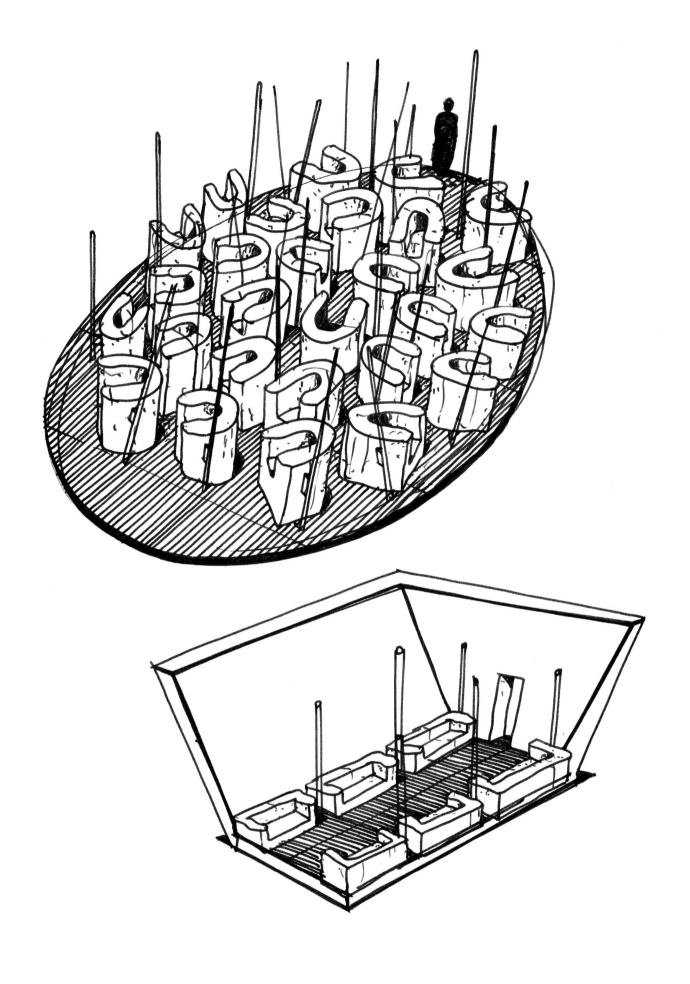

Tannhäuser

Grand romantic opera in three acts by Richard Wagner, libretto by the composer

Staatstheater Braunschweig, 1993; conductor: Anton Zapf, director: Dominik Neuner, sets: Hans Dieter Schaal, costumes: Monika Zeller-Schömig

Hessisches Staatstheater, Wiesbaden, 2001; conductor: Toshiyuki Kamioka, director: Dominik Neuner, sets: Hans Dieter Schaal, costumes: Ute Frühling, dramaturgy: Margrit Poremba

The time: the early 13th century. The Minnesänger Heinrich von Ofterdingen, called Tannhäuser, becomes captivated by the goddess Venus, who has established herself and her retinue in a cave near Eisenach. Venus knows no taboos. It is possible to yield completely to physical lust in her household. But Tannhäuser has now had enough of her. He wants to return to the Wartburg. He is plagued by pangs of religious conscience: »My salvation lies in Mary«. Venus reluctantly lets him go.

Elisabeth, the chaste, virginal woman of the Wartburg, who loves him, is waiting for him. Tannhäuser admits his love to her. The song contest takes place in the great hall of the Wartburg. The landgrave promises his niece Elisabeth to the Minnesänger who sings most beautifully of love. Wolfram von Eschenbach describes a »spring worthy of adoration«, Walther von der Vogelweide adds »If you seek refreshment from the fountain, you must lave your heart, and not your throat …« After these very ambiguous and flowery descriptions of love, Tannhäuser comes to the point. He enthuses about Venus and the wild joys of sexual fulfilment. Everyone is outraged, and the landgrave banishes the breaker of taboos from the country. All that remains for him is a pilgrimage to Rome, where he is to be given absolution.

Elisabeth remains committed to him, despite his unambiguous words. When Tannhäuser returns from Rome, exhausted and depressed, he has to confess that he has not been absolved and that he wants to go back to Venus. At this point Elisabeth's coffin is carried past, and he dies at the side of the maidenly corpse.

It is never made clear why Tannhäuser takes part in the song contest at all, or why in the end he does not stay in Rome or go to another country. His love of Elisabeth is religious in its nature. In reality it is aimed at Mary, the untouchable virgin. To satisfy his sexual urges he can do nothing other than take the path to the heathen cave of the nature goddess Venus, who is a witch in the eyes of the Wartburg community. The world of the spirit is placed high on the Wartburg, that of the instincts deep down in the depths of the earth. This is dramatic symbolism that corresponds to the Christian world picture: love is divine, but sexuality comes from the devil. All the Minnesänger on the Wartburg share this opinion.

Eve and Venus, from the Christian point of view these are the two primal seducers of men. Mary, who conceived and bore the son of God, has to remain a virgin. The first fall of man led to the expulsion from paradise; through Mary, all naturally born children become the result of sinful lust. The two stories leave the Christian singer of verses Tannhäuser no choice; death is the only way out for him.

Tannhäuser entered the realm of Eve-Venus in his search for truth, but he has not gone as far as Baudelaire or Nietzsche. He dies on the border created by the taboo, with one half of his body in the Wartburg and the other in the realm of Venus.

If he were Orpheus, Elisabeth's death would release him creatively. Now he would have an allied soul in the afterlife and could sing of love. If we take a step back and allow Wagner into the picture, then we see that he has become Orpheus. He has written and composed *Tannhäuser*. He has portrayed the icy boundary in sound.

Mary-Elisabeth: for Tannhäuser, this woman is like an angel. And in the Christian imagination angels are light, untouchable forms from the next world, messengers moving between God and man. At the Annunciation, an angel appears to Mary and tells her that she is pregnant. Angels are asexual creatures, neither male nor female. Since the biblical fall of the angels – not all the messengers proved themselves – there have been good and bad, blessed and fallen angels.

Eve-Venus could be a fallen angel. In the Christian imagination of the Wartburg community she entered into a pact with the devil and became a witch. Everyone who comes under her spell is hypnotized by her.

The settings for the action: »1. The Venusberg. Hörselberg near Eisenach. A spacious grotto, stretching as if into infinity in the background because of a turn to the right … 2. The Hall of Song on the Wartburg; in the background is an open view of the courtyard and the valley. 3. Valley below the Wartburg, on the left is the Hörselberg – as at the end of the first act, but with autumn colours …«

In Braunschweig the architecture of the Wartburg was central. The story was told from here. This was the fixed location.

Architecture is built power, each inside wall is a law, each outside wall a ban. Only windows give an open view, for voyeurs as well. Doors are places of transformation: outside one is a different person from the person one is inside. Penetration. Elimination. Closed doors make the house into a prison.

Venus can be everywhere, in the street, in the café, indoors, in museums and theatres, on television and in cinemas as well.

The Venusberg and its grotto were set up in front of the Wartburg set. The stage remained empty in the third scene: we saw a deserted, white area of stage. Snowed up and icy.

The Wartburg hall was central in Wiesbaden as well. The world of Venus was in front of it, and it was possible to look into it from a large window in the hall. Tannhäuser tries to transport his instrument, the grand piano, from one realm to the other. He fails, he has gone too far.

The windows of the hall look out over a tower landscape, white, as though it is made up of snow. Beyond this, in the distance, is Rome, like a blue flower.

Tannhäuser und der Sängerkrieg auf der Wartburg

Große romantische Oper in drei Aufzügen von Richard Wagner, Text vom Komponisten

Staatstheater Braunschweig, 1993; musikalische Leitung: Anton Zapf, Inszenierung: Dominik Neuner; Bühne: Hans Dieter Schaal; Kostüme: Monika Zeller-Schömig

Hessisches Staatstheater, Wiesbaden, 2001; musikalische Leitung: Toshiyuki Kamioka, Inszenierung: Dominik Neuner; Bühne: Hans Dieter Schaal, Kostüme: Ute Frühling, Dramaturgie: Margrit Poremba

Zeit: Anfang des 13. Jahrhunderts. Der Minnesänger Heinrich von Ofterdingen, genannt Tannhäuser, verfällt der Göttin Venus, die sich mit ihren sinnlichen Begleiterinnen in einer Höhle bei Eisenach eingerichtet hat. Venus kennt keine Tabus. In ihrem Etablissement kann man seine körperliche Lust ganz ausleben. Doch ist Tannhäuser ihrer jetzt überdrüssig. Er will zurück zur Wartburg. Religiöse Gewissensbisse plagen ihn: »Mein Heil ruht in Maria«. Unwillig läßt Venus ihn ziehen.

Elisabeth, die keusche, jungfräuliche Wartburgfrau, die ihn liebt, wartet auf ihn. Tannhäuser gesteht ihr seine Liebe. In der großen Sängerhalle der Wartburg kommt es zum Sängerkrieg. Der Landgraf verspricht dem Minnesänger seine Nichte Eilsabeth, der die Liebe am schönsten besingt. Wolfram von Eschenbach beschreibt einen »anbetungswürdigen Brunnen«, Walther von der Vogelweide ergänzt »Willst Du Erquickung aus dem Bronnen haben, mußt du dein Herz, nicht deinen Gaumen laben ...« Nach diesen sehr zweideutigen und blumigen Umschreibungen der Liebe kommt Tannhäuser zur Sache. Er schwärmt von Venus und der wilden Lust an sexueller Erfüllung. Alle sind entsetzt, und der Landgraf verbannt den Tabubrecher außer Landes. Es bleibt ihm nur ein Pilgergang nach Rom, wo er die Absolution erhalten soll.

Elisabeth steht zu ihm, trotz seiner deutlichen Worte. Als Tannhäuser erschöpft und niedergeschlagen aus Rom zurückkehrt, muß er gestehen, daß er keine Absolution erhalten hat und daß er zurück zu Venus will. Da wird der Sarg mit Elisabeth herbeigetragen, und er stirbt an der Seite der jungfräulichen Leiche.

Warum Tannhäuser überhaupt an dem Sängerkrieg teilnimmt, und warum er am Ende nicht in Rom bleibt oder in ein anderes Land geht, bleibt unklar. Seine Liebe zu Elisabeth ist religiöser Natur. Er meint in Wirklichkeit Maria, die Unberührbare. Um seinen Sexualtrieb auszuleben, bleibt ihm nur der Weg in die heidnische Höhle der Naturgöttin Venus, die in den Augen der Wartburggesellschaft eine Hexe ist. Die Welt des Geistes ist hoch oben auf der Burg angesiedelt, die der Triebe tief unten in der Erde. Eine drastische Symbolik, die dem christlichen Weltbild entspricht: Liebe ist göttlich, Sexualität dagegen teuflisch. Alle Minnesänger der Wartburg sind dieser Meinung.

Eva und Venus, das sind aus christlicher Sicht die beiden Ur-Verführerinnen der Männer. Maria, die Gottes Sohn empfangen und geboren hat, muß jungfräulich bleiben. Der erste Sündenfall hat zur Vertreibung aus dem Paradies geführt; durch Maria verkommen alle natürlich gezeugten

Kinder zu Resultaten sündiger Lust. Beide Geschichten lassen dem christlichen Dichter-Sänger Tannhäuser keine Wahl: Ihm bleibt nur der Tod als Ausweg.

Tannhäuser hat auf seiner Wahrheitssuche das Reich der Eva-Venus betreten, aber er ist noch nicht so weit wie Baudelaire oder Nietzsche. Er stirbt auf der Tabu-Grenze, eine Körperhälfte im Wartburgraum, die andere im Reich der Venus.

Wäre er Orpheus, dann würde ihn der Tod Elisabeths schöpferisch lösen. Jetzt hätte er eine verbündete Seele im Jenseits und könnte die Liebe besingen. Treten wir einen Schritt zurück und lassen Wagner ins Bild kommen, dann sehen wir, daß er zum Orpheus geworden ist. Er hat *Tannhäuser* geschrieben und komponiert. Er hat die eisige Grenze zum Klingen gebracht.

Maria-Elisabeth: Für Tannhäuser gleicht diese Frau einem Engel. Und Engel sind nach christlicher Vorstellung lichte, unberührbare Jenseitsgestalten, Boten, die zwischen Gott und den Menschen verkehren. Bei der Verkündigung erscheint in Marias Zimmer ein Engel und sagt ihr, daß sie schwanger sei. Engel sind asexuelle Wesen, weder männlich noch weiblich. Seit dem biblischen Engelssturz – nicht alle Boten haben sich bewährt – gibt es gute und böse, selige und gefallene Engel.

Eva-Venus könnte ein gefallener Engel sein. Sie hat sich in der christlichen Vorstellung der Wartburg-Gesellschaft mit dem Teufel eingelassen und ist zur Hexe geworden. Alle, die in ihren Bannkreis treten, werden von ihr hypnotisiert.

Die Bühnenbild–Orte der Handlung: »1. Der Venusberg. Hörselberg bei Eisenach. Weite Grotte, welche sich im Hintergrund durch eine Biegung nach rechts wie unabsehbar dahinzieht ... 2. Die Sängerhalle auf der Wartburg; im Hintergrunde offene Aussicht auf den Hof und das Tal. 3. Tal vor der Wartburg, links der Hörselberg – wie am Schlusse des ersten Aufzugs, nur in herbstlicher Färbung ...«

In Braunschweig stand die Architektur der Wartburg im Mittelpunkt. Von hier aus wurde die Geschichte erzählt. Sie war der feste Ort.

Architektur ist gebaute Macht, jede Wand ein Gesetz, jede Mauer ein Verbot. Nur Fenster geben die Blicke frei, auch für Voyeure. Türen sind Orte der Verwandlung: Draußen ist man ein anderer als drinnen. Eindringen. Ausscheiden. Verschlossene Türen machen das Haus zum Gefängnis.

Venus kann überall sein, auf der Straße, im Café, in Innenräumen, in Museen und Theatern, im Fernsehen und auch in den Kinos.

Der Venusberg mit seiner Höhle wurde vor das Bild der Wartburg gebaut. Im dritten Bild blieb die Bühne leer: Wir sahen eine leere, weiße Bühnenfläche. Verschneit und eisig.

Auch in Wiesbaden bildete die Wartburg-Halle den Mittelpunkt. Die Venuswelt lag davor und war durch ein großes Fenster von der Halle aus einsehbar. Tannhäuser versucht sein Instrument, den Flügel, von einem Reich zum andern zu transportieren. Er scheitert, hat sich übernommen.

Durch die Fenster der Halle sieht man auf eine Turmlandschaft, weiß, wie aus Schnee gebaut. Dahinter, in der Ferne liegt Rom wie eine blaue Blume.

Salome

Music drama in one act by Richard Strauss, libretto from Oscar Wilde's play of the same name, translated by Hedwig Lachmann and abridged by the composer

Staatstheater Braunschweig, 1994; conductor: Philippe Augin, director: Dominik Neuner, sets: Hans Dieter Schaal, costumes: Monika Zeller-Schömig

Hessisches Staatstheater, Wiesbaden, 1998; conductor: Toshiyuki Kamioka, director: Dominik Neuner, assistant director: Iris Gerath-Prein, sets: Hans Dieter Schaal, costumes: Ute Frühling, dramaturgy: Norbert Abels

The action is set in about 30 AD. Jokanaan (John the Baptist) is being kept captive by Herod Antipas, the Roman governor in Galilee, in a cistern under the palace terrace. In the evening, while celebrations are still under way in the palace, Herod's stepdaughter, Princess Salome, comes out on to the terrace and hears the voice of Jokanaan proclaiming the coming of the Messiah. She is fascinated, and asks to see the prophet. The captain of the guard has Jokanaan brought out, against Herod's express instructions. Salome tries to captivate the prophet, but he has only contempt for her and the rest of the court and goes back down into the cistern.

In the meantime, Herod has appeared on the terrace. He looks lasciviously at Salome and asks her to dance for him. She does not agree to do so until he has promised to give her anything she asks for. After her legendary dance of the seven veils, which is nothing other than a slow striptease, she demands Jokanaan's head from her stepfather. Herod is almost frightened to death. His wife, Herodias, venomously colludes in the request. Herod feels that he has been pushed into a corner and finally gives a reluctant order to behead the prophet. In a wild, hysterical final outburst Salome kisses the cold lips of the murdered man. Herod is so horrified by Salome's cruelty that he has her killed as well.

The whole of the action takes place in a single evening. It is not possible to say how old the real Salome was at this time, biblical scholars assume between fourteen and eighteen. In reality everything could well have happened quite differently. Probably her mother Herodias was the driving force, she had fallen in love with Jokanaan. Oscar Wilde reinterpreted the story, and Richard Strauss introduced new and revolutionary accents, with which he struck a chord in his day. Lolita, the murderous Circe, was born. A dangerous, man-murdering Lulu. Love and sexuality with fatal consequences. A bloody, dangerous game. Something that had previously tended to be ascribed to men – murder through jealousy, revenge, or unrequited love – was now being committed by a woman who was almost a child still. In 1905, when the opera was premièred, this Expressionist bloodthirstiness exploded like a bombshell. King William II was horrified. Where were decency, love and marriage in this? The Berlin censors insisted that the star of Bethlehem should appear at the end of the piece.

In Vienna, the consequences of repressed sexual urges had been investigated by Breuer and Freud before 1900. An inclination towards inhibited prudishness, the negation of female sexuality had led to illness in women in particular. In the late 19th century, doctors' surgeries were full of women suffering from mysterious convulsions and phantom pregnancies.

Against this background, Salome seemed like a primal scream. Yes, that was it! An unstoppable anarchic and primeval force! Its aim: immediate satisfaction of desire, or murder. Reduction to this narrow cycle of action was in tune with the thinking behind Expressionist woodcuts. Of course what was meant here was not love as a noble force, but the sexuality that burgeons with puberty that strives obsessively to possess and could be raging aggression that excludes everything else.

Salome is the exhibitionistic murderess who lasciviously exhibits herself to the gaze of others. She is sacrificed so that we can discover her secret. Before her own death she completes the hysterical death ritual, with Jokanaan's severed head before her on a silver salver: »Ah! thou wouldst not suffer me to kiss thy mouth, Jokanaan. Well! I will kiss it now. I will bite it with my teeth as one bites a ripe fruit. Yes, I will kiss thy mouth, Jokanaan.«

Opera has arrived in its proper expressive region with this final song by Salome: » … only the soprano, the divine one, the heiress of hysterics, whose sewn-up throat now opens at last, and is able to bring forth the most wonderful, ecstatic and unpredictable tones …« (Christina von Braun), only this soprano can express the fatal orgasm. It is a maniac rearing up of all the senses, a final, enormous flare-up – after that the body lies there burned up and ‚fatally exhausted on the ground!

Setting: »A large terrace in Herod's palace, which is adjacent to the banqueting hall. Soldiers are leaning over the parapet. On the right is a massive flight of steps, on the left in the background is an old cistern with a green bronze rim. The moon is shining very brightly.«

The sets in Braunschweig and Wiesbaden showed the large terrace. Indications of architecture suggested the palace rooms around it.

In Braunschweig, Jokanaan's cistern became the second defining motif. Cistern shafts had been driven into the ground all over the terrace. The prophet's voice rang out from them threateningly loudly: everyone but Salome is afraid of Jokanaan, they keep listening to the voice from under the ground: what if he is right, what if the dead really will return?

The terrace is primarily a location for orgies. Here the court meets every evening, eats, drinks, takes its pleasure and gets bored. But this is where the two world views intersect as well: the Romans with their gods and the Jews with their faith. Underneath is the emergent Christian religion (Jokanaan). In addition we have the night and the moon.

In Wiesbaden there were no shafts, just a garden pavilion that had been tipped over at the edge of a swimming-pool. The sense of fear was just the same. The prophet's songs rang out from the cracks and little holes in the floor and on the walls.

Salome

Musikdrama in einem Aufzug von Richard Strauss, Text nach Oscar Wildes gleichnamigem Schauspiel in der vom Komponisten gekürzten Übersetzung von Hedwig Lachmann

Staatstheater Braunschweig, 1994; musikalische Leitung: Philippe Auguin, Inszenierung: Dominik Neuner, Bühne: Hans Dieter Schaal, Kostüme: Monika Zeller-Schömig

Hessisches Staatstheater, Wiesbaden, 1998; musikalische Leitung: Toshiyuki Kamioka, Inszenierung: Dominik Neuner, Regiemitarbeit: Iris Gerath-Prein, Bühne: Hans Dieter Schaal, Kostüme: Ute Frühling, Dramaturgie: Norbert Abels

Die Handlung spielt um das Jahr 30 nach Christus. Jochanaan (Johannes der Täufer) ist von Herodes Antipas, dem römischen Statthalter in Galiläa, in einer Zisterne unter der Palastterrasse gefangengesetzt worden. Am Abend, während in den Palasträumen noch gefeiert wird, betritt die Stieftochter des Herodes, Prinzessin Salome, die Terrasse und hört die Stimme Jochanaans, der die Ankunft des Messias verkündet. Sie ist fasziniert und will den Propheten sehen. Gegen den ausdrücklichen Befehl des Herodes läßt der Hauptmann der Leibwache Jochanaan heraufbringen. Salome versucht, den Propheten zu betören, aber dieser hat nur Verachtung für sie und den ganzen Hofstaat übrig und steigt wieder in die Zisterne herab.

Inzwischen ist Herodes auf die Terrasse gekommen. Mit Lust betrachtet er Salome und bittet sie darum, für ihn zu tanzen. Sie willigt erst ein, nachdem er ihr versprochen hat, alles zu geben, was sie sich wünscht. Nach ihrem legendären Tanz der sieben Schleier, der nichts anderes ist als ein langsamer Striptease, fordert sie als Gegengabe den Kopf Jochanaans von ihrem Stiefvater. Herodes erschrickt fast zu Tode. Geifernd stimmt Herodias, seine Frau, dem Wunsche zu. Er fühlt sich in die Enge getrieben und gibt schließlich widerwillig den Befehl, den Propheten zu köpfen. In einem wilden, hysterischen Schlußgesang küßt Salome die kalten Lippen des Ermordeten. Herodes ist so entsetzt über die Grausamkeit Salomes, daß er auch sie töten läßt.

Alles spielt an einem Abend. Wie alt die wirkliche Salome zu diesem Zeitpunkt war, kann man nicht genau sagen, zwischen 14 und 18 Jahren nehmen die Bibelforscher an. In Wirklichkeit hat sich alles vielleicht etwas anders zugetragen. Wahrscheinlich war ihre Mutter, Herodias, die treibende Kraft, sie hatte sich in Jochanaan verliebt. Oscar Wilde interpretierte die Geschichte um, und Richard Strauss setzte neue, revolutionäre Akzente, mit denen er den Nerv der Zeit traf. Lolita, die tötende Circe war geboren. Eine gefährliche, männermordende Lulu. Liebe und Sexualität mit tödlicher Konsequenz. Ein blutiges, gefährliches Spiel. Was früher eher Männern zugeschrieben wurde – Mord aus Eifersucht, aus Rache oder nicht erfüllter Liebe – wurde jetzt von einer Frau verübt, die fast noch ein Kind war. 1905, als die Oper uraufgeführt wurde, schlug diese expressionistische Blutrünstigkeit wie eine Bombe ein. König Wilhelm II. war entsetzt. Wo blieben hier Anstand, Liebe, Ehe? Die Berliner Zensur verlangte, daß am Ende des Stückes der Stern von Bethlehem aufzugehen habe.

In Wien wurden die Folgen des unterdrückten Sexualtriebs schon vor 1900 von Breuer und Freud erforscht. Die Neigung zu verklemmter Prüderie, die Negation weiblicher Sexualität hatte vor allem bei Frauen zu krankhaften Zuständen geführt. Im ausgehenden 19. Jahrhundert waren die Arztpraxen mit Frauen gefüllt, die unter mysteriösen Krämpfen und Scheinschwangerschaften litten.

Vor diesem Hintergrund wirkte Salome wie ein Urschrei. Ja, das war es! Die anarchische Urkraft, die nicht aufzuhalten war! Ihr Ziel: sofortige Befriedigung der Lust oder Mord! Eine Reduktion auf diesen engen Aktionskreis entsprach dem expressionistischen Holzschnittdenken. Natürlich war hier nicht die Liebe als hehre Kraft gemeint, sondern die pubertär aufkeimende Sexualität, die, obsessiv besitzergreifend, alles andere ausschließende blindwütige Aggression sein konnte.

Salome ist die exhibitionistische Mörderin, die sich lasziv den Blicken der andern ausliefert. Sie wird geopfert, damit wir ihr Geheimnis erfahren. Vor ihrem eigenen Tod vollzieht sie das hysterische Totenritual, den abgeschlagenen Kopf Jochanaans vor sich auf einer Silberschüssel: »Ah! Du wolltest mich deinen Mund nicht küssen lassen, Jochanaan. Wohl! Ich will ihn jetzt küssen. Ich will mit meinen Zähnen hineinbeißen, wie man in eine reife Frucht beißen mag. Ja, ich will ihn küssen, deinen Mund, Jochanaan.«

Mit diesem Schlußgesang der Salome ist die Oper in ihrer ureigensten Ausdrucksregion angekommen: »... nur der Sopran, die Göttliche, die Erbin der Hysterika, deren zugeschnürte Kehle nun endlich geöffnet, die wunderbarsten, ekstatischsten und unberechenbarsten Töne von sich zu geben vermag ...« (Christina von Braun), nur dieser Sopran kann den tödlichen Orgasmus zum Ausdruck bringen. Es ist ein wahnsinniges Aufbäumen aller Sinne, ein letztes großes Auflodern – danach liegt der Körper verbrannt und erloschen, zu Tode erschöpft am Boden!

Bühnenbild-Ort: »Eine große Terrasse im Palast des Herodes, die an den Bankettsaal stößt. Einige Soldaten lehnen über der Brüstung. Rechts eine mächtige Treppe, links im Hintergrund eine alte Zisterne mit einer Einfassung aus grüner Bronze. Der Mond scheint sehr hell.«

Die Bühnenbilder in Braunschweig und Wiesbaden zeigten die große Terrasse. Durch architektonische Andeutungen ließen sich auch die Palasträume ringsum erahnen.

In Braunschweig wurde die Zisterne des Jochanaan zum zweiten bestimmenden Motiv. Überall in der Terrassenfläche waren Zisternenschächte in den Boden getrieben. Aus ihnen hörte man die Stimme des Propheten bedrohlich laut: Alle, außer Salome, haben Angst vor Jochanaan, sie horchen ständig am Boden: Was ist, wenn er Recht hat, wenn die Toten tatsächlich wiederkommen?

Die Terrasse ist primär ein Ort der Orgien. Hier trifft sich der Hofstaat jeden Abend, ißt, trinkt, vergnügt und langweilt sich. Aber dort kreuzen sich auch die Weltanschauungen: Römer mit ihren Göttern und Juden mit ihrem Glauben. Darunter das aufkommende Christentum (Jochanaan). Dazu die Nacht und der Mond.

Im Wiesbaden gab es keine Schächte, dafür einen gekippten Gartenpavillon am Rande eines Swimmingpools. Die Angst-Stimmung war die gleiche. Die Gesänge des Propheten klangen aus den Ritzen und kleinen Löchern im Boden und an den Wänden.

Electra

Tragedy by Richard Strauss in one act, libretto by Hugo von Hofmannsthal. Semperoper, Dresden, 1986; conductor: Hartmut Haenchen, director: Ruth Berghaus, sets: Hans Dieter Schaal, costumes: Marie-Luise Strandt, dramaturgy: Sigrid Neef

Opernhaus Zürich, 1991; conductor: Ralf Weikert, director: Ruth Berghaus, sets: Hans Dieter Schaal, costumes: Marie-Luise Strandt

Theater und Philharmonie Essen, 2000; conductor: Stefan Soltesz, director: Nicolas Brieger, sets: Hans Dieter Schaal, costumes: Uta Winkelsen, lighting: Wolfgang Göbbel, dramaturgy: Kerstin Schüssler

Electra deals with a pathological case as well. Here sexuality and love have an effect not directly, but indirectly, by being suppressed and perverted. The dead father becomes an object of desire, and the mother and the stepfather become targets for hatred.

Agamemnon, King of Mycenae, and his wife Clytemnestra have four children: Iphigenia, Electra, Chrysothemis and Orestes. At the beginning of the Trojan War, in which Agamemnon is involved with the Greek fleet, he sacrifices his daughter Iphigenia to the gods to support his request for fair winds. After his triumphant return ten years later, he is murdered in his bath by his wife and her lover Aegisthus. After this the child Orestes is sent away. Chrysothemis is able to come to terms with the new situation and hopes that she will soon be able to start a family, but Electra is able to think of nothing but avenging her father from the day of the murder onwards.

She races to and fro in the castle courtyard like a wild creature in captivity and fanatically thinks her way into her destructive plans for revenge. She falls prey to mental murderous frenzy, constantly calling upon her dead father, whom she loved immoderately. When she hears that Orestes – for whom she had waited, and who she hoped would carry out the act of revenge – is dead, the digs for the axe and intends to carry out the deed herself. But then the man she had thought dead appears in the courtyard and makes himself known. The rejected one is triumphant and Orestes kills his mother and stepfather. Electra falls down dead after a hysterical final utterance in song.

Electra is a negative heroine, the inmate of a blood-stained castle or a psychiatric institution. How can a woman continue to exist after her own father has been killed by her mother and her mother's lover? How can one live under the same roof as murderers? Electra lives for nothing but revenge, an eye for an eye and a tooth for a tooth. A murder for a murder. Blood vengeance. She does not spare a thought for the fact that this makes her into a murderess herself (even though this murder is not committed by her own hands). She is driven by the fanaticism of an assassin, blindly raging and excluding herself from any reasonable discussion. Her thinking circles its way down into the murder. The world has closed down around her. Eroticism and sexuality have been transformed into hatred, love for her father into mania. »In Electra the individual is cancelled out empirically, in that it is the content of that individual's own life that blows it apart from

the inside. ... Electra is no longer Electra precisely because she devoted herself entirely to being Electra.« (Hugo von Hofmannsthal)

When Hofmannsthal wrote the libretto for Electra he made a precise study of the works of Sigmund Freud, above all the case of Anna O., who was actually called Bertha Pappenheim and had first been treated by Josef Breuer.

»Breuer treated Fräulein Anna O. from December 1880 to June 1882. Her case is now seen as a classical example of hysteria. The patient was an unusually intelligent girl of twenty-one who developed a whole collection of symptoms in the context of her father's fatal illness. She presented a varied pattern of paralysis and contractures, inhibitions and conditions of psychological confusion. This pattern also included serious and complex disturbances of her sight and speech, an inability to eat and a racking cough, for which reason Breuer was brought in ...« (Ernest Jones)

Suddenly one has a feeling that the sicknesses of modern civilization had already been described in the plays of antiquity.

There is only one setting: »The inner courtyard, bordered by the rear of the palace and the low buildings in which the servants live. Maidservants by the well down left. Some of them are overseers. Time: Mycenae, after the end of the Trojan War.«

Electra was presented in three variants in these productions. In Dresden she lives in a tower, inside which – following the wishes of her mother – she is soon to be imprisoned. Her desire is for her faraway brother. She is constantly looking out for him. Up here she feels close to her dead father.

In Zurich the set consisted of a labyrinth of space that could perhaps have been built over ancient walls. The characters are like the inmates of a lunatic asylum.

Things were similar in Essen. The power of the walls was oppressive. The floor had arched upwards. Electra constantly digs in the ground. She is searching like a madwoman for her dead father and the avenging axe.

In all three cases Hofmannsthal's wish that the location should not be given an ancient feel was respected. »The stage set is completely lacking in those columns, those broad flights of steps, all those ancient-style banalities that are more inclined to have a sobering effect than to make a powerfully invocative impression. The chief characteristic of the set should be that it is constricted: it is not possible to escape, the characters are isolated ... Everything takes place in increasing darkness, the piece lasts for just the same time as a slow twilight ...« (Hugo von Hofmannsthal in his notes on *Elektra*).

Elektra

Tragödie von Richard Strauss in einem Aufzug, Text von Hugo von Hofmannsthal. Semperoper, Dresden, 1986; musikalische Leitung: Hartmut Haenchen, Inszenierung: Ruth Berghaus, Bühne: Hans Dieter Schaal, Kostüme: Marie-Luise Strandt, Dramaturgie: Sigrid Neef

Opernhaus Zürich, 1991; musikalische Leitung: Ralf Weikert, Inszenierung: Ruth Berghaus, Bühne: Hans Dieter Schaal, Kostüme: Marie-Luise Strandt.

Theater und Philharmonie Essen, 2000; musikalische Leitung: Stefan Soltesz, Inszenierung: Nicolas Brieger, Bühne: Hans Dieter Schaal, Kostüme: Uta Winkelsen, Licht: Wolfgang Göbbel, Dramaturgie: Kerstin Schüssler

Auch in *Elektra* wird ein pathologischer Fall beschrieben. Hier wirken Sexualität und Liebe nicht direkt, sondern indirekt durch ihre Unterdrückung und Pervertierung. Der tote Vater wird zum Objekt der Begierde, die Mutter und der Stiefvater zum Ziel des Hasses.

Agamemnon, König von Mykene, und seine Frau Klytämnestra haben vier Kinder: Iphigenie, Elektra, Chrysothemis und Orest. Zu Beginn des Trojanischen Krieges, an dem sich Agamemnon mit der griechischen Flotte beteiligt, opfert er seine Tochter Iphigenie den Göttern, um günstigen Fahrtwind zu erbitten. Nach seiner siegreichen Rückkehr zehn Jahre später ermorden ihn seine Frau und deren Geliebter Aegisth im Badezimmer. Anschließend wird das Kind Orest fortgebracht. Während sich Chrysothemis mit der neuen Lage arrangiert und darauf hofft, bald eine Familie gründen zu können, denkt Elektra seit dem Mordtag an nichts anderes, als daran, ihren Vater zu rächen.

Wie ein wildes Tier in der Gefangenschaft läuft sie im Burghof hin und her und steigert sich fanatisch in ihre destruktiven Rachegedanken hinein. Sie verfällt einem gedanklichen Blutrausch, beschwört immer wieder ihren toten Vater, den sie über alle Maßen liebte. Als sie erfährt, daß Orest, auf den sie gewartet und von dem sie erhofft hat, daß er die Blutrache vollenden werde, tot ist, gräbt sie nach dem Beil und will die Tat selbst vollbringen. Da aber tritt der Totgeglaubte in den Hof und gibt sich zu erkennen. Die Ausgestoßene triumphiert: Orest ermordet die Mutter und den Stiefvater. Nach einem hysterischen Schlußgesang bricht Elektra tot zusammen.

Elektra ist eine Negativ-Heldin, die Insassin einer blutgetränkten Burg oder einer Nervenheilanstalt. Wie kann man weiterexistieren, wenn der eigene Vater von der Mutter und ihrem Geliebten ermordet wurde? Wie kann man mit Mördern unter einem Dach zusammenleben? Elektra kennt nur die Rache, Auge um Auge, Zahn um Zahn. Mord gegen Mord. Blutrache. Daß sie dabei selbst zur Mörderin wird (wenn auch am Ende nicht eigenhändig), darüber verliert sie keinen Gedanken. Sie ist getrieben vom Fanatismus eines Attentäters, blindwütig und jedem vernünftigen Gespräch sich verschließend. Kreisend bohrt sich Ihr Denken in den Mord hinein. Die Welt um sie herum ist versunken. Erotik und Sexualität haben sich in Haß verwandelt, Vaterliebe in Wahn. »In Elektra wird das Individuum in der empirischen Weise aufgelöst, indem eben der Inhalt seines Lebens es von innen her zersprengt. ... Elektra ist nicht mehr Elektra, weil sie eben ganz

und gar Elektra zu sein sich weihte.« (Hugo von Hofmannsthal).

Als Hofmannsthal das Libretto zu *Elektra* schrieb, studierte er die Schriften Sigmund Freuds genau, vor allem den Fall Anna O., die eigentlich Bertha Pappenheim hieß und zuerst von Josef Breuer behandelt worden war.

»Vom Dezember 1880 bis zum Juni 1882 behandelte Breuer Fräulein Anna O., die heute als klassischer Fall von Hysterie bekannt ist. Die Patientin war ein ungewöhnlich intelligentes Mädchen von einundzwanzig Jahren, die im Zusammenhang mit der tödlichen Krankheit ihres Vaters eine ganze Kollektion von Symptomen entwickelte. Sie bot ein buntes Bild von Lähmungen und Kontrakturen, Hemmungen und Zuständen von psychischer Verworrenheit. Zu diesem Bild gehörten auch ernste und komplizierte Störungen des Seh- und Sprachvermögens, die Unfähigkeit zu essen und ein quälender Husten, dessentwegen Breuer zu Rat gezogen wurde ...« (Ernest Jones)

Plötzlich hat man das Gefühl, daß bereits in den archaischen Stücken des Altertums moderne Zivilisationskrankheiten beschrieben worden sind.

Es gibt nur einen Bühnenbild-Ort: »Der innere Hof, begrenzt von der Rückseite des Palastes und niedrigen Gebäuden, in denen die Diener wohnen. Dienerinnen am Ziehbrunnen, links vorne. Aufseherinnen unter ihnen Zeit: Mykene nach Ende des Trojanischen Krieges.«

Elektra wurde hier in drei Varianten vorgestellt: In Dresden lebt sie auf einem Turm, in dessen Innenräume sie – nach dem Willen Ihrer Mutter – demnächst gesperrt werden soll. Ihre Sehnsucht gilt dem Bruder in der Ferne. Ständig hält sie nach ihm Ausschau. Hier oben fühlt sie sich ihrem toten Vater nahe.

In Zürich bestand das Bühnenbild aus einem Raum-Labyrinth, das vielleicht über alten Mauern errichtet worden sein könnte. Die Figuren erinnerten an die Insassen einer Irrenanstalt.

In Essen verhielt es sich ähnlich. Die Gewalt der Mauern war erdrückend. Der Boden hatte sich aufgewölbt. Fortwährend gräbt Elektra in der Erde. Wie eine Irre sucht sie den toten Vater und das Beil der Rache.

In allen drei Fällen wurden Hofmannsthals Ermahnungen, den Spielort nicht antikisierend zu gestalten, eingehalten. »Dem Bühnenbild fehlen vollständig jene Säulen, jene breiten Treppenstufen, alle jene antikisierenden Banalitäten, welche mehr geeignet sind, zu ernüchtern als suggestiv zu wirken. Der Charakter des Bühnenbilds ist Enge: Unentfliehbarkeit, Abgeschlossenheit. ... Alles spielt nun bei zunehmender Dunkelheit, die Dauer des Stückes ist genau die Dauer einer langsamen Dämmerung ...« (Hugo von Hofmannsthal in seinen Anmerkungen zu *Elektra*).

Turandot

Dramma lirico in three acts by Giacomo Puccini, libretto by Giuseppe Adami and Renato Simoni
Hessisches Staatstheater, Wiesbaden, 1998; conductor: Enrico Dovico, director: Dominik Neuner, sets: Hans Dieter Schaal, costumes: Ute Frühling, dramaturgy: Margrit Poremba

Salome and Electra become murderesses through unrequited love and a desire for revenge, but Turandot kills on principle. She has sworn to kill all the men who desire her, and for this reason has devised three insoluble riddles. The area around the palace is strewn with men's cut-off heads. Within a year – this is the period covered by the opera – thirteen wooers fall victim to her. It may be that Turandot holds the record as far as operatic killings are concerned. Her hatred of men must be boundless. And yet she constantly finds new victims who are fascinated by her cruel beauty – the taming of the shrew. She plays the sphinx who can talk to men only in riddles. A Salome in the cabinet of mirrors. A femme fatale, with alluring music washing around her. Despite everything, she remains passive, hardly moves.

Whether Turandot really is an erotic femme fatale or a woman who is afraid of men and sexuality remains uncertain. In any case, this is certainly not a normal world of love that is being described here, but a perverse, hysterical world of fear.

The story is set in Peking, in mythological times. Another suitor is to be executed. The people hate the princess because of her cruelty. The crowd attending the execution includes the next prince who admires Turandot's beauty. He too comes forward as a suitor. But to the surprise of all, he is able to solve the riddles. Turandot is furious, she does not want to admit defeat. But at the end she agrees to a marriage, the ice around her melts. But will she change?

Puccini, who was a great lady-killer, loved this woman, as he never ceased to point out. *Turandot* was his last opera. When he travelled to Brussels in 1924 to be operated on for cancer of the larynx, the score, which was not quite complete, was at his side. They found the last notes he jotted down, which referred to the score of Turandot: « … Find melody … less simple than hitherto … then Tristan.«

In the libretto, the instructions about the set are very flowery and decorative. Excerpts: »The walls of the great ›purple city‹: the ›imperial city‹. The massive battlements enclose almost all the scene in a semicircle … A large marquee; the wall of the marquee is strangely decorated with symbolic and fantastic Chinese figures … The curtain rises on the extensive square in front of the palace. A marble staircase almost in the middle … The palace garden: very large, consisting of nothing but undulations in the ground, shrubs and images of the gods in dark bronze …

The picturesque exterior of the imperial palace comes into sight: entirely in white marble on which the rosy reflections of the dawn seem to create glowing flowers …«

The set in Wiesbaden did not take these pompous and kitschy instructions into account in any way. The room did contain an enlarged motif of a rounded Chinese gate, but otherwise the language was essentially functional and geometrical. This meant that the overflowing emotions could develop more effectively.

The gigantic circular doorway in the black rear wall of the room could be closed by a large black disc. According to the position of the disc, cut-out sections were revealed that were reminiscent of different phases of the moon.

In front of the wall were the palace square and the garden, and behind the opening a landscape of ice-floes could be seen: the realm of Turandot. A long walkway extended diagonally across the whole of the stage. It started by the orchestra pit and ended in the landscape of ice-floes. The Princess Turandot appeared on this slightly raised walkway like an icy but beautiful model.

There was a little forest of poles on the front third of the stage. These had the head of the suitors who had already been murdered on top of them.

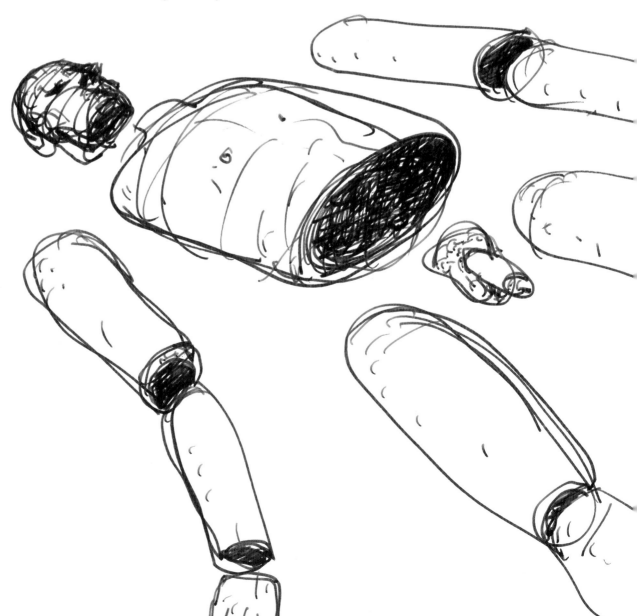

146

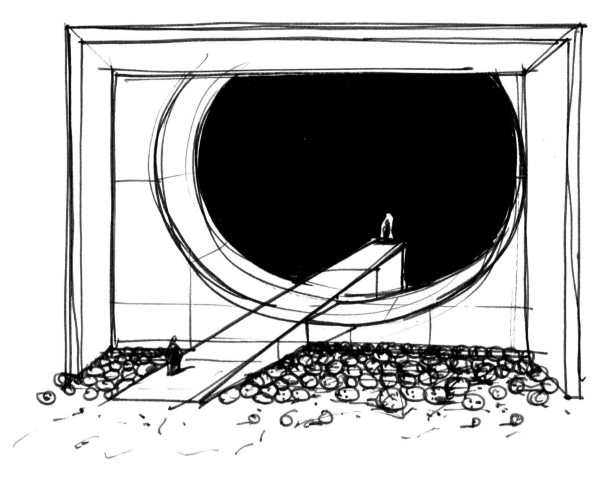

Turandot

Dramma lirico in drei Akten von Giacomo Puccini,
Text von Giuseppe Adami und Renato Simoni
Hessisches Staatstheater, Wiesbaden, 1998;
musikalische Leitung: Enrico Dovico, Inszenierung:
Dominik Neuner, Bühne: Hans Dieter Schaal, Kos-
tüme: Ute Frühling, Dramaturgie: Margrit Poremba

Während Salome und Elektra Mörderinnen aus
verschmähter Liebe und aus Rache geworden
sind, tötet Turandot aus Prinzip. Sie hat sich ge-
schworen, alle Männer umbringen zu lassen, die
sie begehren, und aus diesem Grund drei unlös-
bare Rätsel erdacht. Die Umgebung des Palastes
ist mit abgeschlagenen Männerköpfen übersät.
Innerhalb eines Jahres – diesen Zeitraum beschreibt die Oper – fallen ihr dreizehn Bewerber
zum Opfer. Vielleicht hält Turandot, was das Töten betrifft, in der Operngeschichte den Rekord.
Ihr Männerhaß muß grenzenlos sein. Und dennoch finden sich immer wieder neue Opfer, die
von ihrer grausamen Schönheit fasziniert sind –
der Widerspenstigen Zähmung. Sie spielt die
Sphinx, die mit den Männern nur in Rätseln sprechen kann. Eine Salome im Spiegelkabinett. Eine
Femme fatale, umspült von verlockender Musik.
Trotz allem bleibt sie passiv, bewegt sich kaum.

Ob es sich bei Turandot wirklich um eine erotische Femme fatale handelt oder um eine Frau,
die Angst vor Männern und vor der Sexualität
hat, bleibt ungewiß. Es ist in jedem Fall keine
heile Liebeswelt, die hier beschrieben wird, sondern eine perverse, hysterische Angstwelt.

Die Geschichte spielt in Peking, zu sagenhaf-
ter Zeit. Wieder soll ein Bewerber hingerichtet
werden. Das Volk haßt die Prinzessin wegen ihrer
Grausamkeit. In der Menge, die der Hinrichtung
beiwohnt, steht bereits der nächste Prinz, der die
Schönheit Turandots bewundert. Auch er meldet
sich als Bewerber. Zur Überraschung aller kann er
die drei Rätsel jedoch lösen. Turandot tobt, sie will
sich nicht geschlagen geben. Am Ende aber willigt
sie in eine Hochzeit ein, das Eis um sie schmilzt.
Ob sie sich ändern wird?

Puccini, der ein großer Frauenheld war, liebte
diese Frau, wie er immer wieder betonte. *Turandot* war seine letzte Oper. Als er 1924 nach Brüssel fuhr, um seinen Kehlkopfkrebs operieren zu
lassen, lag die nicht ganz vollendete Partitur neben ihm. Kurz nach der Operation starb der
Komponist. Bei ihm fand man seine letzten Noti-
zen, die der Turandot-Partitur galten: »... Melodie
finden ... weniger einfältig als bisher ... dann Tristan.«

Im Libretto sind die Angaben zum Bühnenbild sehr ausführlich, blumig und dekorativ. Ausschnitte: »Die Mauer der großen ›violetten Stadt‹:
der ›Kaiserstadt‹. Die massigen Zinnen um-
schließen fast die ganze Szene im Halbkreis ...
Ein großer Zeltpavillon; die Zeltwand seltsam ver-
ziert von symbolischen und phantastischen chinesischen Figuren ... Der Vorhang geht über dem
geräumigen Schloßplatz auf. Fast in der Mitte
eine riesige Marmortreppe ... Der Schloßgarten:
sehr ausgedehnt, bestehend aus lauter wellenför-
migen Bodenerhebungen, Gebüschen und Göt-
terbildnissen in dunkler Bronze ...
Die malerische Außenseite des Kaiserpalastes
wird sichtbar: ganz in weißem Marmor, auf dem
die rosigen Reflexe der Morgenröte gleichsam
leuchtende Blumen bilden ...«

Das Bühnenbild in Wiesbaden erfüllte diese
pompös-kitschigen Angaben in keiner Weise. Der
Raum enthielt zwar das vergrößerte Motiv eines
chinesischen Rundtores, aber ansonsten sprach
es eher eine nüchtern-geometrische Sprache.

Dadurch entfalteten sich die überschäumenden
Emotionen wirkungsvoller.

Die riesige kreisförmige Toröffnung in der
schwarzen Rückwand des Raumes konnte mit
einer großen schwarzen Scheibe geschlossen
werden. Je nach Stellung der Scheibe ergaben
sich Ausschnitte, die an Mondsicheln in unter-
schiedlichen Phasen erinnerten.

Vor der Wand lagen Schloßplatz und Garten,
hinter der Öffnung breitete sich eine Eisschollen-
landschaft aus: das Reich der Turandot. Ein langer Laufsteg erstreckte sich diagonal über die
ganze Bühne. Er begann im Bereich des Orches-
tergrabens und endete in der Eisschollenland-
schaft. Auf diesem leicht erhöhten Weg trat die
Prinzessin Turandot auf wie ein eiskaltes, schönes Model.

Im vorderen Dritttel der Bühne gab es noch einen kleinen Stangenwald. Auf den Stangenspit-
zen steckten die Köpfe der bereits Ermordeten.

Lulu

Opera in three acts by Alban Berg based on the tragedies *Erdgeist* and *Die Büchse der Pandora* by Frank Wedekind, orchestration of the last act completed by Friedrich Cerha

La Monnaie, Brussels, 1988; conductor: Sylvain Cambreling, director: Ruth Berghaus, sets: Hans Dieter Schaal, costumes: Marie-Luise Strandt, film projections: Maxim Dessau, dramaturgy: Sigrid Neef

Lulu is Salome's, Electra's and Turandot's modern sister. She uses her seductive powers directly and unscrupulously. A modern child-woman without a mythological past, without an intellectual superstructure, nihilistic, natural and subtle. An ideal victim for male projections. She affects men like a magnet. She has only to appear and they are fascinated, spellbound, and can no longer think of anything else. But this does not lead to any love stories that might make people happy, but to erotic conflicts about relationships, with fatal consequences. Lulu is an object of desire who has a negative effect, and is also a femme fatale.

»›If you love me, you are done for‹, says Godard's Carmen, and thus provides a short but precise character sketch of the femme fatale …« (Carola Hilmes)

A femme fatale has to be puzzling. Her erotic power lies in the fact that she is shrouded in mystery. No one knows where she comes from, perhaps directly from heaven or hell. The road on which she is picked up by Dr. Schön leads out to the flower fields – she is a flower-seller – and to the woods, to the caves where the fairies and witches live.

Alban Berg worked on writing and composing Lulu from 1928 to his death in 1935. Joseph von Sternheim directed *The Blue Angel* with Marlene Dietrich in Berlin in 1929/30. The leading character here is a femme fatale as well, a nihilistic, man-eating woman who thinks only of her body and the pleasures of the flesh. Before her – still in the silent film era – it was Luise Brooks, the very young American in Berlin, who got up to her seductive tricks as Lulu in Georg Wilhelm Papst's films. On seeing these films today it is very easy to understand the enthusiasm that met themes like this in the twenties: for the first time it was possible to talk openly about sexuality, Pandora's box had been opened, the victorious march of women was beginning. Now they had finally emancipated themselves from their 19th century pupation and had broken out free of the swelling bosoms and constricting corsets of the salons – now they were moving out into the open air and into the nocturnal bars of the world's great cities. They stayed up all night, sniffed cocaine and sneered at the petit bourgeois. Otto Dix's pictures show what was happening to bodies and faces at that time.

The story of Lulu is set in Germany, France and England around 1930.

Dr. Schön, an editor-in-chief, has taken Lulu as a lover. In order to put the affair into a bourgeois context, he marries her to the senile medical officer Dr. Goll. While Lulu is sitting for a painter, Dr. Goll bursts into the room in a fit of jealousy and dies of an excitement-induced heart attack. Dr. Schön then marries Lulu to the painter. When he learns of her relationship with Dr. Schön, whom she really loves, he commits suicide.

After Lulu has managed to prevent Dr. Schön from marrying a bourgeois woman, she marries him herself, but starts a relationship with his son Alwa. Dr. Schön tackles her about this. Lulu shoots Dr. Schön dead in the subsequent argument. She is sentenced to life imprisonment. She manages to flee to France with the assistance of dubious friends, including the lesbian Countess Geschwitz. The decline sets in. Her plans for the future collapse, and she runs away again, to London, where she has to eke out a miserable existence as a prostitute. In the end she is murdered by Jack the Ripper, a ghostly and brutal doppelgänger of Dr. Schön.

The settings as described in the libretto: »Prologue in front of the curtain. A spacious but scantily furnished studio. Very elegant salon. Theatre cloakroom. A magnificent German Renaissance hall. A spacious salon in white stucco. A London attic without mansard windows.«

At the end of the second act the libretto suggests a film sequence accompanying the transformation music, showing Lulu's arrest, the interrogation, her trial, the period in prison and her liberation from solitary confinement. Thus the new medium film finds its way into the classical art form of opera.

The set in Brussels did not address all the locations described. In the centre was a high, white space with a large, sensual wave of marble flowing through it. Architecture and landscape intermingled. Frozen emotion. Life on the wrong track, tilted out of the everyday. Concrete furniture and an escalator were concealed within the marble hill. On the summit of the hill stood – in isolation – a porch with a double swing-door. Some fragments of architecture were attached to it, as if ripped out of the context.

Film images were projected on to the big white rear wall of the space from time to time. There were also projections inside the room: on to people, groups of characters, empty pictures and pieces of architecture.

The painter has become a photographer, and later a film-maker as well. He uses Lulu as a model, her face and her body. He can detach his own fantasies from reality with the Lulu who has become an image, and make them appear anywhere at any time. – Though before he can do this he has to black out his dream space, as the fantasies consist only of light and shade. The other men are affected by these images as well. Lulu's decline and tragedy can happen without the images being destroyed.

Lulu

Oper in drei Akten von Alban Berg nach den Tra-
gödien Erdgeist *und* Büchse der Pandora *von*
Frank Wedekind, Orchestrierung des dritten Aktes
vervollständigt von Friedrich Cerha

La Monnaie, Brüssel, 1988; musikalische Lei-
tung: Sylvain Cambreling, Inszenierung: Ruth Berg-
haus, Bühne: Hans Dieter Schaal, Kostüme: Ma-
rie-Luise Strandt, Film-Projektionen: Maxim Des-
sau, Dramaturgie: Sigrid Neef

Lulu ist die moderne Schwester Salomes, Elek-
tras und Turandots. Sie setzt ihre verführerische
Kraft direkt und skrupellos ein. Eine moderne
Kindfrau ohne mythologische Vergangenheit,
ohne geistigen Überbau, nihilistisch, natürlich
und raffiniert. Ein ideales Opfer für männliche
Projektionen. Auf Männer wirkt sie wie ein Magnet. Kaum tritt sie auf, sind sie fasziniert und
gebannt und können an nichts anderes mehr
denken. Aber es kommen keine beglückenden
Liebesgeschichten dabei heraus, sondern erotische Beziehungskämpfe mit tödlichem Ausgang.
Lulu ist ein negativ wirkendes Sehnsuchtsziel
und somit auch eine Femme fatale.

»»Wenn du mich liebst, bist du erledigt‹, sagt
Godards Carmen und gibt damit eine kurze,
aber präzise Charakteristik der Femme fatale ...«
(Carola Hilmes)

Eine Femme fatale muß rätselhaft sein. Ihre
erotische Wirkung besteht darin, daß sie von einem Geheimnis umgeben ist. Man weiß nicht,
woher sie kommt, vielleicht direkt aus dem Paradies oder aus der Hölle. Die Straße, auf der sie
von Dr. Schön aufgelesen wird, führt hinaus zu
den Blumenfeldern – sie ist Blumenverkäuferin –
und zu den Wäldern, in die Höhlen der Natur-
feen und Hexen.

Alban Berg schrieb und komponierte *Lulu*
von 1928 bis zu seinem Tod, 1935. 1929/30 inszenierte Joseph von Sternheim in Berlin *Der Blaue*
Engel mit Marlene Dietrich. Die Hauptfigur ist
ebenfalls eine Femme fatale, eine nihilistische,
männerverschlingende Frau, die nur an ihren Körper und an die Wirkungen des Fleisches denkt.
Vor ihr – noch in der Stummfilmzeit – war es
Luise Brooks, die blutjunge Amerikanerin in Berlin, die als Lulu in den Filmen von Georg Wilhelm
Papst ihr verführerisches Unwesen trieb. Wenn
man diese Filme heute sieht, kann man die Begeisterung, die sich in den zwanziger Jahren mit
solchen Themen verband, sehr gut nachvollzie-
hen: Zum ersten Mal war es möglich, unverhüllt
über Sexualität zu sprechen, die Büchse der
Pandora war geöffnet, der Siegeszug der Frau-
en begann. Nun hatten sie sich endgültig aus
der Verpuppung des neunzehnten Jahrhunderts
gelöst und waren aus den überquellenden und
kostümierten, mit Miedern verschnürten Salons
ausgebrochen – ins Freie ging es und in die
Nachtbars der Metropolen. Man machte die
Nächte durch, schnupfte Kokain und verachtete
die Spießer. Auf den Bildern von Otto Dix kann
man sehen, was damals mit den Körpern und
den Gesichtern geschah.

Die Lulu-Geschichte spielt in Deutschland,
Frankreich und England um 1930.

Der Chefredakteur, Dr. Schön, hat Lulu zu seiner Geliebten gemacht. Um der Sache einen bürgerlichen Rahmen zu geben, verheiratet er sie mit
dem senilen Medizinalrat Dr. Goll. Während Lulu

einem Maler Modell sitzt, dringt Dr. Goll eifersüchtig in den Raum ein und stirbt vor Aufregung an
einem Herzschlag. Anschließend verheiratet Dr.
Schön Lulu mit dem Maler. Als dieser von ihrem
Verhältnis mit Dr. Schön, den Lulu wirklich liebt,
erfährt, begeht er Selbstmord.

Nachdem Lulu erreicht hat, daß Dr. Schön auf
die Heirat mit einer bürgerlichen Frau verzichtet,
heiratet sie ihn selbst, läßt sich jedoch auch auf
ein Verhältnis mit seinem Sohn Alwa ein, worauf-
hin sie von Dr. Schön zur Rede gestellt wird. Bei
einer nachfolgenden Auseinandersetzung er-
schießt Lulu Dr. Schön und wird zu lebenslangem
Zuchthaus verurteilt. Mit Hilfe zwielichtiger Freun-
de, unter denen sich auch die lesbische Gräfin
Geschwitz befindet, gelingt ihr die Flucht nach
Frankreich. Der Abstieg beginnt. Ihre Zukunfts-
pläne zerschlagen sich, und sie flieht weiter nach
London, wo sie ihr Leben kläglich als Prostituierte
fristen muß. Am Ende wird sie von Jack the Ripper, einem gespenstisch-brutalen Doppelgänger
von Dr. Schön, ermordet.

Die Bühnenbild-Orte im Libretto: »Prolog vor
dem Vorhang. Geräumiges, aber dürftig einge-
richtetes Atelier. Sehr eleganter Salon. Garderobe
beim Theater. Prachtvoller Saal in deutscher Renaissance. Ein geräumiger Salon in weißer Stuk-
katur. Eine Londoner Dachkammer ohne Man-
sarden.«

Am Ende des zweiten Akts wird im Libretto
zur Verwandlungsmusik eine Film-Sequenz vorge-
schlagen, die Lulus Verhaftung zeigt, die Untersu-
chungshaft, ihren Prozeß, den Kerker-Aufenthalt
und ihre Befreiung aus der Isolier-Baracke. Damit
hat der Film als neues technisches Medium Ein-
zug in die klassische Kunstform der Oper gehal-
ten.

Das Bühnenbild in Brüssel bediente nicht alle
geforderten Bilder. Im Zentrum stand ein hoher
weißer Raum, der von einer großen, sinnlich ge-
formten Marmorwelle durchspült wurde. Architektur und Landschaft ineinandergebaut. Erstarrte
Emotion. Leben auf der schiefen Bahn, aus dem
Alltag gekippt. In dem Marmorberg steckten Be-
tonmöbel und eine Rolltreppe. Auf dem Gipfel des
Bergs stand – isoliert – ein Windfang mit doppelter
Pendeltür. An dem Gehäuse hingen einige Archi-
tekturfragmente, wie herausgerissen aus dem Zusammenhang.

Auf der großen weißen Rückwand des Raumes
erschienen immer wieder Filmbilder. Es gab auch
Projektionen innerhalb des Raumes: auf Personen,
Figurengruppen, leere Bilder und Architekturteile.

Der Maler ist zum Photographen und später
auch zum Filmemacher geworden. Er benutzt Lulu als Modell, ihr Gesicht und ihren Körper. Mit der
Bild gewordenen Lulu kann er seine eigenen Phantasien von der Realität ablösen, sie jederzeit überall erscheinen lassen – allerdings muß er vorher
seinen Traumraum abdunkeln, die Phantasien bestehen nur aus Licht und Schatten. Auch die anderen Männer werden von diesen Bildern getroffen.
Der Abstieg und die Tragödie Lulus können sich
ereignen, ohne daß die Bilder zerstört werden.

Die Entführung aus dem Serail (Il Seraglio)

Singspiel in three acts by Wolfgang Amadeus Mozart, libretto by Johann Gottlieb Stephanie the Younger based on a play by Christoph Friedrich Bretzner

Theater Lübeck, 1999; conductor: Rüdiger Bohn, director: Jürgen Tamchina, sets: Hans Dieter Schaal, costumes: Beate Tamchina, dramaturgy: Dieter Kroll

Here the characters involved, with the exception of Osmin, the brutal overseer, seem normal and entirely unneurotic.

But first impressions are deceptive. Essentially this is a very brutal story: a woman has been abducted by pirates, together with her maid and her manservant. All three are sold to the harem of Bassa Selim. The conventions of the genre see to it that on stage at least there is no serious use of violence, no injury and also no rape. All the scenes are greatly in love with language and music, so that some almost Dadaist comic scenes occur.

It is not surprising that this opera became Mozart's most successful work for the stage. The plot is a playful reflection on the old problem of love, that can be neither bought, nor stolen, nor forced out of someone. It is an emotion that emerges freely and naturally, and has to be lived like this as well. Here men are constantly ordering women to love them. Blonde, Constanze's maid, is constantly having to fend this off, as love has nothing to do with submission, but is something that both parties involved have the right to enjoy equally. Constanze herself has to contend with demands for love from Bassa Selim. The harem serves as a metaphor for a kind of marriage that seeks to take possession. The female bodies are degraded to the status of goods, and are bought and sold at will. The fact that Bassa Selim still presents himself as a noble person who looks after his women in a kindly fashion should perhaps be seen as a touching kind of Utopia.

The action is set in the 16th century and takes place in the Orient. Bassa Selim's palace is by the sea.

The story begins with the arrival of the noble Spaniard Belmonte, with the intention of liberating his fiancée, Constanze. But outside the palace he meets Osmin, the cruel overseer, who realizes what Belmonte is up to and refuses to admit him. Despite this, Belmonte manages to arrange for Constanze to escape. But Osmin wakes up too early from his drunken stupor and upsets the undertaking. It is only through the kindness of Bassa Selim that they all survive and are able to return home.

Mozart composed *Il Seraglio* in Vienna in 1781, at the age of 25. This was also the time of the dramatic climax of his affair with Konstanze Weber, whom he married three weeks after the première, against his father's wishes. This had all been preceded by the establishment of his own household and the break with the Archbishop of Salzburg. All this turmoil can be clearly heard in the opera.

It is certainly no coincidence that the leading lady in the opera and the real-life fiancée are both called Konstanze. Carl Maria von Weber wrote this about the opera in June 1818: »This lighthearted creation, ablaze with the fullest, luxuriant power of youth, chastely tender in its sensibility, is particularly dear to my personal artistic feeling. I think that I can see in it what everyone's happy youthful years can hold, a heyday that can never again be won in this way, and where irretrievable delights flee away in the eradication of deficiencies.«

The settings: »Act One: square outside Bassa Selim's palace on the seashore. Act Two: Garden at Bassa Selim's palace. On one side is Osmin's home. Act Three: Open space outside Bassa Selim's palace. On one side is the Bassa's palace, opposite are Osmin's apartments, beyond, a view of the sea. It is midnight.«

The set in Lübeck showed a cheerful garden island on which it is pleasant to live. There was a tilted area with conical hedges. A declivity in which it was possible to sit was let into the tilted area, rather like a swimming-pool. Nothing suggested aggression or brutality. Bassa Selim loves his women and he is enthusiastic about architecture and horticulture. Perhaps he is even superior to the Spanish nobleman Belmonte in education and lifestyle?

In the background a backdrop of clouds moved slowly upwards throughout the performance. The daytime sky gradually changed to convey an impression of night, and at the end of the opera the sea appeared beyond the garden. The horizon was beckoning the pardoned loving couples into the distance, towards home

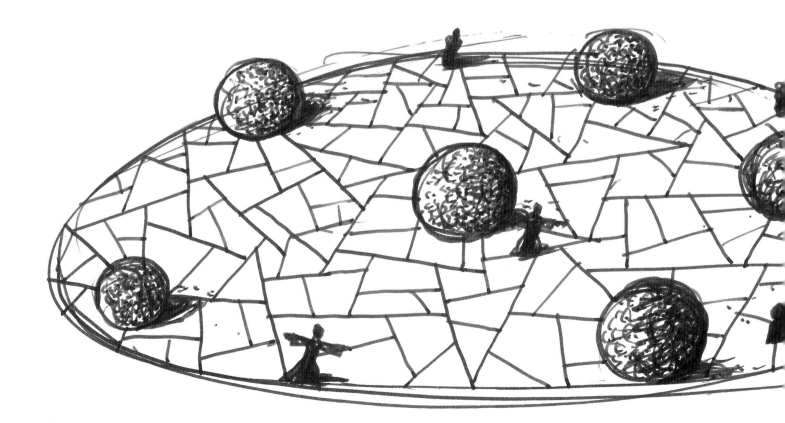

Die Entführung aus dem Serail (Il Seraglio)
Singspiel in drei Akten von Wolfgang Amadeus Mozart, Text von Johann Gottlieb Stephanie d. J. nach einem Bühnenstück von Christoph Friedrich Bretzner

Theater Lübeck, 1999; musikalische Leitung: Rüdiger Bohn, Inszenierung: Jürgen Tamchina, Bühne: Hans Dieter Schaal, Kostüme: Beate Tamchina, Dramaturgie: Dieter Kroll

Hier wirken die handelnden Figuren bis auf Osmin, den brutalen Aufpasser, normal und durch und durch unneurotisch.

Der erste Blick täuscht jedoch. Im Grunde handelt es sich um eine recht grausame Geschichte: Eine Frau ist zusammen mit ihrer Zofe und ihrem Diener von Seeräubern entführt worden. Alle drei werden an den Harem des Bassa Selim verkauft. Daß es, zumindest auf der Bühne, weder zu ernsthaften Gewaltanwendungen, zu Verletzungen und auch zu keiner Vergewaltigung kommt, ist der Konvention des Genres zu verdanken. Alle Szenen sind sehr sprach- und musikverliebt, so daß manchmal fast dadaistisch-komische Situationen entstehen.

Es wundert nicht, daß gerade diese Oper Mozarts erfolgreichstes Werk auf der Bühne wurde. Die Handlung reflektiert spielerisch das alte Problem der Liebe, die man weder kaufen, noch rauben, noch erzwingen kann. Sie ergibt sich als Gefühl naturhaft frei und will auch so gelebt werden. Immer wieder befehlen hier Männer den Frauen, sie zu lieben. Vor allem Blonde, die Dienerin Konstanzes, wehrt sich standhaft dagegen, denn Liebe habe nichts mit Unterwerfung zu tun, sondern sei ein gleichberechtigter Genuß. Konstanze selbst kämpft gegen das Liebesverlangen Bassa Selims. Der Harem dient als Metapher für eine besitzergreifende Form der Ehe. Die weiblichen Körper sind hier zu Waren reduziert, werden gekauft und verkauft, je nach Bedarf. Daß der

Bassa sich dennoch als edler Herr gibt, der seine Damen gütig betreut, ist vielleicht als rührende Utopie zu verstehen.

Die Handlung ist im 16. Jahrhundert angesiedelt und spielt im Orient. Der Palast des Bassa Selim liegt am Meer.

Mit dem Eintreffen des adligen Spaniers Belmonte, der die Absicht hat, seine Braut Konstanze zu befreien, beginnt die Geschichte. Der grausame Wächter Osmin, den er vor dem Palast trifft, ahnt jedoch, was Belmonte im Schilde führt, und verwehrt ihm den Einlaß. Dennoch gelingt es Belmonte schließlich, die Flucht in die Wege zu leiten. Aber Osmin erwacht zu früh aus seinem Rausch und vereitelt das Unternehmen. Nur durch die Güte Bassa Selims überleben alle und können in ihre Heimat zurückkehren.

Mozart hat *Die Entführung aus dem Serail* 1781, mit 25 Jahren, in Wien komponiert. In diese Zeit fiel auch der dramatische Höhepunkt seiner Liebesbeziehung mit Konstanze Weber, die er drei Wochen nach der Premiere heiratete, und zwar gegen den Willen seines Vaters. Vorausgegangen war die Gründung eines eigenen Hausstandes und der Bruch mit den fürstbischöflichen Abhängigkeiten in Salzburg. Man hört der Oper diesen Aufbruch an.

Es ist bestimmt kein Zufall, daß die weibliche Hauptfigur der Oper und die Braut im wirklichen Leben beide Konstanze heißen. Carl Maria von Weber schrieb im Juni 1818 über diese Oper Mozarts: »Meinem persönlichen Künstlergefühle ist diese heitere, in vollster, üppiger Jugendkraft lodernde, jungfräulich zart empfindende Schöpfung besonders lieb. Ich glaube in ihr das zu erblicken, was jedem Menschen seine frohen Jünglingsjahre sind, deren Blütezeit er nie wieder so erringen kann, und wo beim Vertilgen der Mängel auch unwiederbringliche Reize fliehen.«

Die Bühnenbild-Orte: »Erster Aufzug: Platz vor dem Palast des Bassa Selim am Ufer des Mee-

res. Zweiter Aufzug: Garten am Palast des Bassa Selim. An der Seite Osmins Wohnung. Dritter Aufzug: Platz vor dem Palast des Bassa Selim. Auf einer Seite der Palast des Bassa; gegenüber die Wohnung des Osmin; hinten Aussicht aufs Meer. Es ist Mitternacht.«

Das Bühnenbild in Lübeck zeigte eine heitere Garteninsel, auf der es sich angenehm leben läßt. Es gab eine schräge Fläche mit Heckenkugeln. In die Schräge war eine Sitzmulde eingelassen, fast wie ein Swimmingpool. Nichts deutete auf Aggression und Brutalität hin. Der Bassa liebt seine Frauen, und er schwärmt von Architektur und Gartenkunst. Vielleicht ist er dem spanischen Adligen Belmonte an Bildung und Lebensart überlegen?

Im Hintergrund bewegte sich ein Wolkenprospekt während der ganzen Aufführung langsam nach oben. Mit der Zeit ging der Taghimmel in eine Nachtstimmung über, und am Ende der Oper tauchte hinter dem Gartenrund das Meer auf. Der Horizont lockte die begnadigten Liebespaare in die Ferne, der Heimat zu.

Ariane et Barbe-Bleue

Opera by Paul Dukas based on a poem by Maurice Maeterlinck

Châtelet, Théâtre Musical de Paris, 1991; conductor: Eliahu Inbal, director: Ruth Berghaus, sets: Hans Dieter Schaal, costumes: Marie-Luise Strandt, dramaturgy: Frank Schneider

The fascinating idea of this opera lies in the fusion of two utterly different stories, the tale of Ariadne, from ancient mythology, and the 17th century story of Bluebeard.

We remember: the Minotaur is sitting in his labyrinth on Crete. It is a frightening creature, half bull, half man, that feeds on the young men and women who have to be brought to it each year. It is only Theseus, assisted by Ariadne, the daughter of the Cretan king Minos, who succeeds in killing the minotaur. She gives him the famous thread that enables him to find his way back.

The story of Bluebeard was written as a fairytale by Charles Perrault in 1697. In it the knight tests his wife's curiosity by giving her the key to a room that she is not allowed to enter. As she cannot resist temptation she opens the room and is killed by Bluebeard for this disobedience. Five more women suffer the same fate. But the seventh woman is rescued by her brothers.

In Maeterlinck's libretto, King Bluebeard brings a young woman to his fairy-tale castle for the sixth time. No one knows what happened to her five predecessors. They were never seen again after the wedding. Despite being forbidden to do so by Bluebeard, Ariadne searches through all the rooms scarcely before she has got into the castle. After she has found rooms full of precious stones and other treasures behind the doors she goes down into the cellars. Here she finds her predecessors. They are all alive!

She raises the women's spirits and wants to escape from the prison with them. Then Blue-

beard is brought in: he has been captured and bound in the mean time by rebellious peasants from the surrounding area, who now expect that the women will avenge themselves on the lecher. But they cut him free from his bonds and refuse to escape. Only Ariadne goes out into the open, towards the sea. All the rest remain behind.

In Bluebeard, Maeterlinck is describing an anarchic, fairy-tale womanizer, half Minotaur and half Don Giovanni. The women are upset by him and the fabulous wealth amongst which he lives. Ariane embodies the modern, fearless woman on her way to self-determined freedom. She does allow herself to be lured by the king, and perhaps seduced as well, but we entertain the idea that she might be doing it out of sheer curiosity, with the intention of discovering the secret that hovers around Bluebeard and his castle. Perhaps she also intends to avenge herself for years of repression suffered by women. But she does not achieve her aim. The peasants would have been ready to kill the rich parasite, but the captive women save him from the worst. They stand by their oppressor and love their seducer. It is the drama of women who are trapped in a rich marriage. Liberation would mean being plunged into poverty and distress.

Our interpretation in Paris took up this idea, but was surreal rather than realistic overall. We shifted the events to the rooftops of a big city. The rooms were spread around under the gables. The labyrinth had transformed itself into an infinitely large metropolis, in which the Minotaur lived, and owned all the buildings and streets. He was surrounded by boundless luxury. He parked his aeroplanes and ships on the roof, and a fleet of limousines awaited his orders in the garages deep underneath.

Ariane und Blaubart

Oper von Paul Dukas nach einer Dichtung von
Maurice Maeterlinck

Châtelet, Théâtre Musical de Paris, 1991; musi-
kalische Leitung: Eliahu Inbal, Inszenierung: Ruth
Berghaus, Bühne: Hans Dieter Schaal, Kostüme:
Marie-Luise Strandt, Dramaturgie: Frank Schneider

Die faszinierende Idee dieser Oper besteht in der
Verschmelzung zweier grundverschiedener Geschichten, der Ariadne-Geschichte aus der antiken Mythologie und der des Ritters Blaubart aus
dem 17. Jahrhundert.

Wir erinnern uns: Der Minotauros sitzt in seinem Labyrinth auf Kreta. Er ist ein beängstigen-
des Wesen, halb Stier, halb Mensch, das sich
von jungen Frauen und Männern ernährt, die ihm
jedes Jahr gebracht werden müssen. Erst Theseus gelingt es mit der Hilfe Ariadnes, der Tochter des kretischen Königs Minos, den Minotauros
zu töten. Sie gibt ihm das berühmte Wollknäuel
mit, das ihm den Rückweg zeigt.

Die Geschichte des Ritters Blaubart wurde 1697
von Charles Perrault als Märchen niedergeschrie-
ben. Darin prüft der Ritter die Neugier seiner Frau,
indem er ihr den Schlüssel zu einem Zimmer über-
reicht, das sie nicht betreten soll. Sie, die der Ver-
suchung nicht widerstehen kann, schließt das
Zimmer auf und wird für diesen Ungehorsam von
Blaubart getötet. Fünf weitere Frauen erleiden das
gleiche Schicksal. Die siebte Frau jedoch kann von
ihren Brüdern gerettet werden.

In Maeterlincks Libretto bringt König Blaubart
zum sechsten Mal eine junge Frau in sein märchenhaftes Schloß. Niemand weiß, was mit ihren
fünf Vorgängerinnen geschehen ist. Man hat sie
nach der Hochzeit nie wieder gesehen. Trotz
Blaubarts Verbot durchsucht Ariane, kaum ist
sie im Schloß, alle Räume. Nachdem sie hinter
den Türen Zimmer voller Edelsteine und anderer
Schätze gefunden hat, steigt sie hinunter in die
Kellerräume. Dort findet sie ihre Vorgängerinnen.
Alle sind am Leben!

Sie stachelt die Frauen auf und will mit ihnen
aus dem Gefängnis fliehen. Da wird Blaubart ge-

bracht, den die aufständischen Bauern der Umgebung inzwischen gefangen und gefesselt haben. Die Bauern erwarten nun, daß sich die
Frauen an dem Wüstling rächen. Diese aber
durchschneiden seine Fesseln und weigern sich
zu fliehen. Allein geht Ariane hinaus ins Freie,
dem Meer entgegen. Alle andern bleiben zurück.

Maeterlinck beschreibt in Blaubart einen anar-
chischen, märchenhaften Frauenfänger, halb Minotauros und halb Don Giovanni. Die Frauen sind
durch ihn, der in sagenhaftem Reichtum lebt, irri-
tiert. Ariane verkörpert die moderne, unerschro-
ckene Frau auf dem Weg in die selbstbestimmte
Freiheit. Sie läßt sich zwar vom König anlocken,
vielleicht auch verführen, aber man weiß nicht, ob
es nicht nur aus purer Neugier geschieht, mit der
Absicht, das Geheimnis zu lüften, das über der
Burg und Blaubart schwebt. Vielleicht ist es auch
ihre Absicht, sich für die jahrhundertelange Unterdrückung der Frau zu rächen. Aber sie erreicht
ihr Ziel nicht. Die Bauern wären bereit, den reichen Parasiten zu töten, die gefangenen Frauen
jedoch verhindern das Schlimmste. Sie stehen zu
ihrem Unterdrücker und lieben ihren Verführer. Es
ist das Drama der in reichen Ehen gefangenen
Frauen. Befreiung würde Absturz in Armut und
Not bedeuten.

Unsere Interpretation in Paris griff diesen Gedanken auf, war aber insgesamt nicht realistisch
sondern surreal. Wir siedelten das Geschehen
auf den Dächern einer Großstadt an. Die Räume
lagen unter den Giebeln verteilt. Das Labyrinth
hatte sich in eine unendlich große Metropole verwandelt, wo der Minotauros wohnte und lebte
und in der er alle Häuser und Straßen besaß.
Grenzenloser Luxus umgab ihn. Auf den Dächern
parkte er seine Flugzeuge und Schiffe, in den Ga-
ragen tief unten wartete eine Limousinen-Flotte
auf seine Befehle.

Cavalleria rusticana
Melodrama in one act by Pietro Mascagni, libretto by Giovanni Targioni-Tozzetti and Guido Menasci

I Pagliacci
Drama in two acts and a prologue by Ruggero Leoncavallo, libretto by the composer

Bremer Theater, 1998; conductor: Günter Neuhold, director: Dominik Neuner, sets: Hans Dieter Schaal, costumes: Swetlana Zwetkowa, dramaturgy: Norbert Abels

Southern temperaments, fiery passion, jealousy and murder on a large flight of steps between some old, crooked buildings determine the atmosphere of these operas, which are examples of Italian verismo. The plays and operas in this genre are intended to seem as though they had come into being of their own accord. In reality they are much more similar to their predecessors than was intended. Certainly the plots were placed in a village context, and the names of the characters do not have historical roots, but the emotional events were the same as ever. They revolved around tragic love stories that ended fatally as a result of jealousy, as in these two operas.

There is an old tradition of presenting these two short operas on the same evening.

In *Cavalleria rusticana*, Turiddu, a young peasant, comes back from military service to find his former fiancée Lola married to another man, the rich carter Alfio. In order to forget his disappointment and misery, he starts a relationship with Santuzza, one of the village beauties who is still available. But soon he turns his attention to his former fiancée again. Santuzza objects, and insists that he make up his mind. When Lola's husband finds out about Turiddu's liaison with his wife he challenges the adulterer to a duel. Turiddu is killed by Alfio in a dramatic finale.

I Pagliacci: the Italian word pagliaccio means »clown« or »buffoon«. In Goethe's day the »Bajazzo« – which appears in the German title of the piece – was a joker among the tightrope walkers and acrobats. He wore white clothes, a ruff and a pointed hat.

The plot: the leading man in a group of strolling players, Canio, has married a much younger wife, over whom he watches jealously. And indeed the beautiful young Nedda is pursued by a number of suitors. One say she decides to run away with a young lover from the village the troupe is playing in. Disaster strikes on the evening before the planned elopement, during a performance in which Canio is playing the role of the clown.

The clown in the play is jealous of Harlequin, who plays the role of the lover. He asks his wife, who is played by Nedda, to whom he is married in real life, what his name is. Acting and reality now start to become confused. Soon the clown no longer wants to know the name of the lover in the play, but the name of his wife Nedda's real-life lover. He keeps asking her to tell him, and finally stabs her with a dagger when she refuses to reveal the name. The real lover, who is in the audience, rushes on to the stage, but it is too late.

The settings: For *Cavalleria rusticana*: »The main square in the village. In the background on the right is a church with an open door, on the left is the inn and Mother Lucia's house.«

For *I Pagliacci*: »Calabria, near Montalto, on the Feast of the Assumption in about 1870.«

Both plots were shifted to a gigantic flight of stone steps wedged in between two slightly tilted Italian houses. The church stood at the top of the mountain of steps.

Both pieces play on high Catholic feast days. Many people have come out of their houses and witness the tragedies. The atmosphere is turbulent and could have been made for a tangle of emotions and outbursts of jealousy.

I Pagliacci was the last German emperor's favourite opera. Here he did not have to put up with any hysterical perversions, as in *Salome* or *Electra*, but could give himself up entirely to the Italian dream and admire the hot-blooded southerners.

Cavalleria rusticana
Melodrama in einem Akt von Pietro Mascagni, Text von Giovanni Targioni-Tozzetti und Guido Menasci

Der Bajazzo – I Pagliacci
Drama in zwei Akten und einem Prolog von Ruggero Leoncavallo, Text vom Komponisten

Bremer Theater, 1998; musikalische Leitung: Günter Neuhold, Inszenierung: Dominik Neuner, Bühne: Hans Dieter Schaal, Kostüme: Swetlana Zwetkowa, Dramaturgie: Norbert Abels

Südliches Temperament, glühende Leidenschaft, Eifersucht und Mord auf einer großen Treppe zwischen alten, schiefen Häusern bestimmen die Atmosphäre dieser Opern, die als Beispiele des italienischen Verismo gelten. Die Theaterstücke und Opernwerke, die dieser Richtung zuzuordnen sind, sollten wirken, als seien sie von selbst entstanden. In Wirklichkeit unterscheiden sie sich weit weniger von ihren Vorgängern als geplant. Die Handlungen wurden zwar in einen dörflichen Rahmen gestellt, und die Namen der Mitwirkenden hatten keine historischen Wurzeln, aber die emotionalen Vorgänge waren die gleichen wie immer. Im Zentrum standen tragische Liebesgeschichten, die ,wie auch in diesen beiden Opern, durch Eifersucht ein tödliches Ende nehmen.

Beide Kurzopern an einem Abend zu spielen, hat eine alte Tradition.

In *Cavalleria rusticana* findet Turiddu, ein junger Bauer, seine einstige Verlobte Lola bei seiner Rückkehr vom Militärdienst verheiratet mit einem anderen vor, dem reichen Fuhrmann Alfio. Um seine Enttäuschung und Trauer zu vergessen, beginnt er ein Verhältnis mit Santuzza, einer noch freien Dorfschönen. Bald jedoch wendet er sich wieder seiner ehemaligen Verlobten zu. Santuzza wehrt sich und verlangt eine Entscheidung. Als Lolas Ehemann von der Verbindung zwischen Turiddu und seiner Frau erfährt, fordert er den Ehebrecher zum Duell. In einem dramatischen Finale wird Turiddu von Alfio erschlagen.

Der Bajazzo – I Pagliacci: Im Italienischen bedeutet Pagliaccio »Strohsack« und »Hanswurst«. Zur Zeit Goethes war der Bajazzo ein Spaßmacher unter Seiltänzern und Akrobaten. Er trug weiße Kleider, eine Halskrause und einen Spitzhut.

Die Handlung: Der Prinzipal einer Komödiantengruppe, Canio, hat eine sehr viel jüngere Frau geheiratet, die er ständig mit Eifersucht verfolgt. Tatsächlich wird die junge, schöne Nedda von verschiedenen Männern umschwärmt. Eines Tages beschließt sie, mit einem jungen Liebhaber aus dem Dorf, in dem die Truppe gastiert, zu fliehen. Am Abend vor der geplanten Flucht geschieht dann während der Vorstellung, bei der Canio den Bajazzo spielt, das Unheil.

Im Handlungsverlauf des Theaterstücks ist der Bajazzo eifersüchtig auf Harlekin, der die Rolle des Liebhabers verkörpert. Er fragt seine Frau, die von Nedda, seiner wirklichen Gattin, gespielt wird, nach dessen Namen. Spiel und Wirklichkeit beginnen nun miteinander zu verschmelzen. Bald will der Bajazzo nicht mehr nur den Namen des Liebhabers der Theaterhandlung wissen, sondern den des tatsächlichen Geliebten seiner Ehefrau Nedda. Immer wieder fragt er sie danach und ersticht sie schließlich mit einem Dolch, als sie sich weigert, den Namen preiszugeben. Der wirkliche Liebhaber, der sich unter den Zuschauern befindet, stürzt auf die Bühne, kommt jedoch zu spät.

Die Bühnenbild-Orte: Für *Cavalleria rusticana*: »Hauptplatz des Dorfes. Im Hintergrund, rechts, eine Kirche mit offenem Tor, links das Wirtshaus und das Haus von Mutter Lucia.«

Für *Der Bajazzo – I Pagliacci*: »Kalabrien, nahe Montalto, am Fest Mariä Himmelfahrt um 1870.«

Beide Handlungen wurden auf eine riesige Steintreppe verlegt, die sich eingekeilt zwischen leicht gekippten, italienischen Häusern befand. Auf dem »Gipfel« des Treppenberges stand die Kirche.

Beide Geschichten spielen an hohen katholischen Feiertagen: Viele Menschen sind aus ihren Häusern gekommen und werden zu Zeugen der Tragödien. Die Stimmung ist aufgewühlt und wie geschaffen für ein Wirrwarr von Gefühlen und Eifersuchtsausbrüchen.

Der Bajazzo war die Lieblingsoper des letzten deutschen Kaisers. Hier mußte er keine hysterischen Perversionen ertragen, wie in *Salome* oder in *Elektra*, sondern konnte sich ganz dem italienischen Traum hingeben und die Heißblütigkeit der Südländer bewundern.

Leonce und Lena
Comedy by Georg Büchner

Nationaltheater Mannheim, 1989; director: Nicolas Brieger, sets: Hans Dieter Schaal, costumes: Benedikt Ramm, dramaturgy: Jürgen Drescher

Georg Büchner wrote his only comedy, *Leonce und Lena*, in 1836, a love story that really isn't one at all. The two main characters are very young, at an age between childhood, puberty and adolescence. They are surrounded by a sense of initiation, like the protagonists of *The Magic Flute* and *Der Prinz von Homburg*. Private feelings and reasons of state, confusions and a fairy-tale happy ending.

Georg Büchner was born in 1813, the same year as Richard Wagner and Giuseppe Verdi. His life ended in 1837 already. Wagner died in 1883 and Verdi in 1901.

Like Wagner, Büchner started as a revolutionary. He wrote the *Hessischer Landbote* (»Peace to the huts, war to the palaces«). He only just escaped imprisonment. He spent his short life in flight and in exile. Like Mozart, Schubert and Wagner he hated the nobility and the ossified social conditions. The French Revolution made everyone to start to hope that it would be possible to get rid of the monarchy as well. But while Wagner came back to be a servant of princes in later life and Verdi became a national hero of Italian unification, Büchner remained unheard. *Leonce und Lena* was not performed until 1895, *Dantons Tod* until 1902 and *Woyzeck* until 1913.

In 1836 the Cotta press in Stuttgart had announced a comedy competition, for which Büchner wrote *Leonce und Lena*. But it was not ready in time. His manuscript arrived two days after the final delivery deadline. Cotta returned the envelope to Büchner unopened.

Leonce und Lena is a play written between eras, between Romanticism and idealism, between Existentialism and the theatre of the absurd. It seems like a balancing act, like a tightrope walk on time's back. We have a sense of the rip that separates Romanticism from the industrial world of machines. Mechanics lurk everywhere, repetition, machines. In the mechanism, in the roundabout of revolving doors. The point of view is a strange mixture: childish, medical, philosophical, resigned, old and young at the same time. Romanticism in the hospital. The world spirit as a machine, the universe as a piece of clockwork. The love of Leonce, the son of King Peter of Popo and Lena, the daughter of the king of Pipi are seized by is like a lost bird, like a cloud that suddenly comes floating through the room. Both are supposed to marry for reasons of state. But they run away because they do not want to submit to a forced marriage. They meet each other during their flight, without knowing who the other is. They fall in love, and in the end the planned wedding takes place, but under different conditions.

In *Leonce und Lena* Büchner is describing a feeling for life that is full of Weltschmerz and cynically ironic pessimism. The basic mood is boredom.

Leonce is a nihilist. The gods do not wait for Nietzsche and Wagner before they die, they die here in Büchner's plays. Despite all the resignation, love remains as a glimpse of light. But it remains to be seen whether it will be possible to dream up magic that will jolt the couple's future life out of its predetermined mechanics.

The settings: »A garden. A room. A lavishly decorated hall. Candles are burning. A garden. Open field. An inn in the background. The inn on an eminence by a river. Broad view. The garden in front of this. A room. The garden. Night and moonlight. An open square outside King Peter's palace. Great hall. Ladies and gentlemen in their finery. Carefully grouped.«

In Mannheim all the locations were brought together in a single space. There was a fragment of rocky landscape in the foreground. Behind this was a hall with a lot of revolving doors. An absurd place somewhere between palace, hotel lobby and revolving door factory.

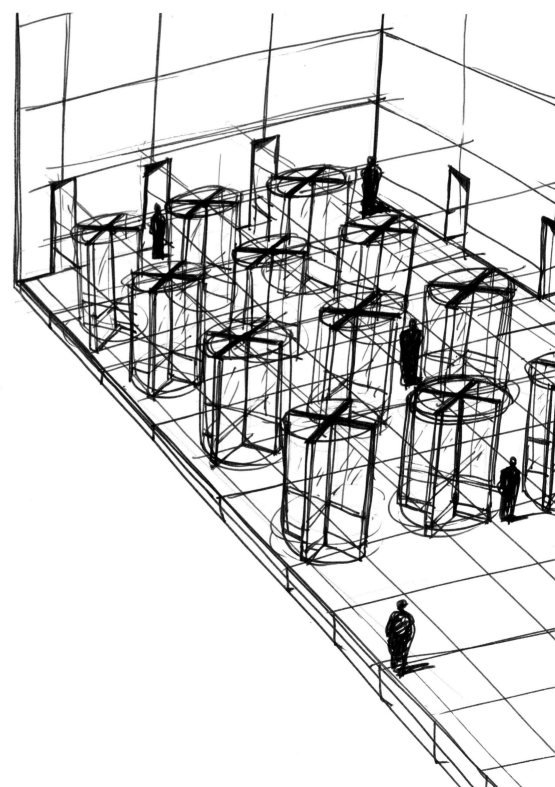

Leonce und Lena

Lustspiel von Georg Büchner

Nationaltheater Mannheim, 1989; Inszenierung: Nicolas Brieger, Bühne: Hans Dieter Schaal, Kostüme: Benedikt Ramm, Dramaturgie: Jürgen Drescher

1836 hat Georg Büchner sein einziges Lustspiel *Leonce und Lena* geschrieben, eine Liebesgeschichte, die eigentlich keine ist. Die beiden Hauptdarsteller sind sehr jung, in einem Alter zwischen Kindheit, Pubertät und Adoleszenz. Ein Hauch von Initiation umgibt sie wie auch die Protagonisten in der *Zauberflöte* und in *Der Prinz von Homburg*. Privates Gefühl und Staatsraison, Verwirrungen und ein märchenhaftes Happy-End.

Georg Büchner wurde 1813 geboren, im gleichen Jahr wie Richard Wagner und Giuseppe Verdi. Bereits 1837 endete sein Leben. Wagner starb 1883 und Verdi 1901.

Wie Wagner begann Büchner als Revolutionär. Er schrieb den *Hessischen Landboten* (»Friede den Hütten, Krieg den Palästen«). Dem Kerker entkam er nur knapp. Sein kurzes Leben verbrachte er auf der Flucht und im Exil. Wie Mozart, Schubert und Wagner haßte er den Adel und die verkrusteten gesellschaftlichen Verhältnisse. Die Französische Revolution ließ in allen die Hoffnung aufkeimen, daß man auch die Monarchie beseitigen könne. Während Wagner sich in seinem späteren Leben jedoch zu einem Fürstendiener zurückentwickelte und Verdi zu einem Nationalhelden der italienischen Einigung aufstieg, blieb Büchner ungehört. *Leonce und Lena* wurde erst 1895 uraufgeführt, *Dantons Tod* 1902 und *Woyzeck* 1913.

1836 hatte der Verlag Cotta in Stuttgart einen Lustspiel-Wettbewerb ausgeschrieben, für den Büchner *Leonce und Lena* verfaßte. Er wurde jedoch nicht rechtzeitig fertig. Sein Manuskript traf zwei Tage nach dem letzten Einlieferungstermin ein. Der Verlag schickte das ungeöffnete Kuvert daraufhin an Büchner zurück.

Leonce und Lena ist ein Stück zwischen den Zeiten, zwischen Romantik und Idealismus, zwischen Existenzialismus und absurdem Theater. Es wirkt wie ein Balanceakt, wie ein Seiltanz auf dem Rücken der Zeit. Man spürt den Riß, der die Romantik von der industriellen Maschinenzeit trennt. Überall lauert die Mechanik, die Wiederholung, die Maschine. Im Räderwerk, im Drehtüren-Karussell. Marionettenhaft. Der Blick ist seltsam gemischt: kindisch, medizinisch, philosophisch, resigniert, alt und jung zugleich. Romantik im Krankenhaus. Der Weltgeist eine Maschine, das All ein Uhrwerk. Wie ein verirrter Vogel, wie eine Wolke, die plötzlich durchs Zimmer schwebt, wirkt hier die Liebe, von der Leonce, Sohn des Königs Peter vom Reiche Popo und Lena, Tochter des Königs vom Reiche Pipi, erfaßt werden. Aus Gründen der Staatsraison sollen beide heiraten. Sie fliehen jedoch, weil sie einer erzwungenen Heirat nicht zustimmen wollen. Auf der Flucht treffen sie aufeinander, ohne zu wissen, wer der andere ist. Sie verlieben sich, und am Ende kommt es zu der geplanten Hochzeit, nur unter anderen Vorzeichen.

In *Leonce und Lena* beschreibt Büchner ein Lebensgefühl voller Weltschmerz und zynisch-ironischem Pessimismus. Seine Grundstimmung ist die Langeweile.

Leonce ist ein Nihilist. Die Götter sterben nicht erst bei Nietzsche und Wagner, sondern hier in den Stücken Büchners. Trotz aller Resignation bleibt als Lichtblick die Liebe. Ob sie das zukünftige Leben des Paares aus seiner vorbestimmten Mechanik herauszaubern wird, bleibt dahingestellt.

Die Bühnenbild-Orte:»Ein Garten. Ein Zimmer. Ein reichgeschmückter Saal. Kerzen brennen. Ein Garten. Freies Feld. Ein Wirtshaus im Hintergrund. Das Wirtshaus auf einer Anhöhe an einem Fluß. Weite Aussicht. Der Garten vor demselben. Ein Zimmer. Der Garten. Nacht und Mondschein. Freier Platz vor dem Schlosse des Königs Peter. Großer Saal. Geputzte Herren und Damen. Sorgfältig gruppiert.«

Alle Orte wurden in Mannheim zu einem Raum zusammengefaßt. Im Vordergrund befand sich ein Stück Felslandschaft. Dahinter lag eine Halle mit vielen Drehtüren. Absurder Ort zwischen Schloß, Hotelhalle und Drehtürenfabrik.

Rigoletto

Melodrama in three acts by Giuseppe Verdi, libretto by Francesco Maria Piave after the play *Le Roi s'amuse* by Victor Hugo

Städtische Bühnen, Münster, 1995; conductor: Will Humburg, director: Dominik Neuner, sets: Hans Dieter Schaal, costumes: Ute Frühling, dramaturgy: Wolfgang Haendeler

The story is set in the 19th century. The duke of Mantua has sought out a new victim for his sexual desires. He does not know that this is Gilda, the secret daughter of the jester Rigoletto. When Rigoletto once more goes too far with his joking, the court kidnap Gilda and take her to the Duke's Court. When Rigoletto discovers where his daughter is, and actually sees her coming out of the Duke's room, he thinks the Duke has dishonoured her and decides to kill the seducer. He commissions the »professional hitman« Sparafucile to do this.

The end of the opera plays on the bank of the river in a dubious inn to which the duke makes his way secretly. In the confusion caused by thunder and lightning, Gilda is murdered instead of the duke. Rigoletto breaks down in despair over the body of his daughter in a rubbish sack.

The settings: »Act One: a magnificent hall in the ducal palace. In the background are doors to other rooms, blazing with magnificently bright light. The gloomy end of a cul de sac. On the left is an attractive house surrounded by a little walled courtyard. In the courtyard are a large, tall tree and a marble bench, in the wall is a door leading to the street, above the wall is a balcony on arches. The door on the first floor leads to the balcony. On the right of the alleyway is the very high garden wall and a wing of the Ceprano palace. It is night. Act Two: Drawing-room in the ducal palace. Two side doors, a large one in the background, which is just closing. Life-size portraits of the Duchess and the Duke hang on either side. An armchair is placed next to a table with a velvet cloth. Act Three: the desolate banks of the Mincio. On the left is a two-storey, semi-dilapidated building. Its façade faces the audience, and an archway gives a view of the ground floor of a rural inn, and also a crude wooden staircase leading to the attic, where a balcony without shutters on the windows reveals a view of a camp bed. In the façade facing the street is a door that opens inwards; there are so many cracks in the wall that it is easy to see from the outside what is happening inside. The rest of the stage shows the gloomy banks of the Mincio, which flows past a partially collapsed embankment in the background; beyond the river is Mantua. It is night.«

So that the opera did not sink without trace in the melodramatic atmosphere, we responded to almost none of Verdi's requirements: We are in a kind of spatial trap. All the characters seem to be the prisoners of their own emotions. They are governed by invisible laws.

At the end the river-bed broods in the sun, empty and dried out. There is no way back. Rigoletto is finally broken.

Rigoletto

Melodrama in drei Akten von Giuseppe Verdi, Text von Francesco Maria Piave nach dem Schauspiel *Le roi s'amuse* von Victor Hugo

Städtische Bühnen, Münster, 1995; musikalische Leitung: Will Humburg, Inszenierung: Dominik Neuner, Bühne: Hans Dieter Schaal, Kostüme: Ute Frühling, Dramaturgie: Wolfgang Haendeler

Die Geschichte spielt im 19. Jahrhundert. Der Herzog von Mantua hat sich ein neues Opfer für seine sexuellen Gelüste ausgesucht. Er weiß nicht, daß es sich um Gilda, die verheimlichte Tochter des Spaßmachers Rigoletto, handelt. Als dieser mit seinen Späßen wieder einmal zu weit gegangen ist, entführt die Hofgesellschaft Gilda und bringt sie an den Hof des Herzogs. Nachdem Rigoletto herausgefunden hat, daß seine Tochter sich bei Hofe aufhält und er sie zudem aus dem Zimmer des Herzogs kommen sieht, glaubt er, der Herzog habe sie entehrt, und er beschließt, den Verführer zu töten. Den Auftrag erhält der »Berufskiller«, Sparafucile.

Der Schluß der Oper spielt am Flußufer in einer zweifelhaften Kneipe, in die sich der Herzog schleicht. Bei Gewitter mit Donner und Blitz wird Gilda statt des Herzogs ermordet. Verzweifelt bricht Rigoletto über den in einen Müllsack gehüllten Leichnam seiner Tochter zusammen.

Die Bühnenbild-Orte: »Erster Akt: Prächtiger Saal im herzoglichen Palast. Im Hintergrund Türen zu anderen Sälen, die prunkvoll hell erleuchtet sind. Das öde Ende einer Sackgasse. Links ein hübsches Haus mit einem kleinen, mit Mauern umgebenen Hof. Im Hof ein großer, hoher Baum und eine Bank aus Marmor, in der Mauer eine Tür, die zur Straße führt, oberhalb der Mauer ein begehbarer Balkon auf Arkaden. Die Tür im ersten Stock führt auf den Balkon. Rechts der Gasse ist die sehr hohe Mauer des Gartens und ein Flügel des Palastes von Ceprano. Es ist Nacht. Zweiter Akt: Salon im herzoglichen Palast. Zwei Seitentüren, eine größere im Hintergrund, die gerade zufällt. Zu beiden Seiten hängen die Porträts der Herzogin und des Herzogs in Lebensgröße. Ein Sessel steht neben dem Tisch mit einer Samtdecke. Dritter Akt: Das öde Ufer des Mincio. Links ein zweistöckiges, halb verfallenes Haus, dessen Front, die dem Zuschauer zugewandt ist, durch einen großen Bogen das Innere eines ländlichen Wirtshauses im Erdgeschoß sehen läßt, sowie eine grob gezimmerte Treppe, die auf den Dachboden führt, wo ein Balkon ohne Fensterläden den Blick auf ein Feldbett freigibt. In der Fassade, die der Straße zugewandt ist, eine Tür, die sich nach innen öffnet; in der Mauer sind so viele Risse, daß man von draußen leicht sehen kann, was im Haus vor sich geht. Der Rest der Bühne zeigt die öde Seite des Mincio, der im Hintergrund hinter einem halb eingestürzten Damm fließt; jenseits des Flusses liegt Mantua. Es ist Nacht.«

Damit die Oper nicht im melodramatischen Gewitter versumpfte, wurde fast keine der Forderungen Verdis bedient: Wir befinden uns in einer Art Raumfalle. Alle Figuren scheinen in ihren Emotionen befangen. Sie werden von unsichtbaren Gesetzen bestimmt.

Am Ende brütet das Flußbett leer und ausgetrocknet in der Sonne. Ein Zurück gibt es nicht. Rigoletto ist endgültig zerbrochen.

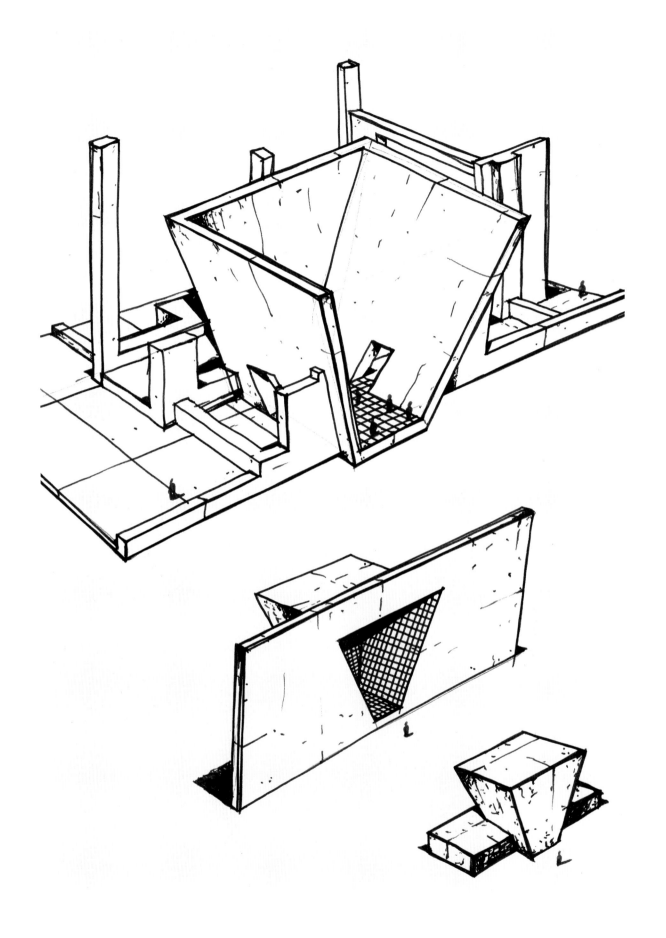

Falstaff

Lyrical comedy in three acts by Giuseppe Verdi, libretto by Arrigo Boito after Shakespeare's *Merry Wives of Windsor* and motifs from *King Henry IV*
Städtische Bühnen Frankfurt am Main, 2000; conductor: Paolo Carignani, director: Katrin Hilbe, sets: Hans Dieter Schaal, costumes: Angelika Rieck, dramaturgy: Peter Ross and Zsolt Horpacsy

In fact he has had the best of his life. His experiences are stored away as memories in his mind and in his belly. He used to be a wild thing, a Casanova. But now, in a world that is ruled by commerce and money, he lies in his armchair like the embodiment of an anachronism, the calm centre in the middle of a great vortex, at the source, where it is possible to get hold of tasty food and good wine. He still enjoys life, even though he is not really up to it any more and is forced to think of mafia-style activities: making other people work, just skimming off the cream himself. Otherwise dully doing nothing, drinking and eating.

This opera is the eighty-year-old Verdi's farewell to the world. All around him nations are building up their armaments, the machines are working, the big cities are growing and losing their nostalgic elegance. His works will still be played, but the opera houses will be like enchanted museums in the middle of an exploding, chaotic world. The new dream palaces are the cinemas, that is where people fight, love and die now. And the orchestras can't be seen any more, their sounds come out of invisible, digitalized spaces.

»Everything is fun on earth, we are born fools.« If we remember that these are the last words that Verdi ever set, then the resigned quality of his basic mood becomes clear. He ends up where he had started, on the surface. Here there is no deeply religious quality, and no belief in the great love, like Wagner. Verdi withdraws completely to the position of the man who has been made a fool of: we are only playing a part, we always write the wrong letters, we are tormented, we are always the losers, all that remains for us is a mask. On the threshold of the 20th century this Falstaff seems like a precursor of Samuel Beckett's nihilistic figures, who are also melancholy waiting figures, never moving from the spot and never arriving.

And then we look at the last photographs of Verdi, and see this obstinate, tight-lipped scrawny old man, looking into the camera with his shoulders down and a resigned expression. My work is over, I will play Verdi once more, for the last time, and then I shall withdraw into the darkness of my rooms.

The settings: »Inside the ›Garter‹ inn. Garden, Ford's house on the left. Groups of trees in the middle ground. Inside the inn again. A room in Ford's house. A little square, on the right is the ›Garter‹ inn. Windsor Great Park. In the centre is Herne's oak. In the background the rampart of a ditch. Thick bushes. Shrubs in bloom. It is night.«

The story is actually set in Windsor in about 1400. Falstaff has set himself up in an inn with his dubious servants. Because he needs money, he writes two love letters to two well-to-do women, both worded the same, for simplicity's sake. Unfortunately the women know each other, show

each other the letters and are outraged, or at least make out that they are. Falstaff is almost discovered by the husband at a rendezvous that one of the two women makes with him. He has to hide in the laundry basket and is thrown into the Thames by the women. But that is not all: half the citizens of Windsor mock and tease him in the moonlight at a second rendezvous.

Our interpretation set the piece in the early 20th century, in a large, run-down hotel in England or Italy. Falstaff has settled into the lobby with his people, by the kitchen door. He can see everything from there. His female antagonists have also set themselves up in the hall: they are running a successful hairdressing salon. The whole plot plays in this hotel.

Falstaff

Commedia lirica in drei Akten von Giuseppe Verdi, Text von Arrigo Boito nach Shakespeares *Die lustigen Weiber von Windsor* und Motiven aus *König Heinrich IV*.

Städtische Bühnen Frankfurt am Main, 2000; musikalische Leitung: Paolo Carignani, Inszenierung: Katrin Hilbe, Bühne: Hans Dieter Schaal, Kostüme: Angelika Rieck, Dramaturgie: Peter Ross und Zsolt Horpacsy

Eigentlich liegt das Leben hinter ihm. Die Erlebnisse haben sich als Erinnerungen in seinem Gedächtnis und in seinem Bauch abgelagert. Früher einmal war er ein wilder Bursche, ein Casanova. Aber heute, in der neuen, nur von Geschäften und Geld regierten Welt, liegt er in seinem Sessel wie der verkörperte Anachronismus, das ruhige Zentrum inmitten eines großen Wirbels, an der Quelle, dort, wo man an schmackhaftes Essen und guten Wein herankommt. Immer noch ist er ein Genießer, auch wenn er es sich eigentlich nicht mehr leisten kann und gezwungen ist, über mafiose Aktivitäten nachzudenken: andere arbeiten lassen, selber nur den Rahm abschöpfen, ansonsten dumpfes Nichtstun, trinken und essen.

Mit dieser Oper verabschiedet sich der 80-jährige Verdi von der Welt. Ringsum rüstet alles auf, die Maschinen arbeiten, die Metropolen wuchern und verlieren ihre nostalgische Eleganz. Man wird seine Werke weiter spielen, aber die Opernhäuser werden wie verzauberte Museen inmitten einer explodierenden, chaotischen Welt sein. Die neuen Traumpaläste sind die Kinos, dort wird heute gekämpft, geliebt und gestorben. Und die Orchester sind nicht mehr zu sehen, ihre Klänge kommen aus unsichtbaren, digitalisierten Räumen.

»Alles ist Spaß auf Erden, wir sind geborene Narren.« Wenn man bedenkt, daß diese Worte die letzten sind, die Verdi vertont hat, wird seine resignierte Grundstimmung deutlich. Er endet dort, wo er begonnen hat: an der Oberfläche. Hier gibt es keine tiefe Religiosität und nicht den Glauben an die große Liebe wie bei Wagner. Verdi zieht sich ganz auf die Position des Genarrten zurück: Wir spielen nur eine Rolle, wir schreiben immer die falschen Briefe, werden gequält, sind immer die Verlierer, uns bleibt nur die Maske. An der Schwelle des 20. Jahrhunderts wirkt dieser Falstaff wie ein Vorläufer der nihilistischen Figuren Samuel Becketts, die auch melancholisch Wartende sind, sich nie von der Stelle bewegen und nie ankommen.

Und dann betrachtet man die letzten Photos Verdis, sieht diesen eigensinnigen, verschlossenen und dürren Greis, der mit hängenden Schultern und resignierter Miene in die Kamera blickt. Das Werk ist vollendet, spiele ich Verdi noch einmal, zum letzten Mal, dann ziehe ich mich endgültig zurück in das Dunkel meiner Räume.

Bühnenbild-Orte: »Im Inneren des Gasthofes ›Zum Hosenbande‹. Garten, links Fords Haus. Baumgruppen im Mittelgrund der Szene. Wieder im Inneren des Gasthofes. Ein Saal in Fords Haus. Ein kleiner Platz, rechts das Gasthaus ›Zum Hosenbande‹. Der Park von Windsor. In der Mitte die große Eiche des Herne. Im Hintergrund der Wall eines Grabens. Dichtes Gebüsch. Blühende Sträucher. Es ist Nacht.«

Die Geschichte spielt eigentlich in Windsor um 1400. Falstaff hat sich mit seinen dubiosen Dienern in einem Gasthof einquartiert. Weil er Geld benötigt, schreibt er an zwei wohlhabende Damen zwei Liebesbriefe, beide gleichlautend, der Einfachheit halber. Leider kennen sich die Damen, zeigen sich die Briefe und sind empört oder tun wenigstens so. Bei einem Stelldichein, das eine von beiden mit ihm vereinbart, wird Falstaff vom Ehemann fast entdeckt. Er muß sich im Wäschekorb verstecken und wird von den Damen in die Themse geworfen. Aber damit noch nicht genug: Bei einem zweiten Rendezvous im Mondenschein veralbert und neckt ihn die halbe Bürgerschaft von Windsor.

Unsere Interpretation verlegt das Stück an den Anfang des 20. Jahrhunderts, in ein großes, heruntergekommenes Hotel in England oder Italien. Falstaff hat sich mit seinen Leuten in dieser Hotelhalle niedergelassen, neben der Küchentür. Von dort aus sieht er alles. In der Halle haben sich auch die weiblichen Gegenspielerinnen festgesetzt: Sie betreiben einen gutgehenden Friseursalon. Die ganze Handlung spielt in dieser Halle.

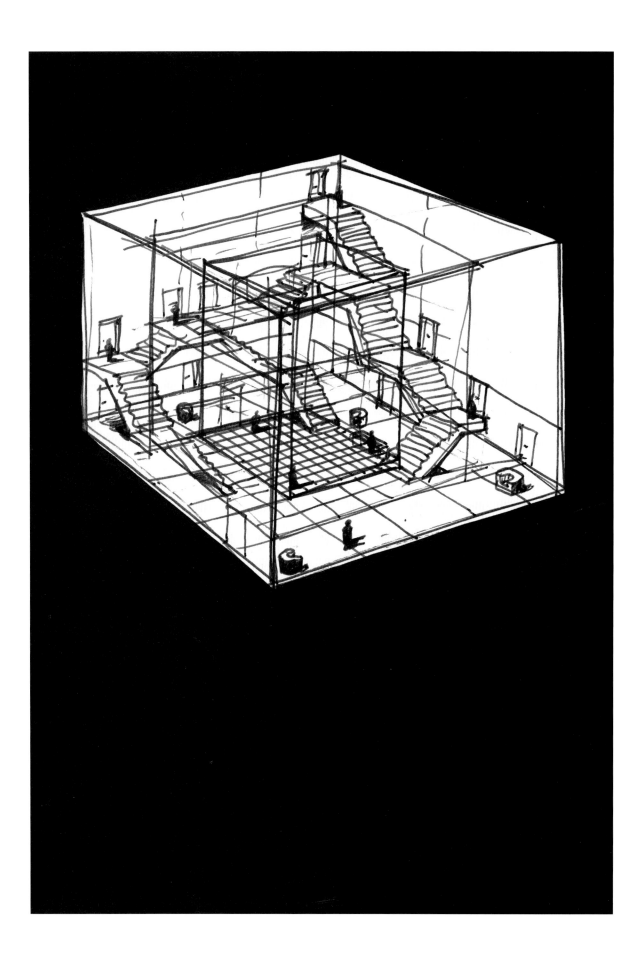

Wozzeck

Opera in three acts by Alban Berg, libretto by the composer based on Georg Büchner's drama *Woyzeck*

Deutsche Staatsoper Berlin, 1984, guest performance at the Teatro San Carlo, Naples, 1985; conductor: Siegfried Kurz, director: Ruth Berghaus, sets: Hans Dieter Schaal, costumes: Marie-Luise Strandt, dramaturgy: Sigrid Neef

Théâtre National Opéra de Paris (Garnier), 1985; conductor: Christoph von Dohnanyi, director: Ruth Berghaus, sets: Hans Dieter Schaal, costumes: Marie-Luise Strandt, dramaturgy: Sigrid Neef

Wozzeck was able to become the classical modern opera of the 20th century partly because of Alban Berg's music, moving to and fro between Expressionism and sensitive atonality, but also because of the simple power of the story. There he is, the modern individual, crushed between external laws, egoism and attacks of anonymity, inner turmoil and the collapsing walls of big cities.

Wozzeck is an architecture opera. The metropolis as a place of events and action. People appear out of niches in walls, rooms and doors like anonymous larvae, they walk along narrow alleyways, look out of windows, move on to bridges and balconies, are lit up and then disappear into the darkness, encounter each other, look at each other, repress, threaten and torment each other, experiment with their »nature«, which they do not understand. They seduce, love and hate each other. They fall over each other and stab each other to death.

Wozzeck is a dance of death, in the middle of a crossroads, an everyday street, in the underpass, at the station, in the industrial quarter, at the point where the city slowly becomes the country.

With *Woyzeck*, Büchner reached the modern age. There are no more palaces and noblemen, no fairy-tale dreams, no Italian landscapes. Now the city shifts into the picture. Coldly and inexorably. Woyzeck spends time here, but is not part of it. He runs around the alleyways and street ravines like a madman. We do not find out anything about his past. He is a plaything for external powers, torn out of his social setting. While Danton and Leonce suffer from boredom like dandies – money is no object, it is simply there – Woyzeck knows only the opposite: he is constantly overwound and overdriven, and races around the world looking for money »like an open razor«.

The plot is based on a real case. On 21 June 1821 a forty-one-year-old hairdresser and wig-maker called Johann Christian Woyzeck, stabbed his mistress, a forty-six-year-old widow to death in a fit of jealousy in the entrance to her home. He was publicly executed in Leipzig market-place on 27 August 1842.

Society is clearly defined in both the play and the opera: there is a captain, a doctor, a drum major, travelling journeymen, a barker and a policeman. Franz Woyzeck is a simple soldier. To feed himself and his child, whom he had – without the blessing of the church – with Marie, he takes on various casual jobs: he cuts withies, he shaves the captain and goes to work for the doctor as a human subject for experiment. Even so he never has any money. Anyone who does not have any money is entirely at the mercy of society and other people who do have money. The pressure on Woyzeck from the outside is great, too great. As he is a dull, uneducated person, who does not have a grip on things and cannot think anything out for himself he reacts to pressure from the outside and to the exploitation of his person not by rebelling actively, but passively, directing the force of his response inwards. He allows his problems to eat into him and cannot find any way out of his inner prison, so that his overtaxed psyche responds morbidly: panic attacks, apocalyptic visions, hallucinations and persecution mania alternate. The walls oppress him, the floor seems like thin ice, the city threatens to collapse on top of him. Like Döblin's Franz Biberkopf and Peter Lorre in Fritz Lang's *M* he is perpetually driven through the labyrinth of the city.

The final disaster comes when Marie betrays him – a single time, because she cannot resist the enticements of the drum major. Instead of turning on the seducer, Woyzeck kills the only being who has given him some support in this city: Marie.

In the opera *Wozzeck* drowns at the end in the pool by which he stabbed Marie, while looking for the murder weapon. He is thus spared being arrested, tried and executed.

The settings: »Room. Open field, with the city in the distance. The city. At the doctor's. Marie's bedroom. Street. Open field. Barrack yard … Woodland path by the pond.«

Short indications of place. Scenes like film takes. Like woodcuts. Without frills or embellishments. Compacted.

Our interpretations in Berlin and Paris worked with images of the big city.

In Berlin the first scene was played in a concrete wall that closed off the proscenium arch. A niche was cut into this. Then the wall was flown out and revealed a view of a city that had partially collapsed. The central building was awry, various floors and the roof were falling apart. A crack ran through the building and later the two halves of the building moved apart. A stretch of motorway with a concrete embankment was revealed. This architectural monster was gradually trucked forward like an attacking tank. Marie was murdered under the motorway, on the concrete embankment. Finally the concrete wall was lowered again and finally closed the urban prison.

The Paris variant worked with similar motifs. Some extra elements were introduced into the set. The first thing to appear behind the concrete wall was the gigantic façade of a building with a staircase cut into it. Niches were sunk into this façade for the individual scenes. The staircase splitted, later opened up and it was only at this point that the actual city architecture could be seen. The façades were at an angle and threatened to collapse on the figures acting out the plot.

Wozzeck

Oper in drei Akten von Alban Berg, Text vom Komponisten nach dem Drama *Woyzeck* von Georg Büchner

Deutsche Staatsoper Berlin, 1984, Gastspiel Teatro San Carlo, Neapel, 1985; musikalische Leitung: Siegfried Kurz, Inszenierung: Ruth Berghaus, Bühne: Hans Dieter Schaal, Kostüme: Marie-Luise Strandt, Dramaturgie: Sigrid Neef

Théâtre National Opéra de Paris (Garnier), 1985; musikalische Leitung: Christoph von Dohnanyi, Inszenierung: Ruth Berghaus, Bühne: Hans Dieter Schaal, Kostüme: Marie-Luise Strandt, Dramaturgie: Sigrid Neef

Daß *Wozzeck* der moderne Opernklassiker des 20. Jahrhunderts werden konnte, liegt zum einen an der raffinierten, zwischen Expressionismus und sensibler Atonalität sich hin- und herbewegenden Musik Alban Bergs, zum anderen aber auch an der einfachen Wucht der Geschichte. Da ist es, das moderne Individuum, das zwischen Fremdbestimmtheit, Ichlust und Anonymitätsanfällen, innerer Zerrissenheit und einstürzenden Großstadtwänden zermalmt wird.

Wozzeck ist eine Architektur-Oper. Die Großstadt als Ereignis- und Handlungsraum. Personen treten wie anonyme Larven aus Wandnischen, Räumen und Türen, sie gehen durch enge Gassen, blicken zu Fenstern hinaus, betreten Stege und Balkone, werden vom Licht getroffen, verschwinden im Dunkeln, begegnen sich, schauen sich an, unterdrücken, bedrohen, quälen einander, experimentieren mit ihrer »Natur«, die sie nicht verstehen. Sie verführen, lieben und hassen sich. Sie stürzen übereinander her und erstechen sich.

Wozzeck, ein Totentanz, mitten auf einer Kreuzung, auf einer alltäglichen Straße, in der Unterführung, am Bahnhof, im Industriegebiet, dort, wo die Stadt langsam in Landschaft übergeht.

Mit *Woyzeck* ist Büchner in der Moderne angekommen. Es gibt keine Schlösser und Adligen mehr, keine märchenhaften Träume, keine italienischen Landschaften. Jetzt rückt die Stadt ins Bild, kalt und unerbittlich. Woyzeck hält sich hier auf, gehört aber nicht dazu. Wie ein Verirrter rennt er durch Gassen und Straßenschluchten. Man erfährt nichts über seine Vergangenheit. Er ist, herausgerissen aus jedem sozialen Gefüge, ein Spielball fremder Mächte. Während Danton und Leonce dandyhaft an Langeweile leiden – Geld spielt keine Rolle, es ist einfach da – kennt Woyzeck nur das Gegenteil: Er ist ständig motorisch überdreht und hastet »wie ein offenes Rasiermesser« durch die Welt auf der Suche nach Geld.

Die Handlung beruht auf einem authentischen Fall. Am 21. Juni 1821 hatte der einundvierzigjährige Friseur und Perückenmacher Johann Christian Woyzeck in Leipzig seine Geliebte, eine sechsundvierzigjährige Witwe, im Hauseingang ihrer Wohnung aus Eifersucht erstochen. Am 27. August 1824 wird er auf dem Marktplatz von Leipzig öffentlich hingerichtet.

Im Stück und in der Oper ist die Gesellschaft klar definiert: Es gibt den Hauptmann, den Doktor, den Tambourmajor, Handwerksburschen, einen Marktschreier und einen Polizisten. Franz Woyzeck ist einfacher Soldat. Um sich und sein Kind zu ernähren, das er – ohne den Segen der

Kirche – mit Marie hat, nimmt er verschiedene Gelegenheitsarbeiten an: Er schneidet Weidenstecken, er rasiert den Hauptmann und verdingt sich beim Doktor als menschliches Versuchsobjekt. Dennoch hat er nie Geld. Wer kein Geld hat, ist der Gesellschaft und den anderen Menschen, die Geld haben, hilflos ausgeliefert. Der Druck von außen auf Woyzeck ist groß, zu groß. Da er ein dumpfer, ungebildeter Mensch ist, der keinen Überblick hat, der nichts zusammen denken kann, reagiert er auf die äußere Bedrängnis und auf die Ausbeutung seiner Person nicht aktiv rebellierend, sondern passiv, nach innen orientiert. Er frißt die Probleme in sich hinein und findet keinen Weg heraus aus dem inneren Gefängnis, so daß seine überforderte Psyche krankhaft reagiert: Anfälle von Angst, von apokalyptischen Visionen, Halluzinationen und Verfolgungswahn wechseln sich ab. Die Wände bedrängen ihn, der Boden erscheint ihm wie dünnes Eis, die Stadt droht auf ihn einzustürzen. Wie Franz Biberkopf bei Döblin und wie Peter Lorre in Fritz Langs *M* treibt es ihn ruhelos durch das Stadtlabyrinth.

Die endgültige Katastrophe tritt ein, als Marie ihn betrügt – ein einziges Mal, weil sie den Verlockungen des Tambourmajors nicht widerstehen kann. Statt sich gegen den Verführer zu wenden, tötet Woyzeck das einzige Wesen, das ihm in dieser Stadt noch Halt gegeben hat: Marie.

In der Oper ertrinkt Wozzeck am Ende in dem Teich, an dem er Marie erstochen hat, bei der Suche nach dem Mordmesser. Verhaftung, Prozeß und Hinrichtung bleiben ihm somit erspart.

Die Bühnenbild-Orte: »Zimmer. Freies Feld, die Stadt in der Ferne. Die Stadt. Beim Doktor. Mariens Kammer. Straße. Freies Feld. Kasernenhof ... Waldweg am Teich.«

Kurze Ortsangaben. Szenen wie Filmeinstellungen. Holzschnittartig. Ohne Schnörkel und Floskeln. Gepreßt.

Unsere Interpretation in Berlin und in Paris arbeitete mit Großstadtbildern.

In Berlin spielte das erste Bild in einer Betonwand, die die Bühnenöffnung verschloß. In diese war eine Raumnische eingelassen. Anschließend fuhr die Wand hoch, und man sah in eine teilweise eingestürzte Stadt. Das zentrale Haus stand schief, Geschoßebenen und Dach waren eingebrochen. Ein Riß spaltete das Haus, und später bewegten sich beide Haushälften auseinander. Im Hintergrund wurde ein Stück Autobahn mit Betonböschung sichtbar. Langsam kam dieses Architektur-Ungeheuer wie ein angreifender Panzer nach vorne gefahren. Der Mord an Marie geschah unter der Autobahn, auf der Betonböschung. Am Schluß senkte sich die Betonwand wieder hinunter und verschloß das Stadtgefängnis endgültig.

Die Pariser Variante arbeitete mit ähnlichen Motiven. Einige Elemente ergänzten das Bild. Hinter der Betonwand erschien zunächst eine riesige Hausfassade mit eingeschnittenem Treppenhaus. Für einzelne Szenen waren Raumnischen in diese Fassade eingesenkt. Das Treppenhaus spaltete sich, fuhr später auseinander, und jetzt erst sah man auf die eigentliche Großstadtarchitektur. Die Fassaden standen schräg und drohten auf die handelnden Figuren einzustürzen.

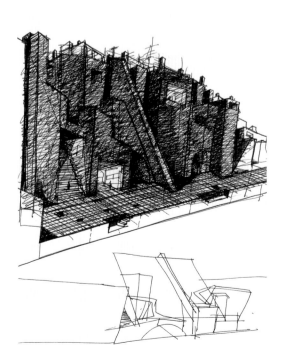

Boulevard Solitude

Lyrical drama in seven scenes by Hans Werner
Henze, libretto by Grete Weil and Walter Jokisch
based on the Abbé Prévost's novel *Manon Lescaut* (1731)
Städtische Bühnen Frankfurt am Main, 1988;
conductor: Bernhard Kontarsky, director: Nicolas
Brieger, sets: Hans Dieter Schaal, costumes:
Jorge Jara, dramaturgy: Norbert Abels, film projections: Hans Peter Böffgen

This is the old story of Manon Lescaut, which
both Puccini and Massenet had already based
operas on. Now the modern metropolis is at the
centre of the events. The action begins in a large
station hall where the student Armand meets
Manon, who is being seen off by her brother. Armand falls in love with the girl and runs away with
her. They live in an attic. Poverty reduces Manon
to selling herself to an older lover. After Manon's
brother has robbed the rich lover's safe, all three
are thrown out into the street. The brother acts
as a pimp between his sister and the rich man's
son. When Manon and Armand meet again, they
are surprised by the old, former lover, and Manon
shoots him. She is taken to prison, and in the
mean time Armand intoxicates himself with cocaine in a low dive. The opera ends with a
grotesque finale. Images swirl past. Manon appears without noticing Armand. The city flows on,
its wheels turn. Rooms move past like cars,
leaves fall; it is raining.

Hans Werner Henze composed *Boulevard
Solitude* in Wiesbaden and Paris in 1950/51. The
opera was first performed in Hanover in 1952.

»›Man is nothing other than what he makes
himself into‹. This was the fundamental axiom in
Sartre's essay ›Is Existentialism a form of human-
ism?‹, which he completed in 1946. Before this,
Camus had asked whether the only freedom
within the absurdity of existence was suicide.
And from then on metaphors of the sealed room
with no way out of it keep appearing, of cold
walls or of failure made into a principle by the
stone that keeps on rolling back. Ultimately the
formula of the greatest possible loneliness in the
key sentence from *Huis Clos*: ›L'enfer, c'est les
autres.‹« (Norbert Abels)

The stage: A kind of mobile city collage was
designed for Frankfurt. In the background was
the façade of a large building with a lot of windows. In front of this was a huge, hall-like showcase with fragments of steps, railway platforms,
roads and lifts. In between were sections of
rooms. The large showcase was on a revolve
and could therefore be shown from all sides. On
each side, off the revolve were two showcase
buildings with built-in shop-windows. These
buildings were mobile and could revolve as well.
New views and architectural compositions
emerged repeatedly.

To all this were added projections of road junc-
tions at night, tall buildings and birds flying past.
Trains could be seen coming in and out of the
station on gauzes. These were also projections.
All the images fell apart almost as soon as they
had formed

Boulevard Solitude

Lyrisches Drama in sieben Bildern von Hans Werner
Henze, Text von Grete Weil und Walter Jokisch nach
dem Roman *Manon Lescaut* des Abbé Prévost
(1731)
Städtische Bühnen Frankfurt am Main, 1998;
musikalische Leitung: Bernhard Kontarsky, Inszenierung: Nicolas Brieger, Bühne: Hans Dieter Schaal,
Kostüme: Jorge Jara, Dramaturgie: Norbert Abels,
Film-Projektionen: Hans Peter Böffgen

Es ist die alte Geschichte über Manon Lescaut,
die bereits von Puccini und Massenet zu Opern
verarbeitet wurde. Jetzt steht die moderne Großstadt im Mittelpunkt des Geschehens. Die Handlung beginnt in einer großen Bahnhofshalle, wo der
Student Armand Manon begegnet, die von ihrem
Bruder zum Zug gebracht wird. Armand verliebt
sich in das Mädchen und flieht mit ihr. Man lebt in
einer Mansarde. Armut bringt Manon dazu, sich an
einen älteren Liebhaber zu verkaufen. Nachdem
Manons Bruder den Tresor des reichen Liebhabers
ausgeraubt hat, werden alle drei auf die Straße geworfen. Der Bruder verkuppelt die Schwester an
den Sohn des Reichen. Als sich Manon und Armand wieder treffen, werden sie von dem alten,
ehemaligen Liebhaber überrascht, und Manon er-
schießt ihn. Sie kommt ins Gefängnis. Inzwischen
berauscht sich Armand in einer Kaschemme mit
Kokain. Die Oper endet mit einer grotesken
Schlußrevue. Bilder wirbeln vorbei. Manon taucht
auf, ohne Armand wahrzunehmen. Die Stadt fließt
weiter, dreht ihre Kreise. Zimmer fahren vorbei wie
Autos, Blätter fallen; es regnet.

Hans Werner Henze komponierte *Boulevard
Solitude* 1950/51 in Wiesbaden und Paris. 1952
wurde die Oper in Hannover uraufgeführt.

»›Der Mensch ist nichts anderes, als wozu er
sich macht‹. So lautet das grundlegende Axiom
Sartres in der 1946 vollendeten Schrift ›Ist der Exis-
tentialismus ein Humanismus?‹ Zuvor noch hat
Camus die Frage gestellt, ob in der Absurdität der
Existenz einzig die Freiheit des Selbstmordes be-
stehe. Immer wieder erscheinen nun Metaphern
des ausweglosen, geschlossenen Raumes, der
kalten Mauern oder des im stets wieder herabrol-
lenden Stein zum Daseinsprinzip gemachten
Scheiterns. Schließlich die Formel größtmöglicher
Einsamkeit in dem Schlüsselsatz aus *Huis Clos*:
›Die Hölle, das sind die anderen.‹« (Norbert Abels)

Die Bühne: Für Frankfurt wurde eine Art mobile
Stadt-Collage entworfen, im Hintergrund eine
große Hausfassade mit vielen Fensteröffnungen,
davor eine riesige, hallenartige Vitrine mit Fragmenten von Treppen, Bahnsteigen, Straßen und Aufzügen, dazwischen Zimmer-Elemente. Die große
Vitrine war auf einer Drehbühne aufgebaut und
konnte sich daher von allen Seiten zeigen. An den
Seiten, außerhalb der Drehbühne, standen jeweils
noch zwei Vitrinenhäuser mit Schaufenster-Einbau-
ten. Auch diese Häuser waren mobil und drehbar.
Immer wieder entstanden neue Durchblicke und
Architekturkompositionen.

Dazu kamen Projektionen von nächtlichen
Stadtkreuzungen, von Hochhäusern und vorbei-
fliegenden Vögeln. Auf Gazevorhängen sah man
Züge ein- und ausfahren. Dies waren ebenfalls
Projektionen. Alle Bilder zerfielen, kaum waren sie
entstanden.

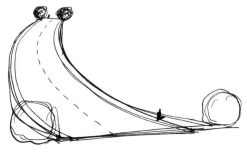

Nachtwache (»Night Watch«)

Composition for the music theatre by Jörg Herchet based on a text by Nelly Sachs

Opernhaus Leipzig, 1993; conductor: Lothar Zagrosek, director: Ruth Berghaus, sets: Hans Dieter Schaal, costumes and properties: Marie-Luise Strandt, dramaturgy: Antje Kaiser

Endgames: »The entire universe has collapsed.« The cities are destroyed, have fallen into disrepair or have decomposed into ruined landscapes. War has passed over them. Now all that is left is night.

This is the point at which this composition for the music theatre starts. It tells the story of Peter and Heinz, who had come under fire in the war and had become part of a nightmare, wounded, bleeding and dying, and this gradually extinguishes them.

A floating piece, somewhere between the world and space, between time and eternity. Dream mechanics. Lyrical images reel through dying egos. Dying as a transitional space and realm of thresholds, in which realities flash into life only as will o' the wisps. Pain and longing for love and redemption, torn out and floating above an icy snowscape.

The settings: »Scene One: Winter night. Snow. The occasional flickering moonbeam. Black branches that come together to form a sort of gallows … There are dark patches on the snow. People who have been shot … Scene Two: Cowshed. A cow is being milked on one side, Heinz is lying on the straw on the other side. Scene Three: Night. Moonlight. Heinz on the path. The path is a hand with black lines of shadow on it … The hand is scarcely perceptible. It just moves from time to time when there is a parting of the ways. Scene Four: Cowshed, as before. Heinz is lying on the straw. Heavy blows can be heard from the smithy. Scene Five: Night. White wood. Gigantic coffin in the centre. Scene Six: Cowshed, as before. Heavy blows. The cow is being milked on one side, Heinz is lying on the straw on the other side. Scene Seven: Threshold. Scene Eight: Heinz wandering in the white wood grown out of his hand. Scene Nine: The iron-barred gate topped with spikes of flaming thorns, Heinz lying in front of it.«

The set in Dresden: Landscape architecture, white as though it has been built out of ice and snow. Deep-frozen elements of the world, ripped out of the action and put together in a new way. A section of hospital corridor with beds. In the corridor, which could also be a coffin, is a gigantic wing whose origin remains uncertain, aeroplane or angel. Beside the wing, a ruined building grows out of the landscape. Fragments of a railway platform and white spheres complete the picture. As well as this, there is a corner with straw (the cowshed). The landscape was set up on the revolve. The dream collage turned slowly. At the end the barred gate was lowered: the smith had been working on it throughout the piece.

»Heinz has silently climbed up the barred gate and is hanging over the spikes: o my creator, o my annihilator, o these knives, o this spitted sun.

Rosalie rushes in and follows Heinz up the barred gate: Heinz, to you, to bleed to death in the sun.«

These are the final words in the composition.

Nachtwache

Komposition für das Musiktheater von Jörg Herchet nach einem Text von Nelly Sachs

Opernhaus Leipzig, 1993; musikalische Leitung: Lothar Zagrosek, Inszenierung: Ruth Berghaus, Bühne: Hans Dieter Schaal, Kostüme und Requisiten: Marie-Luise Strandt, Dramaturgie: Antje Kaiser

Endspiele: »Das ganze Universum ist gestürzt.« Die Städte sind zerstört, zerfallen oder zu Ruinenlandschaften verwest. Der Krieg ist über sie hinweggegangen. Jetzt gibt es nur noch die Nacht.

Hier setzt diese Komposition für das Musiktheater ein. Berichtet wird von Peter und Heinz, die im Krieg angeschossen wurden und verletzt, blutend, sterbend in einen Alptraum geraten, der sie langsam auslöscht.

Ein Stück in der Schwebe, zwischen Welt und All, zwischen Zeit und Ewigkeit. Traummechanik. Lyrische Bilder taumeln durch verlöschende Ichs. Sterben als Übergangsraum und Schwellenreich, in dem die Realitäten nur noch wie Irrlichter aufblitzen. Der Schmerz und die Sehnsucht nach Liebe und Erlösung, herausgerissen und schwebend über einer eisigen Schneelandschaft.

Die Bühnenbild-Orte: »Erstes Bild: Winternacht. Schnee. Zuweilen zuckender Mondstrahl. Schwarze Äste, die zu einer Art Galgen sich fügen … Auf dem Schnee dunkle Flecke. Die Erschossenen … Zweites Bild: Kuhstall. Auf der einen Seite wird eine Kuh gemolken, auf der anderen Seite liegt Heinz auf Stroh. Drittes Bild: Nacht. Mondenschein. Heinz auf dem Wege. Der Weg ist eine Hand mit schwarzen Schattenlinien … Man bemerkt sie kaum. Nur dann und wann bewegt sie sich an einer Wegscheide. Viertes Bild: Kuhstall, wie vordem. Heinz liegt auf dem Stroh. Man hört schwere Schläge von der Schmiede. Fünftes Bild: Nacht. Weißer Wald. Riesenhafter Sarg in der Mitte. Sechstes Bild: Kuhstall, wie zuvor. Harte Schläge. Auf der einen Seite wird die Kuh gemolken, auf der anderen liegt Heinz auf Stroh. Siebtes Bild: Schwelle. Achtes Bild: Heinz wandernd im weißen Wald aus seiner Hand gewachsen. Neuntes Bild: die Gittertür mit flammenden Dornenzacken, Heinz davor liegend.«

Die Bühne in Dresden: Eine Landschaftsarchitektur, weiß wie aus Schnee und Eis gebaut. Tiefgefrorene Elemente der Welt, aus der Handlung herausgerissen und neu zusammengesetzt. Ein Stück Krankenhausflur mit Krankenbetten. Im Flur, der auch ein großer Sarg sein könnte, steckt ein riesiger Flügel, dessen Herkunft unklar bleibt, Flugzeug oder Engel. Neben dem Flügel wächst aus der Landschaft eine Hausruine. Bahnsteigfragmente und weiße Kugeln ergänzen das Bild. Dazu eine Ecke mit Stroh (der Kuhstall). Die Landschaft war auf der Drehbühne aufgebaut. Langsam kreiste die Traumcollage. Am Ende senkte sich die Gittertür herab, an der ein Schmied das ganze Stück über gearbeitet hatte.

»Heinz ist lautlos die Gittertür hochgeklettert, hängt über den Zacken: O mein Schöpfer, O mein Vernichter, O diese Messer, O diese aufgespießte Sonne.

Rosalie stürzt herbei und folgt an der Gittertür hinauf: Heinz zu dir, verbluten in der Sonne.«

Das sind die Schlußworte der Komposition.

Eintagswesen (»Ephemeral Beings«)
Play by Lars Norén
Nederlands Toneel Gent, 1986; director: Guy
Joosten, sets: Hans Dieter Schaal, costumes: Guy
Joosten and Christine Mortier, lighting: Steve Kemp

This too is an endgame. It remains unclear
whether we are watching something that happened way back in the past, whether we are seeing dead people who have been brought back
to life or people who actually are alive today. By
the end they are all dead, each in his own way.
Only the dog on the television screen is alive.
He keeps leaping against bars and barking. His
skeleton lies in front of him, in the real space of
the theatre.

Three couples who are friends with each other,
middle-aged, contemporary working nomads
who hardly have time to see each other during
the week but meet at the weekend in a smart,
modern weekend house. They talk and talk, banalities, old stories, problems with relationships.
More and more alcohol is drunk. The real gradually shifts into the surreal, and the doors to the
subconscious open. The figures become increasingly estranged, become more lonely, and entan-
gled in their memories. Each of them is moving
towards his or her death. Someone leans out of
the window and has disappeared for ever. De-
composition is at work in the midst of life, between the sentences, now.

The white space raft passes on its ghostly
way through the romantic city of Ghent. It floats
on the black canals, past the quays, on which
parked cars are standing like pale mummies.
Burnt trees stoop in front of petrified buildings.
A sunken world. Time burned to ashes.

Eintagswesen
Theaterstück von Lars Norén
Nederlands Toneel Gent, 1986; Inszenierung:
Guy Joosten, Bühne: Hans Dieter Schaal, Ko-
stüme: Guy Joosten und Christine Mortier, Licht:
Steve Kemp

Ein Endspiel auch hier. Es bleibt unklar, ob wir
etwas betrachten, was schon längst vergangen
ist, ob wir wiederbelebte Tote sehen oder wirkliche heute lebende Menschen. Am Ende sind alle
gestorben, jeder auf seine Weise. Nur noch der
Hund im TV-Bildschirm lebt. Er springt bellend
immer wieder gegen ein Gitter. Vor ihm, im realen
Theaterraum, liegt sein Skelett.

Drei befreundete Paare mittleren Alters, zeit-
genössische Arbeitsnomaden, die unter der Wo-
che kaum Zeit haben, sich zu sehen, treffen sich
am Wochenende in einem modernen, schicken
Wochenendhaus. Man redet und redet, Banalitäten, alte Geschichten, Beziehungsprobleme. Der
Alkoholkonsum steigt. Langsam verschiebt sich
die Realität ins Surreale. Türen zum Unterbe-
wußtsein tun sich auf. Die Figuren entfremden
sich, werden einsamer und verstricken sich in Erinnerungen. Jeder geht auf seinen Tod zu. Man
kippt aus dem Fenster und ist für alle Ewigkeit
verschwunden. Die Verwesung arbeitet mitten im
Leben, zwischen den Sätzen, jetzt.

Das weiße Raumfloß treibt gespenstisch weiter
durch die romantische Stadt Gent. Es schwimmt
auf den schwarzen Kanälen, an den Kais vorbei,
auf denen geparkte Autos wie fahle Mumien stehen. Verbrannte Bäume krümmen sich vor Haus-
versteinerungen. Versunkene Welt. Zu Asche verbrannte Zeit.

The Fall of the House of Usher

Opera fragment by Claude Debussy based on Edgar Allan Poe. – Staatstheater Stuttgart, 1996; conductor: Bernhard Kontarsky, director: Christof Nel, sets: Hans Dieter Schaal, costumes: Ilse Welter, dramaturgy: Sergio Morabito

If it were not for Juan Allende-Blin we would no longer have *The Fall of the House of Usher* as a composition by Debussy. The story of his research reads like a thriller. Debussy had been working on it for almost twenty years when he succumbed to his cancer in 1918 at the age of 56. After this, for some mysterious reason, individual pages of the score were spread almost all over the world. Allende-Blin managed to find most of them and fit them together to make a performable operatic fragment.

Debussy identified with Roderick, the decadent main character. As a composer he sensed that there was something absurd about his magical sounds in a world that was arming all around him and finally exploded into the catastrophe of the First World War. In addition to this, he was suffering from cancer, and was unhappily attracted to his stepdaughter.

The plot: Roderick Usher lives with his sister Madeline and a resident doctor in an ancient castle that is slowly falling to pieces. His state of mind is close to madness. He loves his sister, and above all her singing voice. He cannot live without her. The story starts when a friend of his youth turns up at the castle and tries to shake Roderick out of his gloomy frame of mind. The friend is told that Madeline has died in the night, but then she turns up, covered in blood, and takes Roderick out with her into death. The friend departs, horrified.

The setting: »Roderick Usher's room. Large, with a vaulted ceiling. Long, narrow windows high above an oak floor. The walls are hung with gloomy tapestries. On the left is a large fireplace … In the background, three steps lead to a french window with a view of a park, bordered by the stagnant waters of a pond …«

Roderick's inner state is like the outer state of the architecture. For Stuttgart a black ruined space was created, with double walls: there was a second, lighter room with windows behind. The few pieces of furniture stood around in the room like alien beings. A standard lamp gave a false sense of cosiness. A gloomy mood of decay.

Roderick: » … Old stones. Pale stones, what have you made of me? Whether a day goes, another comes, I belong to you. And you know it, you embrace me more firmly every day. Now I am like you, my thoughts eat me up like the winter rain. Old stones, do I have dark sins to atone for that I never committed? What have I done? You know, for you have known me from time immemorial … Do not admit the wings of death … I am afraid … I am afraid!«

Debussy could not complete this opera, and did not want to either. Perhaps it was too close to him: »Be quiet. You want to talk about my next piece: ›La Chute de la Maison Usher‹. It is not finished. When will it be finished? Soon. Never. I know nothing about it.« (Interview by Louis Vuillemin with Debussy on 17 December 1910)

Der Untergang des Hauses Usher

Opernfragment von Claude Debussy nach Edgar Allan Poe

Staatstheater Stuttgart, 1996; musikalische Leitung: Bernhard Kontarsky, Inszenierung: Christof Nel, Bühne: Hans Dieter Schaal, Kostüme: Ilse Welter, Dramaturgie: Sergio Morabito

Ohne Juan Allende-Blin gäbe es den *Untergang des Hauses Usher* als Debussy-Komposition nicht mehr. Die Geschichte seiner Recherche liest sich wie ein Kriminalroman. Debussy hatte bald zwanzig Jahre lang an diesem Werk komponiert, bis er 1918 im Alter von 56 Jahren seinem Krebsleiden erlag. Danach wurden die Einzelblätter aus unverständlichen Gründen fast über die ganze Welt verstreut. Allende-Blin gelang es, die meisten davon wieder aufzuspüren und zu einem aufführbaren Opernfragment zusammenzufügen.

Debussy identifizierte sich mit Roderick, der dekadenten Hauptfigur. Als Komponist spürte er, daß sein Klangzauber etwas Widersinniges hatte, in einer Welt, die ringsum aufrüstete und schließlich mit dem Ersten Weltkrieg katastrophal explodierte. Hinzu kam das Leiden an der Krebskrankheit und die unglückliche Neigung zu seiner Stieftochter.

Die Handlung: Roderick Usher lebt mit seiner Schwester Madeline und einem Hausarzt in einem uralten, langsam zerfallenden Schloß. Sein Gemütszustand nähert sich dem Wahnsinn. Er liebt seine Schwester, vor allem ihre Singstimme. Ohne sie kann er nicht leben. Die Geschichte setzt ein, als ein Jugendfreund im Schloß auftaucht und versucht, Roderick von seinen düsteren Gedanken zu befreien. Man sagt dem Jugendfreund, daß in der Nacht Madeline gestorben sei, aber dann taucht sie blutüberströmt auf und nimmt Roderick mit hinaus in den Tod. Entsetzt reist der Jugendfreund ab.

Der Bühnenbildraum: »Das Zimmer Roderick Ushers. Großer Raum mit Deckengewölbe. Lange, schmale Fenster hoch über einem Fußboden aus Eichenholz. Die Wände mit düsteren Wandteppichen bespannt. Links ein großer Kamin … Im Hintergrund führen drei Stufen zu einer Fenstertür, durch die man in einen Park blickt, der von fauligen Wassern eines Teichs begrenzt wird …«

Der innere Zustand Rodericks entspricht dem äußeren der Architektur. Für Stuttgart wurde ein schwarzer Ruinenraum aufgebaut, zweischalig: dahinter lag ein zweiter hellerer Raum mit Fenstern. Wie fremde Wesen standen die wenigen Möbel im Raum. Eine Stehlampe täuschte Gemütlichkeit vor. Düstere Stimmung des Verfalls.

Roderick: »… Alte Steine. Fahle Steine, was habt ihr aus mir gemacht? Ob ein Tag geht, ein anderer kommt, ich gehöre euch. Und ihr wißt es, mit jedem Tag umklammert ihr mich fester. Jetzt gleiche ich euch, meine Gedanken zerfressen mich wie euch der Winterregen. Alte Steine, habe ich dunkle Sünden zu büßen, die ich nicht beging? Was habe ich getan? Ihr wißt es, denn ihr kennt mich seit jeher. … Laßt die Flügel des Todes nicht herein … ich habe Angst … ich habe Angst!«

Debussy konnte und wollte diese Oper nicht zu Ende komponieren. Vielleicht war sie ihm zu nahe: »Schweigen Sie. Sie wollen auf mein nächstes Stück zu sprechen kommen: ›La Chute de la Maison Usher‹. Es ist nicht fertig. Wann es fertig wird? Bald. Niemals. Ich weiß darüber nichts.« (Interview von Louis Vuillemin mit Debussy am 17. Dezember 1910)

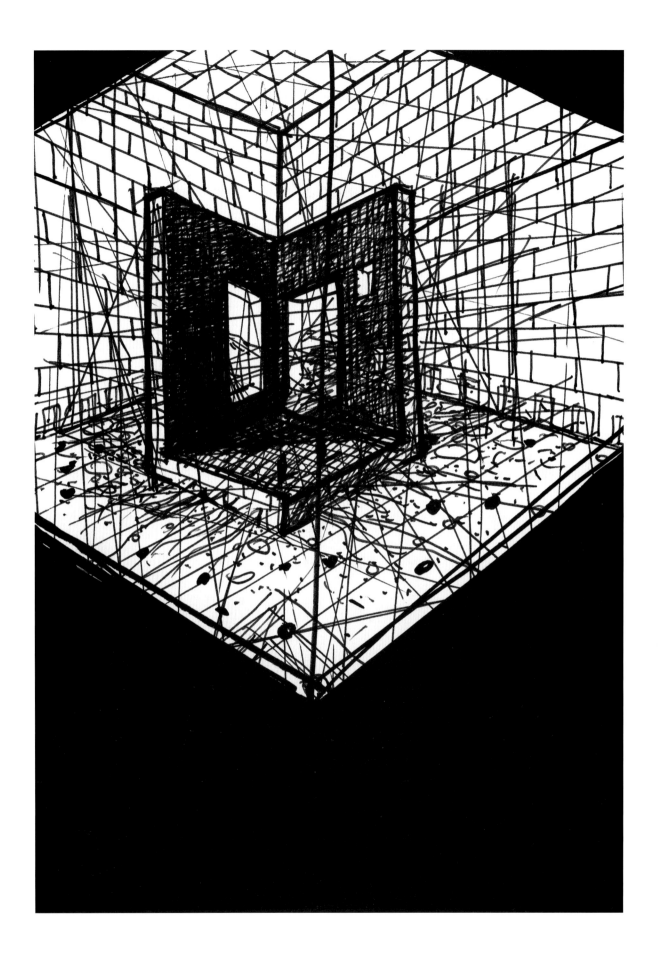

Doktor Faust

Poem for music in two preludes, an interlude and three main scenes by Ferruccio Busoni, libretto by the composer

Oper Nürnberg, 1998; conductor: Philipp Auguin, director: Jürgen Tamchina, sets: Hans Dieter Schaal, costumes: Beate Tamchina

Ferruccio Busoni was born in 1866 in Empoli in Italy and died in Berlin in 1924. He was fascinated by German culture throughout his life, probably because his mother was a German. He worked on *Doktor Faust* from 1914 to his death. With it he wanted to create nothing less than a symbiosis of southern and northern ways of feeling and thinking. He wrote the libretto for his main work himself, modelling it on an old puppet play. Goethe's *Faust* was an influence as well.

Busoni was not able to complete his *Doktor Faust* himself, and never saw it on stage. The work was first performed only a year after he died, completed by his pupil Philipp Jarnach, on 23 May 1925 at the Staatsoper in Dresden.

In Faust he had found a character that he could put to music and bring to life, someone who strives for the absolute in his innermost being, half universal scholar, half artist. Faust is not content with the everyday, he wants everything, universal knowledge and total life. In order to dream himself into this absolute space he has to enter into the devil's pact with Mephistopheles. By doing this he steps outside the existing cultural edifice. Outside there is no more good and evil, no top and no bottom. Space and time are

masses that he has totally at his disposal. His adventure in space and time has something of the quality of an intoxicated dream. The universe is in him and he is in the universe. A space traveller in the world of absolutely free thought. He is little disturbed by the fact that this makes him into a liar and a magician, a cynical seducer and a murderer. He has long since left all taboos behind him.

The fall comes abruptly: the journey was short, perhaps it lasted only a few seconds. The end remains a pitiful one, a death in the street.

Busoni developed his own theory of composition that in the field of opera resisted Italian Verismo in particular. His aim was absolute artificiality, he wanted a world of appearances and magic mirrors.

This is also why he went back to the old puppet play. He did not want to create anything new and revolutionary, but to revive the old stories in all their woodcut-like artificiality.

The plot: Faust is visited by three students in his Wittenberg study, who present him with a book. When they suddenly disappear, he realizes that they were messengers from an alternative world. Then Mephistopheles appears, and Faust signs his pact with the devil. After a soldier is murdered, the journey through time takes him to the court of Parma. Here Faust appears as a great magician, abducts the duchess and reappears in Wittenberg. His allotted span ends after a wild scene in an inn. He dies in a snowy street in Wittenberg. A naked youth comes out of the circle that has formed around him and walks through the snow into the town.

The libretto prescribes the following settings: »In front of the curtain. Study. High Gothic room, half library and half alchemist's kitchen ... Ancient Romanesque chapel in the minster. Bare grey walls, wooden pews, a crucifix ... The ducal park in Parma ... Inn in Wittenberg ... A snowy street in Wittenberg. On the left is one of the entrances to the minster. Round the corner, on the same wall, a life-size crucifix with a step in front of it. It is night.«

Our interpretation in Nuremberg was based on the concepts of time travel and the magic mirror.

The state represented a kind of spaceship, made up of several metallic, frame-like bulkheads arranged one behind the other. These could also be seen as planes in a mirror. A street running through the entire space connected the mirror images with each other. In the background a large window opened up on to the universe. Various elements were moved into this space from scene to scene: medieval gables, castle towers, tables, chairs, horses. There was also a kind of magic chest with a round projection screen that could be moved on rails from upstage right down to the orchestra pit. Faces appeared on the screen, body parts and the figures conjured up by Faust's magic: King Solomon, the Queen of Sheba, Samson and Delilah, Salome and Jokanaan (in the Parma scene).

The spectators were supposed to feel that they were floating through the universe in the spaceship, and that all our memories were accommodated in the belly of the ship – architectural, scientific and artistic. Consciousness space. Memory space. Fantasy space.

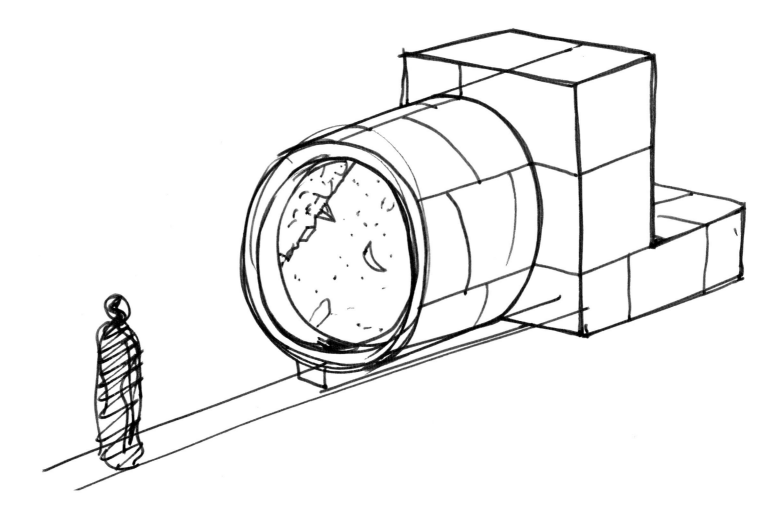

Doktor Faust

Dichtung für Musik in zwei Vorspielen, einem Zwischenspiel und drei Hauptbildern von Ferruccio Busoni, Text vom Komponisten

Oper Nürnberg, 1998; musikalische Leitung: Philipp Auguin, Inszenierung: Jürgen Tamchina, Bühne: Hans Dieter Schaal, Kostüme: Beate Tamchina

Ferruccio Busoni, der 1866 im italienischen Empoli geboren wurde und 1924 in Berlin starb, war Zeit seines Lebens von der deutschen Kultur fasziniert, was wahrscheinlich auch daran lag, daß seine Mutter Deutsche war. Mit dem Musikstück *Doktor Faust*, an dem er von 1914 bis zu seinem Tode arbeitete, wollte er nicht weniger als eine Symbiose aus südlichen und nördlichen Gefühls- und Denkweisen schaffen. Den Text zu seinem Hauptwerk hat er selbst nach dem Vorbild eines alten Puppenspiels verfaßt. Auch Goethes *Faust* stand Pate.

Busoni konnte seinen *Doktor Faust* nicht mehr selbst vollenden und hat ihn nie auf der Bühne gesehen. Erst ein Jahr nach seinem Tod wurde das Werk mit den Ergänzungen seines Schülers Philipp Jarnach am 23. Mai 1925 an der Dresdner Staatsoper uraufgeführt.

Mit Faust konnte er eine Figur vertonen und zum Leben erwecken, die im Innersten nach dem Absoluten strebt, halb Universalgelehrter, halb Künstler. Faust gibt sich nicht mit dem Alltäglichen zufrieden, er will alles, das universale Wissen und das totale Leben. Um sich in diesen Absolutheitsraum hineinzuträumen, muß er den Teufelspakt mit Mephistopheles eingehen. Er verläßt damit das vorhandene Kulturgebäude. Außerhalb gibt es kein Gut und Böse mehr, kein Oben und kein Unten. Raum und Zeit sind eine beliebig handhabbare Verfügungsmasse. Seine Zeit- und Abenteuerreise hat etwas von einem Rauschgifttraum. Das Weltall ist in ihm, er ist im Weltraum. Ein Raumfahrer der absolut freien Gedankenwelt. Daß er dabei zum Lügner und Zauberer wird, zum zynischen Verführer und zum Mörder, stört ihn wenig. Alle Tabus hat er längst hinter sich gelassen.

Der Absturz folgt abrupt: Die Reise war kurz, vielleicht nur sekundenlang. Das Ende bleibt kläglich, ein Tod auf der Straße.

Busoni hat eine eigene Kompositionslehre entwickelt, die sich im Opernbereich vor allem gegen den italienischen Verismo wendet. Sein Ziel war die absolute Künstlichkeit, er wollte die Scheinwelt und den Zauberspiegel.

Deswegen griff er auch auf das alte Puppenspiel zurück. Er wollte nichts revolutionär Neues schaffen, sondern die alten Geschichten in ihrer holzschnittartigen Künstlichkeit wiederbeleben.

Zur Handlung: In seiner Wittenberger Studierstube erhält Faust Besuch von drei Studenten, die ihm ein Buch übereichen. Als sie plötzlich verschwunden sind, weiß er, daß sie Boten der Gegenwelt waren. Dann erscheint Mephistopheles, und er unterschreibt den Teufelspakt. Nach der Ermordung eines Soldaten geht die Zeitreise an den Hof von Parma. Dort tritt Faust als großer Zauberer auf, entführt die Herzogin und erscheint wieder in Wittenberg. Nach einer wilden Schenkenszene endet seine Frist. Er stirbt auf einer verschneiten Straße in Wittenberg. Ein nackter Jüngling steigt aus dem Kreis, der sich um ihn gebildet hat, und geht durch den Schnee in die Stadt hinein.

Das Libretto schreibt folgende Bühnenbildorte vor: »Vor dem Vorhang. Studierstube. Hoher gotischer Raum, halb Bibliothek und halb alchemistische Küche ... Uralte romanische Kapelle im Münster. Kahle graue Wände, Holzbänke, ein Kruzifix ... Der herzogliche Park zu Parma ... Schenke in Wittenberg ... Verschneite Straße in Wittenberg. Links einer der Eingänge zum Münster. Um die Ecke, an der nämlichen Mauer, ein lebensgroßes Kruzifix mit Kniestufe davor. Es ist Nacht.«

Unsere Interpretation in Nürnberg ging von den Begriffen der Zeitreise und des Zauberspiegels aus.

Der Raum stellte eine Art Raumschiff dar, gebildet durch mehrere hintereinander gestaffelte, metallische, rahmenartige Schotten. Diese konnte man auch als Spiegelebenen sehen. Eine den ganzen Raum durchragende Straße verband die Spiegelbilder miteinander. Im Hintergrund öffnete sich ein großes Fenster, das den Blick in das Weltall freigab. In diesen Raum schoben sich von Szene zu Szene verschiedene Elemente: mittelalterliche Giebel, Burgtürme, Tische, Stühle, Pferde. Es gab auch eine Art Zauberkiste mit runder Projektionsfläche, die auf einer Schiene von hinten bis vorne zum Orchestergraben fahren konnte. Auf der Fläche erschienen Gesichter, Körperteile und die von Faust herbeigezauberten Figuren: König Salomo, die Königin von Saba, Samson und Dalila, Salome und Jochanaan (im Parma-Bild).

Dem Zuschauer sollte das Gefühl vermittelt werden, er schwebe mit dem Raumschiff durch das All, und im Bauch des Schiffes sei unser gesamtes Erinnerungsgut – architektonisch, wissenschaftlich und künstlerisch – untergebracht. Bewußtseinsraum. Erinnerungsraum. Phantasieraum.

Tristan und Isolde

Music drama in three acts by Richard Wagner, libretto by the composer

Hamburgische Staatsoper, 1988; conductor: Zoltan Pesko, director: Ruth Berghaus, sets: Hans Dieter Schaal, costumes: Marie-Luise Strandt, dramaturgy: Sigrid Neef

Guest performance at the Teatro Comunale di Bologna, 1996; conductor: Christian Thielemann

And to finish, Richard Wagner again with his most extreme work: great love as an ecstatic religion for the universe. It is not a god whose praises are being sung here, but the longing for redemption in the other, in the beloved opposite. There is no banal everyday world any more, there is only Tristan and Isolde and an absolute desire to fuse one another, physically-erotically and psychologically-mentally. This highest rapture, this epitome of soaring can exist only in death. The absolute cannot put up with getting up in the morning, washing, showering, eating, taking the rubbish out, talking banalities, this absolute wants to be silent for ever and for ever in the cosmos, in death.

Tristan had been sent to Ireland by King Mark to woo Isolde on his behalf and bring her back. During the sea crossing, Tristan and Isolde decide to seek death because Isolde feels that she has been betrayed by Tristan. But instead of a death potion her intimate friend hands them a love potion. The effect is conclusive: the two fall into each other's arms in the grip of complete erotic passion. But Tristan has to take King Mark's betrothed to him in Cornwall. But after this, Tristan and Isolde meet each other again – at night. They are discovered. Seeking death, Tristan hurls himself on to his assailant's sword. Seriously wounded, he spends his last days at his ancestral castle in Brittany. When Isolde and King Mark appear, Tristan rips all the bandages from his body and bleeds to death. Isolde sings herself to death in ecstatic rapture.

The settings: »Act One: a tent-like chamber on the foredeck of a ship, lavishly hung with tapestries, completely closed in the background at the beginning, at the side a narrow flight of steps leads down to the rest of the deck. Act Two: garden with tall trees outside Isolde's chambers, to which steps rise at the side. Light, pleasant summer night. A burning torch is placed by the open door. Act Three: Castle garden. On one side is a high castle, on the other a low parapet, interrupted by a watchtower; in the background is the castle gate. It is to be assumed that the site is on top of a cliff; apertures reveal a broad view of the sea stretching to the horizon. The whole scene exudes an air of abandonment, badly cared for, here and there damaged and overgrown. In the foreground, on the inner side, Tristan is lying, in the shade of a great lime tree, sleeping on a couch, stretched out as if lifeless …«

Our interpretation in Hamburg made no attempt at realism. Psychological spaces. Romantic feelings caught up in the force of reality, the mechanism, the turbines of the night. Nature exists only as a cosmos. On earth it has disappeared completely under steel skins.

Tristan music is the music of the future, composed transcendence, euphoric longing for the joint death in the cosmos. Tristan and Isolde love

their ecstasy and Richard Wagner's music. They are music-eroticists. They would be nothing without music. With it they are everything in the eternal night of the cosmos. Their nocturnal love is the new religion. The moon is their companion, the sun their enemy.

The end: The moon has crashed, the romanticism is destroyed. The lovers have been killed by their own desire. The planets circle on indifferently above the ruins of romanticism.

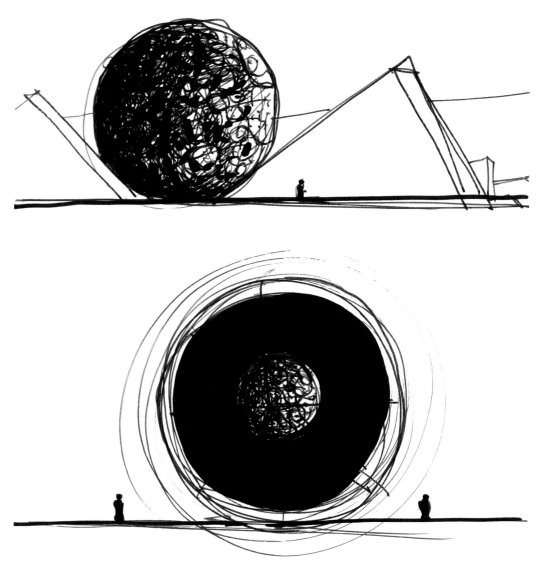

Tristan und Isolde

Handlung in drei Aufzügen von Richard Wagner, Text vom Komponisten

Hamburgische Staatsoper, 1988; musikalische Leitung: Zoltan Pesko, Inszenierung: Ruth Berghaus, Bühne: Hans Dieter Schaal, Kostüme: Marie-Luise Strandt, Dramaturgie: Sigrid Neef

Gastspiel im Teatro Comunale di Bologna, 1996; musikalische Leitung: Christian Thielemann

Zum Schluß noch einmal Richard Wagner mit seinem extremsten Werk: Die große Liebe als ekstatische Weltall-Religion. Kein Gott wird hier besungen, sondern die Sehnsucht nach Erlösung im andern, im geliebten Gegenüber. Es gibt keinen banalen Alltag mehr, es gibt nur noch Tristan und Isolde und die absolute Sehnsucht, miteinander zu verschmelzen, körperlich-erotisch und seelisch-geistig. Dieses höchste Glück, dieses Schweben schlechthin kann es nur im Tod geben. Das Absolute duldet kein morgendliches Aufstehen, Waschen, Duschen, Essen, Müll rausbringen, Banalitätsreden, dieses Absolute will schweigen für immer und ewig im Weltall, im Tod.

Als Brautwerber hat Tristan für König Marke Isolde aus Irland geholt. Auf der Überfahrt suchen die beiden den Tod, weil sich Isolde von Tristan verraten fühlt. Statt eines Todestranks verabreicht ihre Vertraute ihnen jedoch einen Liebestrank. Die Wirkung ist durchschlagend: Mit voller erotischer Wucht fallen sie sich in die Arme. Aber Tristan hat die Braut bei König Marke in Cornwall abzuliefern. Danach treffen sie sich jedoch weiterhin – nachts. Sie werden entdeckt. Den Tod suchend, stürzt sich Tristan in das Schwert seines Angreifers. Schwer verletzt verbringt er seine letzten Tage auf seinem Stammschloß in der Bretagne. Als Isolde und König Marke auftauchen, reißt sich Tristan alle Verbände vom Körper und verblutet. Isolde singt sich in ekstatischer Verzückung zu Tode.

Die Bühnenbild-Orte: »Erster Aufzug: Zeltartiges Gemach auf dem Vorderdeck eines Seeschiffes, reich mit Teppichen behangen, beim Beginn nach dem Hintergrunde zu gänzlich geschlossen, zur Seite führt eine schmale Treppe in den Schiffsraum hinab. Zweiter Aufzug: Garten mit hohen Bäumen vor dem Gemach Isoldes, zu welchem, seitwärts gelegen, Stufen hinaufführen. Helle, anmutige Sommernacht. An der geöffneten Türe ist eine brennende Fackel aufgesteckt. Dritter Aufzug: Burggarten. Zur einen Seite hohe Burggebäude, zur anderen eine niedrige Mauerbrüstung, von einer Warte unterbrochen; im Hintergrunde das Burgtor. Die Lage ist auf felsiger Höhe anzunehmen; durch Öffnungen blickt man auf einen weiten Meereshorizont. Das Ganze macht den Eindruck der Herrenlosigkeit, übel gepflegt, hie und da schadhaft und bewachsen. Im Vordergrunde, an der inneren Seite, liegt Tristan, unter dem Schatten einer großen Linde, auf einem Ruhebett schlafend, wie leblos ausgestreckt ...«

Unsere Interpretation in Hamburg suchte keinen Realismus. Es sollten innere Zustände dargestellt werden. Seelenräume. Romantische Gefühle, die in die Gewalt der Realität geraten, in das Räderwerk, in die Turbinen der Nacht. Natur gibt es nur noch als Weltall. Auf der Erde ist sie ganz unter Stahlhäuten verschwunden.

Tristan-Musik ist Zukunftsmusik, komponierte Transzendenz, euphorische Sehnsucht nach dem gemeinsamen Sterben im Weltall. Tristan und Isolde lieben ihre Ekstase und die Musik Richard Wagners. Sie sind Musik-Erotiker. Ohne Musik wären sie nichts. Mit ihr sind sie alles in der ewigen Nacht des Alls. Ihre nächtliche Liebe ist die neue Religion. Der Mond ist ihr Gefährte, die Sonne ihr Feind.

Das Ende: Der Mond ist abgestürzt, die Romantik vernichtet. Das Liebespaar ist von der eigenen Sehnsucht erschlagen worden. Über dem Trümmerfeld der Romantik kreisen die Planeten teilnahmslos weiter.

Hans Dieter Schaal in conversation with Frank R. Werner

Werner: When did you start to take an interest in theatre, in opera, in set design, how did it all come about?

Schaal: I was lucky enough to be a schoolboy in Ulm when the legendary Hübner team was at the municipal theatre there. I saw famous productions by Zadek (of Brendan Behan's *The Hostage*, for example), by Johannes Schaaf and Alfred Kirchner. It was usually Wilfried Minks who designed their sets. I was very enthusiastic, and wrote about them in our school magazine. But of course enthusiasm is not enough. After vain attempts to have a stage design commissioned while I was studying architecture in Hanover and Stuttgart, I decided that this practical side of things was dead as far I was concerned. The door to theatre as a real field did not open for me until 1982, when Klaus Zehelein rang me up to ask me if I would like to do the designs for Hector Berlioz's *The Trojans* at the Frankfurter Oper.

Werner: What had made him think of you?

Schaal: My books. After graduating I had published *Wege und Wegräume*, *Ulm Neu* and *Architektonische Situationen*. Zehelein inferred from the drawings that I was the right man for the theatre and the opera.

Werner: The theatre field is just one theme among many for you. Your view of the world is encyclopaedic. Nevertheless the fleeting location that is the stage seems to appeal to something fundamental in you.

Schaal: A stage set creates a new kind of reality, a second surreal world that has a great deal to do with images in the mind. The stage is a magic box, a mental space in which things that are otherwise concealed become visible. It is possible to stage pictorial and architectural dramas, secretly in the background, almost incidentally. Blocks of disaster and islands of happiness break in as though people had just been dreaming about them. The pictorial spaces are visible to the audience, but they cannot walk into them or touch them.

Werner: How do you go about things in concrete terms when you are commissioned to design a stage set for material you are not familiar with. How do you approach the subject from case to case?

Schaal: Obviously you start working on the material, and the dramaturg helps you with that. There are a lot of meetings. You come up with suggestions, work on a certain way of looking at or interpreting things and finally design a space or a sequence of pictorial spaces that will provide the best context for the play or the opera to make its maximum effect. What remains important is the subjective interpretation. How does this material, this music affect me today? What does the play trigger for me? What do I think about that? Later the audience have to sense and see this attitude that lies behind the sets. Art comes about when everything fuses into a powerful whole and the work comes to life as it never has before.

Werner: How do you see the role of the temporary space-image, the »temporary world«, if you like? I mean, does it have a dominant or a »servant« role? Is there a fundamental difference between sets for the theatre and sets for the opera?

Schaal: The opera tends more towards surreal emotion and drama, it is essentially a theatrical medium that has taken off. Music makes everything float. Theatre is more earthbound, and also inclines more towards realism, despite all the possible poetry. It is possible to argue about whether the set should be reticent or play a particular part. As a pictorial thinker the sets are almost all that I can remember when I think back, I always forget the plots.

Werner: When you work your way into a stage play, an opera libretto, a ballet choreography, and offer directors, actors and audience spatial dream »locations«, then you are helping to determine part of the course of the action and the requirements of the production. Wouldn't it in fact make better sense to let the designer direct the show from the outset? Or do you see advantages in restriction?

Schaal: The designer does direct indirectly, he determines the location, the atmosphere, he provides ways of appearing and disappearing. Handling actors, singers and dancers is a very different job.

Werner: Who have been the directors you've found it most satisfying to work with hitherto? And why?

Schaal: My favourite director will always be one who makes best use of the space I put at his or her disposal, who absorbs it completely and works creatively in it. Of course it was exciting working with Ruth Berghaus, but other directors I've worked with have also been able to handle my spaces. Christof Nel, Nicolas Brieger, Niels-Peter Rudolph, Arila Siegert, Dominik Neuner, Jürgen Tamchina, Katrin Hilbe, Martin Schüler, Guy Joosten ... they all discover different possibilities, they all develop their own aversions and preferences. I always find it a stimulating dialogue.

Werner: Have your experiences as an exhibition and landscape designer or architect stood you in good stead when designing stage sets, or vice versa? Are these three fundamentally different trades, or do they complement each other?

Schaal: I am always fascinated by cross-connections: a stage set in a garden, showcases on stage. All the media involve concealing and revealing, describing and exaggerating, poeticizing, romanticizing and building up a violent charge. At exhibitions you have no control over how visitors behave, how they move around and look at things, and the same applies to parks and gardens. It is only in the theatre that everything is rehearsed, the light comes up at the appointed moment, the singer sings her aria here and everything contributes to producing the best possible image. To this extent theatre is a space demanding obedience on the one hand (for the performers above all) and on the other hand it is also a dream-like condition. This is related to chance in reality, to the state of openness on the one hand and a planned state on the other.

Werner: Has your appearance on the scene as someone who »crept in by the back door« (and extraordinarily successfully at that) ever caused you any problems?

Schaal: The advantage of my late entrance to the stage design sphere was above all that I had time to let my ideas mature. The experimental phase, just fiddling around and trying things out, happened off stage. So to this extent there weren't really any problems.

Werner: Are you mentally and artistically comfortable with the job of creating »space-time architecture« not in real time, but in the form of shortened, compressed or highly abbreviated temporary images? Do you not slow down, ritualize, spiritualize, dream the diffuse and the subliminal to make them into quite contemplative, archetypal places that could sometimes hold their own within the architectural reality of the outside world?

Schaal: Yes, certainly. Sometimes you do dream of translating certain things into urban reality. Every morning when you step to the window the town is the same, nothing has changed, only the light and the weather. Of course there are building sites. But it is still exciting to imagine a town that can change: all the buildings on wheels, ships and revolves, façades suspended from gigantic cranes, soft buildings, hard buildings, dancing buildings, empty and hollow buildings. Light games, projections. It occurs to me that there is no German city – with one exception – that still has a ruin from the last war, which I think is a pity. Eiermann's idea of preserving the bomb-damaged Gedächtniskirche in the middle of Berlin turns out to be more and more brilliant the further we get away from the time when all this happened. One German city should have been preserved completely in its damaged condition. One would have been enough.

Werner: What is the role of artificial, staged light, that is to say staged lighting for your sets? To what extent do you involve yourself in the subject of lighting?

Schaal: Lighting is very important. The stage as such is dark, a black box. It is incredibly exciting to see these spaces that have been set up for a particular piece being brought to life by lighting.

Werner: How do you handle – if it is unavoidable – naturalistic elements, bright colours, picturesque moments, pseudo-historical costumes, folklore etc?

Schaal: My style moves between geometrical reduction and expressionist emphasis. Naturalistic corners, zones or suggestions crop up from time to time (baths, living rooms or elements of external town, for example). But realistic naturalism, of the kind used in films, for example, does not work in the theatre any longer. It seems unsophisticated and bourgeois. And nature itself – leaves, trees, rocks etc. – won't do either. Elements like this are always a bit of an embarrassment on stage. The stage is an art-space, everything is artificial. History and historical echoes do occur in my work, however, folklore does not, of course.

Werner: Has the peepshow view, the view with a shortened perspective, the view over a diagonal plane influenced or changed the rest of your artistic output since you started working in the theatre? Surely this way of looking at things has both its positive and its negative aspects?

Schaal: Yes, that certainly did influence me. How precisely I can't say. I think in the theatre that the main factor is concentration. And the vanishing point is always the most important concentration

Hans Dieter Schaal im Gespräch mit Frank R. Werner

Werner: Seit wann besteht dein Interesse am Theater, an der Oper, am Bühnenbild, wie kam es dazu?

Schaal: Ich hatte das Glück, meine Schulzeit in Ulm zu verbringen, als das legendäre Hübnerteam am dortigen Stadttheater wirkte. Ich habe damals die berühmten Inszenierungen von Zadek (beispielsweise *Die Geisel* von Brendan Behan) von Johannes Schaaf und Alfred Kirchner gesehen. Meist war es Wilfried Minks, der dafür die Bühnenbilder schuf. Ich war begeistert und schrieb darüber in unserer Schülerzeitung. Aber Begeisterung reicht natürlich nicht aus. Nach vergeblichen Versuchen, während meines Architekturstudiums in Hannover und Stuttgart, an einen Bühnenbild-Auftrag zu kommen, habe ich diese praktische Seite für mich beerdigt. Erst ein Anruf von Klaus Zehelein 1982, der mich fragte, ob ich die Ausstattung zu den *Trojanern* von Hector Berlioz an der Frankfurter Oper übernehmen wolle, öffnete mir die Tür in den realen Theaterbereich.

Werner: Wie ist er auf dich aufmerksam geworden?

Schaal: Durch meine Bücher. Ich hatte nach dem Studium *Wege und Wegräume*, *Ulm Neu*, und *Architektonische Situationen* veröffentlicht. Zehelein hat aus den Zeichnungen geschlossen, daß ich der Richtige für das Theater und die Oper sei.

Werner: Der Bereich Theater ist für dich nur ein Thema von vielen. Dein Blick auf die Welt ist enzyklopädisch. Trotzdem scheint der flüchtige Ort der Bühne etwas Wesentliches in dir anzusprechen.

Schaal: Das Bühnenbild schafft eine neue Art von Realität, eine zweite surreale Welt, die sehr viel mit Bildern im Kopf zu tun hat. Der Bühnenraum ist eine Zauberkiste, ein Seelenraum, in dem Dinge sichtbar werden, die sonst verborgen sind. Es lassen sich Bild- und Architekturdramen inszenieren, heimlich im Hintergrund, wie nebenher. Die Katastrophenblöcke und die Glücksinseln brechen herein, als hätte man gerade von ihnen geträumt. Die Bildräume sind für die Zuschauer zwar sichtbar aber unbetretbar und unberührbar.

Werner: Wenn du den Auftrag erhältst, ein Bühnenbild zu einem dir nicht ganz geläufigen Stoff zu erschaffen, wie gehst du dann konkret vor? Wie näherst du dich dem Sujet von Fall zu Fall?

Schaal: Du beschäftigst dich mit dem Stoff, der Dramaturg oder die Dramaturgin hilft dir dabei. Es gibt zahlreiche Treffen. Man erarbeitet Vorschläge, feilt an einer bestimmten Sehweise und Interpretation und entwirft schließlich einen Raum oder eine Bildraumfolge, von der man glaubt, daß in ihr das Stück oder die Oper am besten zur Wirkung kommt. Wichtig bleibt die subjektive Interpretation. Wie wirkt der Stoff, die Musik heute auf mich? Was löst das Stück in mir aus? Wie stehe ich dazu? Der Zuschauer muß später die Haltung spüren und sehen, die hinter den Bildern steht. Kunst kommt dann zustande, wenn sich alles zu einem kraftvollen Ganzen fügt und das Werk lebt wie nie zuvor.

Werner: Wie siehst du die Rolle des temporären Raum-Bildes, der »Welt auf Zeit«, wenn man so will? Das heißt, kommt ihr eine dominierende oder eine »dienende« Aufgabe zu? Besteht dabei ein wesentlicher Unterschied zwischen Bühnenbildern für das Theater und solchen für die Oper?

Schaal: Die Oper neigt mehr zu surrealem Pathos, sie ist in sich ein abgehobenes Medium für das Theater. Musik läßt alles schweben. Theater ist bodenständiger, neigt meist auch mehr zum Realismus, bei aller möglichen Poesie. Ob sich das Bühnenbild eher zurückhalten oder eine bestimmende Rolle spielen soll, darüber kann man sich streiten. Ich als Bilderdenker kann mich fast nur an Bühnenbilder erinnern, wenn ich zurückdenke, die Handlungen habe ich vergessen.

Werner: Wenn du dich in ein Sprechtheater, ein Opernlibretto, eine Tanzchoreographie einarbeitest und Regisseuren, Akteuren und Zuschauern traum-räumliche »Verortungen« anbietest, dann bestimmst du ja einen Teil der Handlungsabläufe, der Regievorgaben mit. Wäre es da nicht von vornherein sinnvoller, den Bühnenbildner auch immer Regie führen zu lassen? Oder siehst du in der Beschränkung auch Vorteile?

Schaal: Der Bühnenbildner führt indirekt Regie, er bestimmt den Ort, die Atmosphäre, er gibt Möglichkeiten des Auftretens und des Verschwindens vor. Der Umgang mit Schauspielern, Sängern und Tänzern ist ein ganz anderes Metier.

Werner: Mit welchen Regisseurinnen, welchen Regisseuren hast du bisher am fruchtbarsten zusammengearbeitet? Und warum?

Schaal: Der liebste Regisseur ist mir derjenige, der meine Räume am besten benutzt, der sie ganz in sich aufnimmt und in ihnen kreativ wird. Man sieht und spürt das. Natürlich war die Arbeit mit Ruth Berghaus aufregend, aber auch die anderen Regisseure, mit denen ich gearbeitet habe, konnten mit meinen Räumen etwas anfangen. Christof Nel, Nicolas Brieger, Niels-Peter Rudolph, Arila Siegert, Dominik Neuner, Jürgen Tamchina, Katrin Hilbe, Martin Schüler, Guy Joosten ... jeder entdeckt andere Möglichkeiten, jeder entwickelt eigene Aversionen und Vorlieben. Für mich ist das immer wieder ein anregender Dialog.

Werner: Kamen dir bislang deine Erfahrungen als Ausstellungs- und Landschaftsgestalter bzw. Architekt beim Entwerfen von Bühnenbildern zugute, oder umgekehrt? Sind das drei grundverschiedene oder komplementäre Metiers?

Schaal: Mich reizen die Querverbindungen sehr: ein Bühnenbild im Garten, Vitrinen auf der Bühne. Alle Medien haben zu tun mit Zeigen und Verbergen, mit Beschreibung und Übertreibung, mit Poetisierung, Romantisierung und gewaltsamer Aufladung. Bei Ausstellungen hast du nicht in der Hand, wie sich die Besucher verhalten, wie sie gehen und schauen, auch in Gärten und Parks nicht, nur im Theater ist alles einstudiert, das Licht leuchtet an der geplanten Stelle auf, die Sängerin singt hier ihre Arie, alles ist optimiert zum bestmöglichen Bild. Insofern ist das Theater einerseits ein Gehorsamsraum (vor allem für die Darsteller), zum anderen auch ein traumhafter Zustand. Das hat mit dem Zufall in der Realität zu tun, mit dem Aggregatszustand der Offenheit einerseits, der geplanten Hermetik andererseits.

Werner: Hat dir dein Auftreten in der Szene als »Seiteneinsteiger« (noch dazu als ein außerordentlich erfolgreicher) je Probleme bereitet?

Schaal: Der Vorteil meines späten Einstiegs in den Bühnenbildbereich war vor allem der, daß ich Zeit hatte, meine Überlegungen ausreifen zu lassen. Die Experimentierphase, das bloße Herumprobieren geschah im Verborgenen. Insofern kann man nicht von Problemen sprechen.

Werner: Kommt dir der Job des Erschaffens einer »Raum-Zeit-Architektur« nicht in Echtzeit, sondern in Gestalt geraffter, komprimierter oder extrem verkürzter Bilder auf Zeit mental, künstlerisch entgegen? Verlangsamst, ritualisiert, spiritualisiert, träumst du das Diffuse, Unterschwellige nicht zu ganz kontemplativen, archetypischen Orten, die mitunter auch in der architektonischen Realität draußen genauso Bestand haben könnten?

Schaal: Ja, bestimmt. Man träumt manchmal davon, manches auch in die Realität der Stadt zu übersetzen. Jeden Morgen, wenn du ans Fenster trittst, ist die Stadt die gleiche, nichts hat sich verändert, nur das Licht und das Wetter. Natürlich gibt es Baustellen. Aber es ist schon spannend, sich eine Stadt vorzustellen, die sich verändert: alle Häuser auf Rädern, Schiffen und Drehscheiben, Fassaden hängen an riesigen Kränen, weiche Häuser, harte Häuser, tanzende Häuser, leere und hohle Häuser. Lichtspiele, Projektionen. Mir fällt auf, daß es in keiner deutschen Stadt mehr – mit einer Ausnahme – eine Ruine aus dem letzten Krieg gibt, was ich schade finde. Eiermanns Idee, die Gedächtniskirche in ihrem zerstörten Zustand mitten in Berlin zu konservieren, entpuppt sich heute, je weiter wir uns vom Zeitpunkt der Ereignisse entfernen, als immer genialer. Man hätte eine deutsche Stadt ganz in ihrem zerstörten Zustand erhalten sollen. Eine hätte genügt.

Werner: Welche Rolle spielt das künstliche, inszenierte Licht, sprich die Bühnenbeleuchtung für deine Bilder? Wie weit mischst du dich in das Thema Licht ein?

Schaal: Licht ist sehr wichtig. Der Bühnenraum an sich ist ja dunkel, eine black box. Es ist unglaublich spannend, diese für das jeweilige Stück aufgebauten Räume mit Licht zum Leben zu erwecken.

Werner: Wie gehst du – wenn es unumgänglich ist – mit Naturalismen, Buntheit, dem Pittoresken, historisierenden Kostümen, der Folklore usw. um?

Schaal: Mein Stil bewegt sich zwischen geometrischer Reduktion und expressionistischer Zuspitzung. Es gibt immer wieder naturalistische Ecken, Zonen oder Andeutungen (Bäder, Wohnzimmer oder Elemente der äußeren Stadt zum Beispiel). Aber realistischer Naturalismus, wie er im Film oft eingesetzt wird, funktioniert im Theater nicht mehr. Das wirkt bieder und spießig. Und Natur selbst – Blätter, Bäume, Felsen usw. – geht auch nicht. Auf der Bühne wirken diese Elemente immer peinlich. Bühne ist ein Kunstraum, alles ist künstlich. Geschichte und historische Anklänge dagegen kommen bei mir schon vor, Folklore natürlich nicht.

Werner: Hat der Guckkasten-Blick, hat der perspektivisch verkürzte Blick, hat der Blick über die schräge Ebene dein übriges künstlerisches Schaffen seither beeinflußt, verändert? Denn diese Art zu sehen hat ja durchaus positive und negative Aspekte.

Schaal: Ja, das hat mich bestimmt beeinflußt. Wie genau, kann ich nicht sagen. Ich denke, im

point. We are individuals – one person – we have only one line of vision, we can pursue only one city offers variety, falls apart into thousands of images, all at the same time, that is certainly entertaining, but it can get on your nerves as well, and creates confusion. Every statement remains a superficial splinter, there is nothing but the surface.

Werner: Wouldn't you prefer to design sets for a total theatre, a lake stage you can see into from at least three sides (like Bregenz, for example), rather than a proscenium stage. And if so, why?

Schaal: No, I can pick up what I just said before here: the clearly defined location – here am I, and there is the stage – means that points of view cannot get muddled up. Here you can achieve the kind of concentration that isn't possible in the city. The city is total theatre, the proscenium stage is the opposite. A cult place as well. A thousand people are sitting and looking at an image, at a hole, in anticipation – of what?

Werner: What did you do at the time you first started working for Ruth Berghaus that was so fundamentally different from what your stage designer colleagues were doing? Because if you hadn't done something differently the specialist world wouldn't have become aware of you all of a sudden. And has something of this »doing things differently« survived until today?

Schaal: I can't really say that myself. Perhaps it was the architectural aspect that hadn't been so radically present before. And at that time I also picked up more on the tradition of the 20s (Russian Revolutionary art and the Bauhaus) than the art movements that were prevalent in the 80s. It would be interesting to follow all these connections through some time – and to do the same for exhibition design and landscape architecture as well.

Werner: Why is it that in almost all your stage designs (and in your exhibition designs as well) you use para- or proto-architectural landscapes or settings, often supported by a suggestion of concrete, beams, shades of grey in grey, and white space-containers?

Schaal: For me that is the specific element of the architectural aspect, it is simply part of my style. Style in fact means limitation. Constriction. You deny yourself certain things and develop a formal language within the restrictions you have imposed upon yourself.

Werner: Are there any limits for you as a set designer (for example if you had to design a completely empty space)? And if you can identify any boundaries like this, then where and why?

Schaal: I have already described the limits. But you redefine them with each design. Empty space is interesting as well. To a certain extent it is the starting point for almost every train of thought. Perhaps one limit would be – it has just occurred to me: designing a conventional, traditional stage set. They do still crop up, these spaces, in Romance countries in particular, with backcloths, sunbeams, Italian piazzas and ancient columns. The opera audience is very conservative and dreams backwards. This has to do with the »good old days«, but let's not say any more about that.

Werner: Would you prefer to design more realistic film sets, moving sequences of images, rather than stylized, static stage landscapes? Where do you see the main qualitative difference between film and stage sets, apart from the fact that on the stage you of course have to deal with living, real bodies in »temporarily real« space?

Schaal: That subject is dealt with in the body of this book. Of course film and television are the up-to-date medium for the 21st century. I would very much like to work in this field. I have in fact written a book about film and architecture, and addressing these themes was central to my work in the Berlin film museum. It strikes me incidentally that there is no comparable theatre museum. We do not take the medium of the stage set seriously as an artistic discipline. That is certainly a mistake. In film – with the exception of Science Fiction films – realistic design has become generally accepted. But that does not have to remain the case. I can definitely imagine that there will be films again sometime that are more artificial and dreamy than they are today.

Werner: What is the source of the almost »priestly« suggestive power, the dramatic impact of your sets in the context of the particular plots they serve?

Schaal: I can scarcely say that myself. If it is true, so much the better. Perhaps it is because of the serious approach that has become so rare today and the radical concentration on a very few elements?

Werner: In your stage sets, how do you tackle the »forbidden look«, the voyeuristic attitude, the look that has been desecrated by breaking a taboo (for example concentration camps or Fascism)?

Schaal: Concealing and revealing plays a key role in my designs. And concealing is often the more important of the two. I do not wish to be an exhibitionist. Each scene is an open wound. Provocation and the breaking of taboos are part of this. And I have always been someone who crosses borders as well.

Werner: What part does the concept of »assimilation« have to play in your stage designs?

Schaal: I am very interested in that. I want to see the aggression that someone develops when faced with my walls, and I want to see the affection as well. Assimilation arises as a result of habit. If we see things frequently, we become familiar with them and internalize them. We are enslaved to doors and windows. Only our beds take us in silently every evening, warmly and cosily. All other elements are our external opposites. In my garden designs I am often confronted with vandalism: things are daubed with paint, pulled down, set on fire, rubbish is thrown at them etc. – what am I supposed to say about that, actually it should please me, but in all honesty …

Werner: My third-from-last question: why do you think your »scenae« always have something fateful or fundamental about them, regardless of their being fixed in terms of time and subject?

Schaal: Yes, that is probably because of my preference for tragic aspects. I like melodrama, and I am sceptical about happy endings. I am interested in failure and things coming to an end. Dance-of-death stories.

Werner: And picking up at precisely that point, the last question but one: why are your designs always so serious? Or put another way: how do you handle things that are light, fragile, ethereal, or with absurd, ironic, humorous material?

Schaal: I don't know either. Fundamentally I like funny things, I like humour, and above all irony. Perhaps I should work on that a bit harder.

Werner: A final, somewhat provocative question to someone who has been building exhibition architecture, designing parks, constructing installations and realizing buildings as well as working in theatres for a long time now: could it be that the stage world is actually more interesting, more exciting and ultimately more realistic for you as well than the world out there, because it has more options and connotations to offer? If yes, why precisely? And if it really is the case, which world do you live in?

Schaal: Like museums, theatres are protected fortresses. There are official figures at every end and turn, tearing your ticket or taking your coat. You feel safe here. Your architectures are guarded like serious offenders. Everything that you set up outside – I was just talking about this – is unprotected and at the mercy of the public, and thus vulnerable and open to destruction. It does not belong to anyone, it is fair game. What does that mean? The city in a state of latent civil war, protected bubbles of space inside it in which it is possible to dream?

Despite all the split quality, it is perhaps really the case that the theatre and the opera – along with museums and galleries – are the last reservations in which it is possible to reflect about being human, fate, love, hatred, life and death. Art and cult still belong together here. Opened up as in a laboratory, expanded in the manner of a workshop. Near to the power station that drives us all.

Theater geht es vor allem um Konzentration. Und der Fluchtpunkt ist immer noch der wichtigste Konzentrationspunkt. Wir sind Individuen – eins – wir haben einen Blickstrahl, können nur ein Bild und eine Geschichte verfolgen, und das ist gut so. Die Stadt bietet Disparatheit, zerfällt in tausende von Bildern, gleichzeitig, das unterhält zwar, ist aber auch nervig und führt zu einem Zustand der Verwirrtheit. Jede Aussage bleibt oberflächlicher Splitter, es gibt nur die Oberfläche.

Werner: Würdest du Bühnenbilder nicht viel lieber für ein Totaltheater, eine wenigstens von drei Seiten her einsehbare Seebühne (beispielsweise Bregenz) entwerfen als für Guckkästen. Wenn ja, warum?

Schaal: Nein, da kann ich anknüpfen, an das, was ich gerade gesagt habe: Durch die klare Ortsdefinition – hier bin ich, und dort ist die Bühne – vermischen sich die Standpunkte nicht mehr. Jetzt kann die Konzentration eintreten, die in der Stadt nicht herrscht. Die Stadt ist das Totaltheater, das Guckkastentheater ist das Gegenteil. Ein Kultort auch. Tausend Menschen sitzen und schauen auf ein Bild, auf ein Loch, in Erwartung – von was?

Werner: Was hast du seinerzeit, als deine Zusammenarbeit mit Ruth Berghaus begann, so grundlegend anders gemacht als deine damaligen Bühnenbildner-Kolleginnen und -Kollegen? Denn sonst wäre die Fachwelt ja nicht schlagartig auf dich aufmerksam geworden. Und was ist von diesem »Andersmachen« bis heute geblieben?

Schaal: Das kann ich selbst nicht sagen. Vielleicht war es der Architektur-Aspekt, den es in dieser Radikalität bisher nicht gab. Ich habe damals auch eher bei der Tradition der 20er Jahre (Russische Revolutionskunst und Bauhaus) angeknüpft als bei den in den 80er Jahren herrschenden Kunstströmungen. Es wäre interessant, all diesen Querverbindungen einmal nachzugehen – wie ja auch bei der Ausstellungsgestaltung und der Landschaftsarchitektur.

Werner: Aus welchen Gründen benutzt du in nahezu allen deinen Bühnenbildern (wie auch in deinen Ausstellungsgestaltungen) para- oder proto-architektonische Landschaften bzw. Setzungen, häufig unterstützt durch die Suggestion von Beton, Balken, Grau in Grau, und weißen Raumbehältern?

Schaal: Das ist für mich das Spezifische des Architektur-Aspekts und gehört eben zu meinem Stil. Stil heißt ja Beschränkung. Einengung. Man verbietet sich gewisse Dinge und entfaltet seine Formensprache innerhalb der selbst gesetzten Grenzen.

Werner: Bestehen für dich Grenzen als Bühnenbildner (etwa wenn du den absolut leeren Raum zu gestalten hättest)? Wenn du für dich solche Grenzen siehst, dann wo und warum?

Schaal: Die Grenzen habe ich bereits beschrieben. Aber mit jedem Entwurf definiert man sie neu. Auch der leere Raum ist interessant. Er steht in gewisser Weise immer am Anfang fast aller Überlegungen.

Eine Grenze wäre vielleicht, – fällt mir gerade ein: ein konventionelles, traditionelles Bühnenbild zu entwerfen. Es gibt sie immer noch, diese Räume, vor allem in den romanischen Ländern, mit Stoffattrappen, Sonnenstrahlen, italienischen Piazzen und antiken Säulen. Das Opernpublikum ist sehr konservativ und träumt rückwärts. Das

hat zu tun mit der »guten alten Zeit«, aber darüber wollen wir nicht weiter sprechen.

Werner: Würdest du es vorziehen, realistischere Filmkulissen, bewegte Bildsequenzen an Stelle stilisierter, statischer Bühnenlandschaften zu gestalten? Wo siehst du den qualitativen Hauptunterschied zwischen Film- und Bühnenbildern, einmal abgesehen davon, daß du es auf der Bühne natürlich immer mit lebenden, realen Körpern im »kurzzeitrealen« Raum zu tun hast?

Schaal: Das Thema wird im Text des Buches behandelt. Natürlich ist das Film- und TV-Medium das zeitgemäße Medium für das 21. Jahrhundert. Die Arbeit in diesem Bereich würde mich sehr reizen. Ich habe ja ein Buch über Film und Architektur geschrieben, und bei der Arbeit im Filmmuseum in Berlin stand die Auseinandersetzung mit diesen Themen im Mittelpunkt. Es fällt mir übrigens auf, daß es kein vergleichbares Theatermuseum gibt. Das Medium des Bühnenbildes wird als Kunstdisziplin bei uns nicht ernst genommen. Das ist bestimmt ein Fehler. Im Film hat sich – abgesehen von Science-Fiction-Filmen – die realistische Ausstattung durchgesetzt. Aber das muß ja nicht so bleiben. Ich kann mir durchaus vorstellen, daß es auch mal wieder Filme gibt, die etwas künstlicher und traumverlorener sind als heute.

Werner: Woher kommt die fast »priesterliche« Suggestivkraft, die dramatische Nachwirkung vieler deiner Bilder im Kontext mit den jeweiligen Handlungen?

Schaal: Das kann ich selbst kaum sagen. Wenn es so ist, umso besser. Vielleicht liegt es an der heute so selten gewordenen Ernsthaftigkeit und an der radikalen Konzentration auf die wenigen Elemente!?

Werner: Wie gehst du in deinen Bühnenbildern, mit dem »verbotenen Blick«, der voyeuristischen Attitüde, dem durch Tabubruch (zum Beispiel KZ oder Faschimus) entweihten Blick um?

Schaal: Verbergen und Zeigen spielt bei meinen Entwürfen eine wesentliche Rolle. Wobei das Verbergen machmal wichtiger ist. Man will ja kein Exhibitionist sein. Jede Szene ist eine offene Wunde. Provokation und Tabubruch gehören dazu. Ich bin immer auch ein Grenzgänger.

Werner: Welche Rolle spielt der Begriff der »Einverleibung« in deinen Bühnenbildentwürfen?

Schaal: Das interessiert mich sehr. Ich will die Aggression sehen, die jemand gegen meine Wände entwickelt, und ich will auch die Zuneigung sehen. Einverleibung entsteht durch Gewohnheit. Was wir oft sehen, lernen wir kennen und verinnerlichen wir. Wir sind Sklaven von Türen und Fenstern. Nur unsere Betten nehmen uns schweigsam jeden Abend in sich auf, warm und anschmiegsam. Alle anderen Elemente sind unser äußeres Gegenüber. Bei meinen Gartenentwürfen werde ich oft mit Vandalismus konfrontiert: Da wird beschmiert, abgerissen, angezündet, mit Müll beworfen usw. – was soll ich dazu sagen, eigentlich sollte mir das gefallen, aber ehrlich gesagt …

Werner: Drittletzte Frage: Was glaubst du, warum deine »Scenae« ungeachtet ihrer zeitlichen und thematischen Fixierung eigentlich immer etwas Schicksalhaftes oder Fundamentales an sich haben?

Schaal: Ja, das liegt wahrscheinlich an meiner Vorliebe für die tragischen Aspekte. Ich liebe das

Melodrama, dem Happy-End gegenüber bin ich skeptisch. Mich interessiert das Scheitern und Untergehen. Totentanz-Geschichten.

Werner: Daran unmittelbar anschließend, die vorletzte Frage: Warum sind deine Entwürfe eigentlich immer so ernst? Anders herum gefragt: Wie gehst du mit dem Leichten, Fragilen, dem Ätherischen bzw. dem Skurrilen, Ironischen, Humoristischen um?

Schaal: Ich weiß auch nicht. Im Grunde liebe ich das Witzige auch, den Humor und vor allem die Ironie. Vielleicht muß ich in diesem Bereich noch mehr arbeiten.

Werner: Letzte etwas provozierende Frage an Jemanden, der außerhalb von Bühnenhäusern ja auch seit langem Ausstellungsarchitekturen baut, Parks anlegt, Installationen baut und Gebäude realisiert: Könnte es sein, daß die Bühnenwelt für dich eigentlich die interessantere, aufregendere und letztendlich auch realistischere Welt ist als die da draußen, weil sie viel mehr Optionen und Konnotationen bereit hält? Wenn ja, genauer warum? Und wenn dem wirklich so ist, in welcher Welt lebst du dann?

Schaal: Die Theater sind genauso wie die Museen beschützte Burgen. Wärter stehen an allen Ecken, Kartenabreißer und Garderobieren. Hier bist du sicher. Deine Architekturen sind bewacht wie Schwerverbrecher. Alles, was du draußen aufbaust – ich sprach gerade davon – ist der Öffentlichkeit schutzlos ausgeliefert und damit verletzbar und zerstörbar. Es gehört niemandem, ist Freiwild. Was heißt das? Die Stadt als Zustand des latenten Bürgerkriegs, in ihr beschützte Raumblasen, in denen geträumt werden kann?

Bei aller Gespaltenheit ist es vielleicht wirklich so, daß das Theater und die Oper – neben den Museen und Galerien – die letzten Reservate sind, in denen nachgedacht werden kann über das Menschsein, das Schicksal, Liebe, Haß, Leben und Tod. Kunst und Kult gehören hier noch zusammen. Laborartig aufgebrochen, in Werkstattmanier erweitert. Gefühlsbaustellen. Nahe dem Kraftwerk, das uns alle antreibt.

Photo credits / Photonachweis

Barbara Aumüller 134.2, 135.3
Mara Eggert 36, 53.1, 54.2, 56.3, 57.4, 58.5
Alexander Focke 105.2, 105.3
Ines Gellrich 216.3, 217.4, 219.5
Thomas Huther 86.3, 86.4, 87.5, 87.6, 87.7
Arwid Lagenpusch 48.1, 49.2, 50.3
Hans Jörg Michel 63.2, 64.3, 69.2, 70.3, 71.4,
    74.2, 75.3, 76.4, 80.2, 82.3
Jaques Moatti 186.5, 186.6, 187.7, 187.8
Bettina Müller 112.3, 112.4, 112.5, 113.7, 113.6,
    116.3, 117.4, 118.5, 119.6, 148.3, 149.4
Jörg Landsberg 164.2, 165.3
Stefan Odry 177.3
Oper Nürnberg 208, 212.2, 212.3, 213.4
Jaap Pieper 152.2, 152.3
Anita Pinggera 172.2, 172.3, 173.4
Hans Dieter Schaal 20.1, 21.2, 23.3, 28.1, 30.3,
    40.3, 83.4, 83.5, 101.2, 101.3, 139.4, 139.5,
    158.1, 159.3, 160.4, 168.2, 169.3, 200.1, 202.3,
    203.4
A. T. Schaefer 190.3, 192.4, 193.5, 206.2
Schlegel & Egle 143.2
Bernd Schmidt 144.3, 144.4, 144.5, 145.6,
    145.7, 145.8
Robert Söllner 130.2, 131.3
Georg Soulek 106, 121.2, 122.3
Staatsoper, Vienna/Wien 126.3, 127.4
Städtische Bühnen Frankfurt 178.4, 179.5
Maria Steinfeldt 26, 34.3, 34.4, 35.5, 53.1, 90.1,
    91.2, 92.3, 93.4, 142.1, 180, 184.2, 185.4,
    194, 198.2, 199.3, 199.4
Theater Lübeck 41.4, 41.5, 44.2, 45.3, 156.3,
    157.4
Joachim Thode 216.3
Axel Zeininger 44.2, 45.3, 46.4, 46.5, 47.6, 47.7
Nanette Zimmermann 96.2, 96.3, 96.4, 97.5,
    97.6, 97.7